THE POLITICAL ECONOMY
OF RUSSIA

THE POLITICAL ECONOMY OF RUSSIA

Edited by Neil Robinson

ROWMAN & LITTLEFIELD PUBLISHERS, INC.
Lanham • Boulder • New York • Toronto • Plymouth, UK

Published by Rowman & Littlefield Publishers, Inc.
A wholly owned subsidiary of The Rowman & Littlefield Publishing Group, Inc.
4501 Forbes Boulevard, Suite 200, Lanham, Maryland 20706
www.rowman.com

10 Thornbury Road, Plymouth PL6 7PP, United Kingdom

British Library Cataloguing in Publication Information Available

Library of Congress Cataloging-in-Publication Data

The political economy of Russia / edited by Neil Robinson.
    pages ; cm
  Includes bibliographical references and index.
  ISBN 978-1-4422-1074-5 (cloth : alkaline paper) — ISBN 978-1-4422-1075-2
(paperback : alkaline paper) — ISBN 978-1-4422-1076-9 (electronic)
  1. Economics—Political aspects—Russia (Federation) 2. Economic development—
Political aspects—Russia (Federation) 3. Russia (Federation)—Economic policy—1991–
4. Russia (Federation)—Politics and government—1991– —Economic aspects.
I. Robinson, Neil, 1964–
  HC336.27.P654 2013
  330.947—dc23
                                                                    2012017127

Printed in the United States of America

For Maura, Sáoirse, and Mani

Contents

Figures

Tables

1

Introduction

The Political Problems of Russian Capitalism

Neil Robinson

THE ECONOMY HAS BEEN CENTRAL to the development of the Russian political system over the past twenty years. Economic structure and struggles over economic policy and property have been at the heart of political development, influencing the structure of political competition, the institutional form of the Russian state, popular attitudes toward democracy and rule, the rule of law, and Russia's place in the world. In the 1990s, it looked as if economics was "in command" in Russia, as the state appeared to have been captured by business interests. In the first decade of the new century, it looked as if the reverse was true: "state capture" had been replaced by "business capture" as the political system under President Vladimir Putin reasserted itself.[1] These images of Russia, which are common in both academic and popular discourses on the country, do not, however, tell the whole truth about the development of both politics and economics in the country and the overlap between them. The power of business was not as strong in the 1990s as talk of oligarchy might lead us to believe, and, conversely, the power of the state in the 2000s is not as strong as pictures of Vladimir Putin striding about bare chested doing manly things might cause us to think. Russia's political and economic systems and the nexus of relations between them have continually evolved and will continue to evolve into the future.

This book looks at the main themes in this story of intertwined political and economic development to make some contribution to our knowledge of Russia's political economy. The themes covered are deliberately broadly chosen. It looks at how politics and economics have impacted each other in Russia through historical and comparative lenses and how international factors have influenced the development of Russia's political economy. We look at private agriculture, the issues that surround demographic crisis, and the struggles over property and taxation. Because of this wide-ranging focus, the approach taken in this book is not a methodologically proscriptive one: political economy in this volume is not, as it is in some accounts, the application of economic methodology to the study of politics.[2] Methodologically, the positions adopted here draw on a wide range of the larger set of positions that can be found in the broader fields of comparative and international political economy as they have developed historically.[3] Neither is any level of analysis accorded a privileged position in this volume conceptually or analytically; the development of Russia's political economy is dealt with at both its domestic and its international levels, and Russia is looked at as a case and comparatively. The aim of this book, therefore, is not to promote any particular angle on Russia's political development but rather to bring together discussions on different issues in the development of Russia as a politicoeconomic system to see how political and economic inequalities and structures shape one another and the social, economic, and political possibilities that result from this mutual development.

Even with this in mind, there is a problem that runs through the chapters of the book that needs to be brought up at the start. This is the question of what kind of capitalism Russia is developing. This is confronted directly in several chapters and indirectly in the rest. No consensus emerges on the answer to this question, although there is consensus over the political problems of Russian capitalism and the political character of Russian capitalism. There are problems of policy: How do you design policies to cope with demographic crisis? How do you encourage the spread of private agriculture to revitalize the post-Soviet countryside? Can Russia develop strategies that enable it to take advantage of its power as an energy producer in creative ways that build partnership with its customers? There are also problems of political control, of stabilizing revenue flows, of ending corruption and practices like raiding to assist economic development, and of balancing economic development needs and political stability.

These two sets of questions are obviously related to one another. In the longer run, the nature of Russian capitalism will be determined by the success that the Russian political system has in developing solutions to its economic problems. But the development of Russian capitalism itself will determine whether solutions can be found and, if they are found, whether they can be implemented to any general effect. It is the general effect that is important. The Russian political system, like the Soviet system before it, has great capacity to order a specific development. Stalin could command the rapid construction of an atomic arsenal, Khrushchev could order that space flight be made a priority, and Dmitri Medvedev can order that some fields outside Moscow be transformed into a high-tech business park and financial hub. Despite their success, however, Stalin and Khrushchev could not diffuse the achievements of their pet projects through the Soviet economy as a whole. The question is, can Vladimir Putin be successful where general secretaries of the Communist Party of the Soviet Union, Boris Yeltsin, Putin's first presidential term, and his successor were not?

There is no one answer to this problem in the chapters of this book. Instead, there are versions of the two main answers that we can find both in the literature generally on Russia and in Russian political discourse. These two answers reflect different beliefs about what a "political capitalist" system is and what it can do. A political capitalist system is distinct from the types of capitalism that we know in the global West. There is always political regulation of these types of capitalism; indeed, the way in which this regulation is enforced is one of the key factors that determines what type of capitalism we live under.[4] In a political capitalist system, the degree of regulation is quantitatively and qualitatively different. Other varieties of capitalism do not subordinate the profit motive to political logics routinely except in times of national emergency;[5] the economic logic of the market is regulated, but the purpose of regulation is to ensure the reproduction of that logic. In political capitalist systems, this is not the case, nor is it routinely and automatically so. The profit motive is secondary to political logics. Both views of political capitalism presented in this book and that exist in wider commentary on Russia accept that Russia, as a form of political capitalism, has subordinated the profit motive to political logics. The difference between them concerns what they believe these logics are and can be.[6]

The first belief about political capitalism is that it can lead to the creation of a developmental state. This view of political capitalism was most clearly expressed by Alexander Gerschenkron in his classic analysis of late development. Late developers, Gerschenkron argued, do not have time to build the social and economic institutions that create development in early developing nations. These institutions take time to develop organically, time that late developers, if they are not to be left even further in the wake of early modernizers, do not have. They therefore simulate the development of the social and economic institutions necessary for development. The body that does this simulating is the state. Instead of waiting for a financial sector to develop over time and for that financial sector to direct investment into economic activity that creates development, the state does it. Using the political authority that it has and its systems of resource extraction and allocation, the state takes resources from what Gerschenkron called "old wealth" and redistributes it from consumption to investment. The logic of politics that supplants the market logic of profit seeking is economic development, therefore, and the state represents and acts for a general social interest, the interest that all its citizens have in securing economic growth.[7]

The second belief about political capitalism is not so positive. Some states may be lucky enough to secure a developmental state in which the political class sorts out the institutional development needed to create economic growth and then channels resources through those institutions to achieve such progress. But other states (and probably the majority) are not so lucky. In these examples of political capitalism, the political logic that subordinates the profit motive is not directed to fulfilling a general social interest in economic progress but rather is concerned with the private interests—economic and political—of political agents. Property rights and control over privately held resources are not encroached on to ensure investment rather than consumption but are encroached to change who has the right to that consumption. The state itself is seen as an economic resource to be consumed in this version of political capitalism and as a result is fragmented. The state in this view does not represent a common interest (albeit imperfectly since there is never a universally accepted version of what the common interest is and deciding that it is perhaps anyway impossible). What emerges is "a privilege-centered polity where de facto control over assets is asserted by means of fragmented and personalized enforcement mechanisms. The boundaries of the state are porous and liable to be transgressed by social predators, and the de-bureaucratization of the public domain resulted in diminished levels of stateness."[8]

The developmental state model reflects the idea that there was a watershed in Russia's post-Soviet development when the "chaos" of the 1990s under Boris Yeltsin was replaced by the "order" of the 2000s under Vladimir Putin and his "successor" Dmitri Medvedev.[9] This shift from chaos to order was accompanied by the expansion of the Russian state's role in the management of some leading Russian corporations and the creation of new state corporations in areas of national economic interest. Together, order, imposed by the Kremlin's curtailment of political competition, and the expanding role of bureaucrats in economic management at the apex of the economy led, so the argument goes, to state capitalism. Variations of this argument have been made academically and in popular commentary on Russia since the early 2000s.[10] This view of the world was given a further boost by the global economic crisis. While severe in its immediate impact in Russia, it was not as severe as the crisis in other parts of the world. This has led some to argue that the global crisis is actually a specific crisis of an ideological model of capitalism: neoliberalism. This makes the Russian "model" more attractive, and it has been portrayed at one leading edge of a global rise of state capitalism.[11]

While it is to be hoped that Russia does develop economically and beyond oil and gas, it is not clear that this view of political capitalism as some sort of developmental state capitalism tells the whole story. State capitalism is a very loose category. It has positive connotations as well as negative ones, as Gerald Easter points out in his chapter. Easter associates it with "concessions" rather than development.[12] Further, one could add that it is unclear whether state capitalism is something that exists as a form of political economy in Russia or whether it is a project, something to be created to address developmental goals. Moreover, it is not clear that any move to state capitalism has come about because of changes in the state and its capacity to govern the economy; the features of state capitalism in Russia could as well (and probably better) be described as the result of changed relations between the political regime and economic actors rather than as a change in the state's management capacity and ability to direct economic growth and change, a point we will return to throughout the book.

Russia's political capitalism is thus very ambiguous. As a form of state capitalism, it is often described less as something that exists and more as something that might be emerging; Russian state capitalism is frequently described as having latent properties as much as actual ones that can be analyzed. This enables the analyst to impute characteristics to it without their fully being there. Hence, state capitalism is frequently seen as having some of the properties of corporatism, for example, and state corporatism, despite the specific meaning of that term, is sometimes used as a synonym for it since there are no distinguishing features for either.[13] This tension between what is and what might be and between what is and what might be a good route from current circumstances runs throughout Russian and foreign debates about the future. It points to the central paradox of Russia's political economy as it has developed and confronted its Soviet legacies. The Soviet system left a society that wanted economic change and hence reform but that was not able to achieve it. Reform was thus doomed to be a narrowly political enterprise: it was conceived by a small group of people who were theoreticians rather than representatives of social constituencies, enacted by them in relative social isolation, and its fate was determined by a political struggle that was detached in the main from the day-to-day lives of the Russian people. The failure of reform ensured that this social disconnection between the desire for change and active social agency to achieve it has endured. When Vladimir Putin—on the eve of his first accession to the presidency in December 1999—argued that Russian's view of the state was different from that of Europeans and North Americans because Russians saw the state as their main hope for change, he was stating an unfortunate truth.[14] It was unfortunate, first, because it was hard to see what other vehicle there was that could deliver change and, second, because there were so many faults with the state that it was hard to see it as a vehicle roadworthy enough to undertake the hard reform journey. It remains the case that the state is still probably the main vehicle through which change will come and that it needs major repair in order to deliver change consistently.

The Structure of the Book

The problems of the Russian state and the kind of capitalism over which it presides and of whether it can create a good form of political capitalism will be returned to throughout this book. As has already been mentioned, the reason for the centrality of the state and for the political problem of Russian economic change lies in the legacies of the Soviet Union. We start, therefore, with an examination of the contexts that have shaped the development of Russia's political economy, Soviet legacies, and the policy choices that have been made since the collapse of communism in 1991. The intention in the next chapter is not to provide an exhaustive account of either the Soviet economy or all the twists and turns that have occurred in Russian policy-making and economic thinking over the past two decades. Rather, it is to highlight that there have been some common problems that confronted Soviet leaders at the end of the Soviet Union and Russia's postcommunist leaders. These are, first, that Russia is relatively backward economically in comparison to other economically successful states. This relative backwardness is a legacy of the Soviet system, has endured throughout the post-Soviet period, and is now the focus of policy discussions about "modernization." Modernization is not just about diversifying the Russian economy so that it is less dependent on energy exports (a theme that is picked up in several of the book's chapters). It is also—unavoidably and no matter what—about catching up with one's rivals.[15] The problem of catching up is not a new one, and neither is the problem that confronts politicians anxious to promote policies for closing the gap on other economically successful states. Who is to actually close the gap? Recognizing that you have a problem is one thing; being able to do something about it another. While Russians are frequently in favor of modernization as a society, Russia has proven to be resistant to change. The roots of this resistance again go back to Soviet legacies, to the ways in which the command-administrative system created by central planning and its discontents created dense networks of interest that could not see if they had an interest in the success of reform. This meant that efforts at reform ran aground in the 1990s, and political power was compromised by an ongoing fiscal crisis. The chapter describes the economic structures that emerged during this period, how they endured into the 2000s despite the consolidation of political power that took place under Putin, and how they remain to be overcome by the policies of modernization. Again, the problem of reform, for modernization as for market reform before it, is who will work to close the gap created by relative backwardness. The initiative comes from the political system, but what interest do economic actors have in it: how do they respond to it given the political constraints that they operate under? Suggestions have been made as to what the answers to these questions are, but how they will be developed into answers (and by whom) remains to be decided.

The chapters by Gerald Easter and Richard Sakwa explore some of the issues raised in the second chapter at greater length and confront the political problems of the Russian economy head on. Easter's chapter looks at the problems that Russia has had changing its systems of taxation and securing the fiscal stability of the Russian state. These problems and how politicians have dealt with them are telling of the nature of the relationship between political authorities and private interests. Easter argues that revenue generation can be broken down into two general approaches: revenue can be either taken or traded for. Taking revenue relies on coercion; trading for revenue requires that some public goods are returned by the state for the revenue that it receives and that some mechanisms—generally democratic institutions— are put in place to decide what those goods are and to arbitrate whether their provision is sufficient. Reform in the 1990s tried to move from the old Soviet taking model—where the state essentially skimmed off resources from the economy as property owner—to a trading model of taxation. This failed because of opposition and because the state had no great store of resources to trade with; the population and elites rejected what looked to be a one-sided deal. This plunged the state into fiscal crisis, a situation that was relieved only when Putin moved to a taking model of revenue generation, with a tax structure to match. This tax structure is a simplified one that relies on the state's control over the legal system and threat to work; it does not involve the forms of tax collection—income taxes, for example—associated with trading and its attendant political institutions.[16] This has had a fundamental effect on the transitional economy, Easter argues. It has eased the fiscal crisis of the Russian state but at the cost of economic development. Taking has made the Russian economy a form of what Easter calls "concession capitalism," a bad form of political capitalism that comprises "a kind of "upstairs-downstairs" economy in which upstairs is found strategic industries in the form of large corporations that remain directly or indirectly subordinated to the state sector, while downstairs is found mass-consumption retail and trade in the form of small and medium-size enterprises that are organized into a regulated private sector. In this "concessions capitalism," property rights in major economic interests are held as concessions from the state, concessions that are made on personal terms between members of the political and economic elites. Such concessions are easily revoked.

The theme of insecure and politically contingent property rights is examined in more depth in Sakwa's chapter. Sakwa looks at the relationship between *reiderstvo* (raiding) and what he calls Russia's "dual state," a form of "constitutional-patrimonialism" in which the organizational integrity and capacity of the state are low and office holding is proprietorial and often involves misappropriation of state and social resources.[17] Raiding is the hostile takeover of one firm by another. This form of hostile corporate takeover is frequently political in its initiation and procedures in Russia. Raiding takes place against firms whose management has displeased political authorities to the advantage of firms whose management is politically pliant. Raiding involves the active and sometimes corrupt participation of state officials. Takeover bids are accompanied by specious legal proceedings, tax audits (often by armed tax police), and judicial rulings that are politically directed in favor of the authorities' corporate allies. This form of corporate takeover is possible, Sakwa argues, because of the character of the Russian political system. Its "dual state" is made up of a formal, constitutional order where there are laws, rules, and bureaucratic procedures drawn up to regulate the conduct of both political and economic life. Within these, however, there is another, administrative state where actual administration is dominated by patrimonialism, factional struggles, and Byzantine maneuverings, for influence over policy and the presidency. This parallel world of politics generates raiding but also stymies the development of both the political and the economic system: powerful elite groups have an interest in arresting the course of reform in order that the advantages they gain from raiding and influence peddling, gains that bring little to the mass of the Russian population, are not lost. Sakwa illustrates his points through a discussion of two cases of raiding: the Yukos case, which is the most famous instance of a politically motivated revenge attack against a disloyal corporate management, and the Togliattiazot case, a paradigmatic case of a politically sanctioned property grab. Raiding, Sakwa argues, has contributed to the holding back of Putin's efforts at re-creating a developmental state (to replace the Soviet one). Dmitri Medvedev's accession to the presidency represented an effort to redirect this desire for a new political authority that could create sustainable and diverse economic growth. This solution to the dual state and the economic practices that it encourages has not worked, however. This, of course, explains both the constant linkage of modernization, the Medvedev mantra, to discussions of political change. These discussions, heavily promoted by Medvedev's allies in bodies like the

Institute for Contemporary Development, did not bear much practical fruit except to give grist to the rumor mill about divisions in the Kremlin.[18]

The focus of the next two chapters is slightly different from Easter's and Sakwa's, but they reinforce some of the points that are made therein. Linda J. Cook examines the efforts made to deal with the demographic crisis that Russia is facing into over the next decades. This crisis has its roots in Soviet social problems, Russian lifestyle, and contemporary economic development. It is an economic and a security problem for Russia. It will weaken Russia's ability to exploit its territory economically because of low population density and a contracting working-age population and will mean that Russia is unable to populate large parts of its territory.[19]

During the 1990s, these problems were beyond the control of government, as the economic crisis robbed it of the means to forge policy solutions and probably the will to do so as well. Since 2000, the issue has been tackled, however, as the state has had the financial wherewithal to incentivize prenatal policies. Moreover, Russia has been an attractive destination for migrant labor that can make up the shortfall caused by population shrinkage among Russian citizens. The latter need to be regulated, and the effects of pronatalist and maternalist employment practices need to be monitored because of their labor market effects. Cook finds that government responses have not been particularly effective. Partly, this is not the government's fault. As she points out, pronatalist policies are generally not an effective means of dealing with falling birthrates and population decline since they do not deal with the structural factors that underpin such problems. Some examination of the past might have told the Russian government this: similar pronatal and maternalist policies and subsidies were not successful in Soviet times. Still, Cook shows, pronatal and maternalist concerns have begun to shape a whole raft of social policy issues and have also begun to impinge on women's control of their reproductive rights. They might also be counterproductive as well as unsuccessful since they might, if they drift in a more conservative, neofamilial direction, constrict women's entry into the workforce, lowering even further the available workforce.

Immigration is a novel issue for Russia both because it has no great experience of it from its past and because it is both a labor force and a demographic issue. As elsewhere in Europe, however, the policy area is seen as a law-and-order issue and is distorted in public discourse by xenophobia. The rioting by football fans in Moscow in December 2010 was the public, violent end of a spectrum of social and official intolerance, which creates a vicious circle, perpetuates illegality, encourages the growth of the shadow economy, creates stereotypes, and weakens the chances of using migration as a means of rectifying population shrinkage. As with policies on birthrates, migration policy is unlikely to solve labor supply problems in Russia, therefore. This will bring future costs to Russia both in terms of the effect that labor shortages will have on economic growth and in terms of the security problems that they cause.

Stephen K. Wegren looks at the development of private agriculture, seeing how government policies, food output, the popularity of private farming, and landholdings have influenced the development of the sector. Private agriculture has begun to develop more as policy has developed since the mid-2000s to support private farmers and as government leaders have supported private farming to improve national food security and broaden the range of exports. They have had some success, as Russia has become a grain exporter again. However, at the same time, the development of private farming, while improving, shows the uneven patterns of development of a sector of the Russian economy. This uneven development is an issue in other areas of the economy too and raises questions about the ability of the Russian state to construct policies that deliver the development of a national economic space. Again, as with pronatal policies, incentives to develop private farming really took off in the mid-2000s after poor performance in the 1990s. There was a connection then between economic growth elsewhere and the development of policy and hence to export earnings from energy. Both the pronatal policies that Cook writes about and the increased support provided to private farmers depended on the changes to revenue collection that Easter discusses. The increased resource allocations made to private farming built on policy frameworks that had been put in place earlier but that do not seem to have been effective when state financing was more stretched, as it was in the 1990s and first years of the 2000s. But, as has been mentioned, the results are uneven. There are a few "superwinners," including large agricultural complexes that are also geographically clustered in a few regions. The government has accepted the importance of private farmers, again as with demographics, in part because of security issues and in part because the expansion of private farming makes it an area that needs greater political monitoring.

Andrew Barnes's chapter looks in more detail and comparatively at the place of Russia in the global economy. As is pointed out in chapter 2, hydrocarbons are the major sector of the Russian economy, the sector that is more economically productive and most linked into the global economy. The price of oil has been of fundamental importance to Russia's economic survival and recovery over the postcommunist period; control over oil has been the most politically contentious subject both at home and abroad. The size of Russia's oil economy and its importance for its neighbors also means that Russian oil is a foreign policy issue. Most of the commentary on Russian oil since the end of the Yeltsin presidency and the cooling of relations between President Putin and the West has been concerned with Russia's use of energy as a foreign policy weapon. It would be stupid to deny that energy has been used as a weapon on occasion by Russia, in particular during its disputes with Belarus and Ukraine, and that this has raised hackles in the rest of Europe. It would also be stupid to deny that Russia seeks some advantages geopolitically and commercially from its oil reserves and that it is helped in this by the West's avaricious consumption of oil and growing Chinese demand for energy on Russia's eastern borders. Accepting that Russia has attempted to leverage its oil wealth is, however, not the same as buying into the idea that Russia has achieved great power because of its energy wealth or that power can be achieved only through the use of oil as a weapon and as a proxy for military power. This view generally portrays Russia as an "energy superpower."[20] The argument has an emotional resonance and seems to square an analytical circle by bringing together two propositions. The first proposition is that oil wealth and democratic failure are generally associated with one another since oil brings a "resource curse" that dooms democracy to failure.[21] The second proposition is that consolidated democracies have good relations with each other but difficult relationships with states that are having problems making a democratic transition stick.[22] Thus, Russia has oil and therefore problems with democratization and hence poor relations with the democratic world, poor relations that are expressed through its use of the one weapon it has: energy. While this is a satisfying equation, it depends on too many assumptions: it is, for example, difficult to believe that Russia would be a democracy without oil. Moreover, the idea that Russia is an energy superpower is a suspect one. Russia's gains from using energy as a weapon have been few, and the concept itself makes little sense.[23]

Barnes's chapter picks up on this line of argument and develops it in new ways. Instead of repeating arguments about Russian foreign policy objectives, Barnes looks at Russia as a part of the world oil system. He argues that Russia's dependence on oil economically makes it very hard for the country to use supply as a weapon. While other states might be dependent on Russia for supply, Russia is dependent on those states for revenue. Mutual dependency does not mean that Russia has no means of leveraging its energy wealth to greater advantage, however. While cutting supply might have limited and short-term benefits for Russia (and leave longer-term reputational damage in its wake), Russia can have greater influence economically and politically if it uses its energy wealth to shape the oil futures markets. This potential should not be seen negatively—or at least not just negatively—Barnes argues. Russian power on the global futures market might generate resources for Russia and help price stability in the world oil market more generally. Barnes's chapter reminds us, therefore, that the development of Russia's political economy contains more options than might seem to be the case if we view its international engagements as confrontational and do not look at the full range of possibilities that exist within the global economy.

Paul T. Christensen's chapter looks at Russia from the perspective of world systems theory. This theory argues that there is a division of the global economy into core, semiperipheral, and periphery areas. The development of the international system is shaped by the competition and interaction between these areas as well as between the states within them. Russia has always been a semiperipheral state.[24] Such states are marked out by their sharing some of the characteristics of core states, such as higher levels of development, but also by their resistance to the developmental models offered by the core. Semiperipheral states do not benefit from the economic lead enjoyed by core states—the relative backwardness of Russia discussed in chapter 2 being a case in point—and are also not integrated into the political structures and conventions shared by core states. In reaction and also as a means of catching up and ending their subaltern status, they seek different paths of development to the core states. Sometimes, this search takes the form of resistance across the full spectrum of socioeconomic life, as in the Russian Revolution; at other times, divergence from the core pattern is more muted.

Christensen puts Russia's place at the semiperiphery in historical perspective and discusses the concept of semiperipherality generally, noting that it was not only the case that prerevolutionary Russia was in the semiperiphery but also that the Soviet Union remained connected to the global capitalist economy and dependent on it as a semiperipheral country. This conclusion restates the argument made in chapter 2 about the relative economic backwardness of the Soviet Union. Christensen argues that post-Soviet policies did not change the structure of the Russian economy or its relationship with the global economy. His chapter then focuses on the social dimensions of this, arguing that Russia's place in the global economy has had a negative effect on the development of Russian society as a politically responsible structure. The demands of development at the semiperiphery have helped squeeze Russian society and social organization despite the phenomenal flowering of associational life of the late 1980s and 1990s.

Finally, in chapter 9, the book returns to the question of the character and political problems of Russian capitalism and its prospects. The authors of this book's chapters all recognize that Russia has a form of political capitalism. The intention under Putin and Medvedev has been to develop a form of political capitalism that is developmental. However, it is open to question how far they have managed to do this and what their future prospects are. Although there have been significant changes in Russian politics in the 2000s, these have not led to a rejuvenation of the state as an agent of economic change, and it is a matter of conjecture as to whether it can become such an agent under current global economic conditions.

Notes

1. Andrei Yakovlev, "The Evolution of Business-State Interaction in Russia: From State Capture to Business Capture?," *Europe-Asia Studies* 58, no. 7 (2006): 1033–56.

2. Barry R. Weingast and Donald A. Wittman, "The Reach of Political Economy," in *The Oxford Handbook of Political Economy*, ed. Barry R. Weingast and Donald A. Wittman (Oxford: Oxford University Press, 2006), 3.

3. For overviews, see Ronald H. Chilcote, *Theories of Comparative Political Economy* (Boulder, CO: Westview Press, 2000), and Mark Blyth, ed., *Routledge Handbook of International Political Economy (IPE): IPE as a Global Conversation* (London: Routledge, 2010).

4. Peter A. Hall and David Soskice, "An Introduction to the Varieties of Capitalism," in *Varieties of Capitalism: The Institutional Foundations of Comparative Advantage*, ed. Peter A. Hall and David Soskice, 1–70 (Oxford: Oxford University Press, 2001).

5. Venelin I. Ganev, "Postcommunist Political Capitalism: A Weberian Interpretation," *Comparative Studies in Society and History* 51, no. 3 (2009): 648–74.

6. For discussions of varieties of capitalism and postcommunism, see Ganev, Postcommunist Political Capitalism"; David Lane, "Emerging Varieties of Capitalism in Former State Socialist Societies," *Competition and Change* 9, no. 3 (2005): 221–41; David Lane and Martin Myant, eds., *Varieties of Capitalism in Post-Communist Countries* (Basingstoke: Palgrave, 2007); and Martin Myant and Jan Drahokoupil, *Transition Economies: Political Economy in Russia, Eastern Europe, and Central Asia* (London: Wiley, 2011). On Russia specifically, see David Lane, "What Kind of Capitalism for Russia? A Comparative Analysis," *Communist and Post-Communist Studies* 33, no. 4 (2000): 485–504, and Philip Hanson and Elizabeth Teague, "Russian Political Capitalism and Its Environment," in Lane and Myant, *Varieties of Capitalism in Post-Communist Countries*, 149–64.

7. Alexander Gerschenkron, *Economic Backwardness in Historical Perspective: A Book of Essays* (Cambridge, MA: The Belknap Press of Harvard University Press, 1962), 13.

8. Ganev, "Postcommunist Political Capitalism," 72.

9. David Lane, "From Chaotic to State-Led Capitalism," *New Political Economy* 13, no. 2 (2008): 177–84.

10. Ryabov, cited in Richard Sakwa, *The Quality of Freedom: Khodorkovsky, Putin, and the Yukos Affair* (Oxford: Oxford University Press, 2009), 344; A. Radygin, "Rossiya v 2000–2004 godakh na puti k gosudarstvenomy kapitalizmu?," *Voprosy ekonomiki* 4 (2004): 42–65; Anders Åslund, "Russia's Energy Policy: A Framing Comment," *Eurasian Geography and Economics* 47, no. 3 (2006): 321–28; Ovsey Shkaratan, "The Russian Transformation: A New Form of Etacratism?," in *The Transformation of State Socialism. System Change, Capitalism or Something Else?*, ed. David Lane, 143–58 (Basingstoke: Palgrave Macmillan, 2007); Lane, "From Chaotic to State-Led Capitalism"; T. Kim, "Bringing the State Back In? Rise of State Capitalism in Russia," paper presented to the PSA annual conference, April 2009, Manchester, United Kingdom.

11. See the arguments in National Intelligence Council, *Global Trends 2025: A Transformed World* (Washington, DC: U.S. Government Printing Office, 2008), and

Ian Bremmer, "The Return of State Capitalism," *Survival* 50, no. 3 (2008): 55–63, and "State Capitalism Comes of Age," *Foreign Affairs* 88, no. 3 (2009): 40–55.

12. For a positive reading, see Lane, "From Chaotic to State-Led Capitalism."

13. Lane, "From Chaotic to State-Led Capitalism"; Peter Rutland, "The Oligarchs and Economic Development," in *After Putin's Russia: Past Imperfect, Future Uncertain*, ed. Stephen K. Wegren and Dale R. Herspring, 159–82 (Lanham, MD: Rowman & Littlefield, 2010).

14. Vladimir Putin, "Rossiya na rubezhe tysyachiletii," in *Plan Prezidenta Putina: Rukovodstvo dlya budushchikh prezidentov Rossii* (Moscow: Evropa, 1999), 321.

15. Boris Makarenko, "Vozmozhna li v Rossii modenizatsiya?," *Pro et Contra* 12, no. 5–6 (2008): 35.

16. See also Scott Gehlbach, *Representation through Taxation: Revenue, Politics, and Development in Postcommunist States* (New York: Cambridge University Press, 2008).

17. Neil Robinson, *Russia: A State of Uncertainty* (London: Routledge, 2002) 5–15.

18. Institute for Contemporary Development, *Rossiya XXI veka: Obraz zhelaemogo zavtra* (Moscow: Ekon-Inform, 2010).

19. For specific analysis of some of these problems, see Michael Bradshaw and J. Prendergast, "The Russian Heartland Revisited: An Assessment of Russia's Transformation," *Eurasian Geography and Economics* 46, no. 2 (2005): 83–122.

20. Marshall Goldman, *Petrostate: Putin, Power, and the New Russia* (Oxford: Oxford University Press, 2008).

21. Michael L. Ross, "The Political Economy of the Resource Curse," *World Politics* 51, no. 2 (1999): 297–322. For evaluations of Russia as "resource cursed," see M. Steven Fish, *Democracy Derailed in Russia: The Failure of Open Politics* (Cambridge: Cambridge University Press, 2005), chap. 5; William Tompson, "A Frozen Venezuela? The Resource Curse and Russian Politics," in *Russia's Oil and Natural Gas: Bonanza or Curse?*, ed. Michael Ellman, 189–212 (London: Anthem Press, 2006); and Vladimir Gel'man, "Introduction: Resource Curse and Post-Soviet Eurasia," in *Resource Curse and Post-Soviet Eurasia*, ed. Vladimir Gel'man and Otar Marganiya, 1–22 (Lanham, MD: Lexington Books, 2010).

22. Edward D. Mansfield and Jack Snyder, "Democratization and the Danger of War," *International Security* 20, no. 1 (1995): 5–38.

23. Peter Rutland, "Russia as an Energy Superpower," *New Political Economy* 13, no. 2 (2008): 203–10.

24. For a recent discussion of "semiperiphery," see Owen Worth, "Whatever Happened to the Semi-Periphery?," in *Globalization and the "New" Semi-Peripheries*, ed. Owen Worth and Phoebe Moore, 9–24 (Basingstoke: Palgrave Macmillan, 2009). For other discussions of Russia, see Michael J. Bradshaw and Nicholas J. Lynn, "After the Soviet Union: The Post-Soviet States in the World System," *Professional Geographer* 46, no. 4 (1994): 439–49; Boris Kagarlitsky, *Periferiinaya imperiya: Tsikly russkoi istorii* (Moscow: Agoritm, 2009); and Rick Simon, "Upper Volta with Gas? Russia as a Semi-Peripheral State," in Worth and Moore, *Globalization and the "New" Semi-Peripheries*, 120–37.

2

The Contexts of Russia's Political Economy

Soviet Legacies and Post-Soviet Policies

Neil Robinson

THIS CHAPTER PLACES THE DEVELOPMENT of contemporary Russian political economy in its historic setting. The chapters that follow deal with specific issues to do with Russia's political economy and its place in the world and in comparison to other postcommunist systems. Understanding these issues requires us to have some idea of the range and intensity of the problems that Russia and its leaders have faced. This chapter deals with these issues by reviewing what Russia has tried to overcome as it moved away from communism in the 1990s and what problems were thrown up as this movement took place. It is not a complete history of the Soviet economic experiment or of Soviet-style economic systems,[1] nor is it a complete description of economic reform and the technical dimensions of economic policy.[2] Instead, it looks at the relative backwardness of late Soviet economy and the nature of economic power within this social structure. It then looks at how efforts to deal with these legacies reshaped rather than destroyed them and what this has meant for the administrations of Presidents Boris Yeltsin, Vladimir Putin, and Dmitri Medvedev.

Soviet Legacies

The collapse of the Soviet Union in 1991 also meant the end of its economic system as mechanism for the organization of production and the distribution of goods, services, and welfare. There was therefore a powerful need to develop a new form of economy as the Soviet Union collapsed, but the tasks of economic reformers were complicated by the legacies of the Soviet economy. These legacies are interrelated but can be best described as, first, relative economic backwardness in comparison to advanced capitalist economies and, second, an antireform (and hence antimarket) social structure and system of economic exchange.

Soviet Relative Economic Backwardness

The Soviet Union's relative economic backwardness to its capitalist rivals both drove its economic development and was a product of that development. The Soviet Union embarked on rapid economic development in the late 1920s in order to catch up with its capitalist enemies in as short a period of time: it was, as Stalin famously put it in 1931, "50 or 100 years behind the advanced countries. We must make good this distance in 10 years. Either we do it, or we shall go under."[3] In many key respects the Soviet Union did catch up: it developed from a primarily agricultural to a primarily industrial and urban economy, and it went from a position of military weakness to one of equality in terms of its destructive nuclear capacity. However, the very mechanisms that it used to achieve rapid growth and secure a degree of economic parity with "the advanced countries" led it to lag behind them once again by the late 1970s (and possibly even earlier than this).

The reason for this was that central economic planning, the economic system developed by the Soviet Union to overcome its backwardness, was both impossible to operate and practically resistant to change. The result was that the Soviet Union locked in a model of economic development that was over time less able to ensure growth. Planning was impossible to operate because it was not logistically possible to centrally direct all the economic actions involved in a complex economy, producing a wide range of goods and responding to a broad range of social and political needs: the amounts of information that needed to be collated and aggregated and the amounts of orders that needed to be drawn up and distributed were simply too large to manage.[4] Indeed, the Soviet Union never had a properly planned economy in the sense that its planners could match up productive capacity, investment, and other inputs (raw materials and labor) to deliver all the economic outputs that society and political authorities desired. Planners directly planned and controlled a very small part of economic production; in the late 1980s, Hewitt estimated that planners controlled the output and distribution of 20,000 products of the estimated 24 million produced in the Soviet economy.[5] Since the planning of production was not feasible for all products, for most producers economic plan targets were arbitrary. Plans were set to meet political goals and were not always mindful of what was economically possible; this was a command-administrative economy rather than a planned one. This created negative incentives for producers and their supervisors. If the plan was not set with an eye on what was possible, it was not in the interests of producers to reveal their real production capacity. Instead, producers had an incentive to underestimate what they could produce and overestimate what they needed to achieve plan targets. By doing this, they made sure that they could always meet targets, which would be lower than they had the capacity to produce. Those charged with supervising the economy—party leaders and industrial ministries—had an incentive to collude with these practices since they were judged not on the basis of the efficiency with which they fulfilled the plan but rather on the simple fact of its fulfillment.

The problems of planning were not a problem when there were abundant and cheap labor reserves and raw materials. But eventually these began to dry up. This affected both the rate of growth, which began to slow down from the 1960s on, and the ability of the Soviet Union to keep up with other advanced industrial economies. Figure 2.1 shows the growth of output that could be secured from each worker and the amount of new capital per worker recovered in the 1950s after the war years of the 1940s. It did not reach the heights of the 1930s, when coercion ensured that wage rates were very low, but growth was substantial. But this was the high tide of the Soviet economy: thereafter, whether we use official Soviet figures or the much lower recalculations by later Russian economists like those of Grigorii Khanin in Figure 2.1, economic growth went into decline.

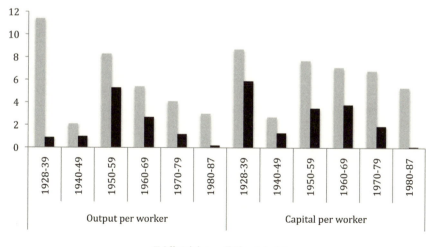

FIGURE 2.1
Growth Rates in the Soviet Economy, 1928–1987 (average annual percent). *Source:* Adapted from the data in William Easterly and Stanley Fischer, "The Soviet Economic Decline," *World Bank Economic Review* 9, no. 3 (1995): 343.

At this point, the Soviet system should have changed its pattern of growth from an extensive pattern to an intensive one; growth from increasing the amount of labor and resources used in the economy would have been succeeded by growth from increased efficiency of resource use, higher labor productivity, and greater returns on investment. Again, Figure 2.1 shows that this did not happen. Both the planning system and the economic bureaucracy prevented it. Economic reform in the post-Stalin era was halfhearted and stymied by powerful vested bureaucratic interests.[6] As reform was halfhearted, it could not overcome the logic of the planning system that encouraged overestimating production needs and underestimating potential output. This meant that demand for investment was high but that returns on it were poor. Structurally, the Soviet economy suffered from "investment hunger," as the great economist critic of central planning János Kornai put it; leaders demanded growth, and firms and their managers had "soft budget constraints" (discussed later in thus chapter) and knew that "liquidation will not follow from any faulty investment decisions, however high the costs and financial losses may be."[7] Rates of investment in the Soviet Union and its allies—and particularly of industrial investment—far exceeded investment in advanced capitalist countries and grew more rapidly over time and at a faster rate than the growth of gross domestic product (GDP).[8] Excessive demand for investment meant that although the rate of investment as a percentage of GDP was high in the Soviet Union, there was a general shortage of investment as resources were spread thinly between competing interests, especially after military production and prestige projects such as aerospace had taken their large cut from the investment budget. The effect of this was to delay the completion of investment projects for roughly twice as long as was the norm in capitalist economies.[9] Windfalls, such as the high revenues earned in the 1970s from oil sales after the OPEC price spikes, drained away. The revenue generated by Soviet energy sales went a considerable way to subsidizing industrial production and increases in living standards at a time when the rest of the industrialized world was closing down inefficient plants and seeking to rationalize industrial production through job cuts, efficiency drives, and technological modernization.[10] The Soviet Union, in contrast, pursued technological innovation slowly and haphazardly and sought to maintain social stability through broadening the social contract between regime and people based on incremental improvements in living standards.[11] Indeed, such was the demand for the capital that oil wealth made available that the Soviet economic system began to kill its golden egg–laying goose: demands for resources from other sectors meant that the oil sector did not get enough investment to renew itself. The Soviet Union did not develop new energy sources during the boom years of the early 1970s or improve efficiency in the energy sector to keep energy costs low. By the time that crisis hit the energy sector at the end of the 1970s, the technological level and organization of the energy sector had deteriorated to such a level that the investment needed to head off a crisis was enormous and threatened to deprive *all* other industrial sectors of new investment in the early 1980s.[12]

In these circumstances, the Soviet Union could only fall behind and become relatively backward in comparison to other industrialized states. Its very nature meant that "in effect [it] was frozen in place as the other world economies progressed."[13] The Soviet economy was "modern" in that it was largely industrialized and supported a welfare state, but it was not innovative or competitive. Apart from space flight and lasers—and even here Soviet comparative advantages soon flagged—the Soviet Union did not lead in any of the technological innovations made after World War II.[14] These innovations—in computing, telecommunications, energy, material, and medical sciences—were to transform economies in the 1980s and afterward, but the Soviet Union and hence Russia were left behind. The only area that the Soviet Union had a comparative advantage in was energy production; other sectors of its manufacturing economy were not competitive in the world economy.[15] Only 4 percent of Soviet plant was on a technological par with world standards by 1991.[16] Consequently, the Soviet Union was not able to develop as an economic power in the world. Relative backwardness and soft budget constraints combined to make Soviet goods unsalable on world markets. Much Soviet industrial production created "negative value-added goods," manufactured objects worth less on world markets than the raw materials and labor used to produce them.[17] Only about 7 to 8 percent of Soviet production was of "world standard," that is, exportable outside the Soviet bloc countries, by the late 1980s.[18] Consequently, the Soviet Union increasingly had the foreign trade structure of an industrially undeveloped state. Its exports were mainly raw materials rather than industrial goods to which value had been added in the process of their transformation from raw materials into manufactured objects. In 1950, the Soviet Union exported more consumer goods (4.9 percent of exports) than energy products (3.9 percent of exports); by 1987, however, 46 percent of Soviet exports were from the energy sector.[19] Not surprisingly, and despite its energy sales, the Soviet Union was a peripheral player in world trade. In 1990, it accounted for only 2.1 percent of exports in the world economy and 2.3 percent of imports—less than Belgium, the Netherlands, and Italy and a long way behind the United States and Japan.[20]

The Antireformism of Soviet Social Structure and Economic Exchange

The Soviet leadership was well aware of their growing relative backwardness in comparison to advanced capitalist economies. A section of the elite began to note the occurrence of what they called a "scientific-technological revolution" in Western economies in the 1970s and called for the Soviet Union to emulate it.[21] Obviously, none of these appeals or initiatives bore fruit. Some of the reasons for this have been mentioned already: the power of industrial ministries and bureaucracies was too great, and the planning system was too intractable. Some things can be deduced from what we have said: de-Stalinization removed the gross threat of coercion from the economic policy toolbox. But economic reform was also stymied by the weakness of tools and agents to promote change.

The absence of tools for reform and agents to carry it out does not fit with how we think of the Soviet system traditionally and what we know about social attitudes at the end of the Soviet period. We think of Soviet society traditionally as a highly organized and directed society. Its rulers should, then, have been able to force change through using the power and ubiquity of the Communist Party of the Soviet Union, with its branches in every significant economic enterprise and directorate. Society was also receptive to change at the end of the Soviet period. The collapse of the Soviet regime clearly demonstrated a need for systemic change, and public opinion poll data consistently showed "majority support for a market economy" in the last years of Soviet power and immediately thereafter.[22] Either the political system or social forces, in other words, should have been able to bring about economic reform. In practice, however, the political system was weak, and public opinion was not uniform and was not (and still is not) able to translate into concrete, positive political practice. The reason for this is that the Soviet economic system encouraged highly particularistic relationships between economic actors over common and universal ones. This was also disempowering of society since much of the population was dependent on people in positions of power in the economy; resources that people had that might have been used to support reform efforts were also devalued. The main reason for this was the nature of economic exchange and how that exchange determined value. National, capitalist markets largely set the value of goods impersonally; both buyers and sellers of goods have choices as to where they trade; the price of goods is largely determined by overall levels of supply and demand and takes account of costs of production, labor, and raw materials that went in to their production; and, finally, the value of a good is expressed in a common, generally accepted unit of exchange: money. An act of economic exchange in a market thus has a *common* or *universal* character with all other exchanges in a national economy. Goods of a similar type can be purchased for roughly the same price across a national market and for the same, commonly accepted unit of exchange: money. One type of good can be compared to another because it is possible to judge its relative worth in monetary terms; market exchange and the value of goods and property are thus fairly transparent. Resources—land, raw materials, labor power, factories, and shops—possessed by a person or group can be valued in terms of money, and the income that they generate can be compared and evenly taxed by the state across the economy. The ability to develop economic power depends on the possession of money since this is necessary to purchase more property, invest, and so on. Economic activity that does not take account of costs (measured in money) and demand (the estimation of which creates an idea of what monetary return can be expected by producing and supplying a good) cannot break even or be profitable; anyone engaging in such activity may expect to go bankrupt.

The Soviet system was very different to this both in its usual operation from the 1920s on and in its legacy.[23] Goods in the Soviet economy had a monetary value assigned by the state. Prices were arbitrarily determined by central planners without regard for the costs of supply—what a product might cost in terms of raw material, labor, and so on—and without regard to demand. Political priorities mattered more than economic costs. Production was subsidized; prices and the monetary value of goods were often nominal. Since prices were set arbitrarily, no accurate profit-and-loss calculations could be made of economic activity. If a firm made a "loss" and had a deficit of rubles caused by overspending or poor efficiency, the result was not bankruptcy. Credit came not from a commercial lending organization concerned with making a profit but rather from the state, which cared only about fulfilling the plan. For this reason, it was often asserted that Soviet enterprises only had "soft budget constraints."[24] If an enterprise spent more than its budget allowed, it did not face the hard constraint of not having any more money to spend, a situation in a market economy that would mean an end to economic activity (bankruptcy). More "soft" credit would be made available to the "bankrupt" firm so that it could trade from the state in the form of increased subsidy, investment would continue through the mechanism of the plan, tax obligations to the state could be waived, and so on. This soft credit would generally not have to be returned to the state and did not incur interest payments. Money did not, therefore, fully play an effective accounting function as it might in a market; success and failure were not measured in monetary terms. There were also strict political limits to what could be done with money. The state owned or controlled all significant property and resources, and development priorities and investment were determined and controlled through the planning system. Money earned either by a firm or by an individual could not be used to consolidate control over economic activity by the purchase of more land, machinery, or business outlets, and shortages meant that money could not, by and large, be used to buy up consumer goods.

Money was thus largely detached from economic activity in the Soviet system. Along with shortages and planning inefficiencies, this helped to create one other difference between the Soviet and a market economy. Most distribution of goods and services took place in the Soviet Union through plan allocations, but there was an alternative system of exchange in the Soviet system parallel to the planning system with its nominal assignments of monetary value to goods. Value was assigned to goods and services by the actors involved in an exchange in economic exchanges outside the planning system (such as black-market deals) or to supplement it (the unofficial exchanges arranged by party-state officials and economic managers to compensate for breakdowns in the plan). As a result, these transactions were *particularistic*; each exchange and the value of goods exchanged were, unlike exchanges in a national market economy, unique to that exchange. Again, and as in the official system, these transactions took place without reference to what goods had cost to make, what someone else might pay for them, or what price the state had formally attached to them. Particularistic exchanges were highly personal, based on acquaintance, mutual affinity, and trust rather than on a desire to make profit and avoid loss, as in monetized exchanges in capitalist economies.[25] The value of goods was secondary to the value assigned to them through personal relations and such things as considerations of the political power of traders (bureaucrats, party officials, and economic managers), the value of being connected to them, and the favors that such connections might bring in the future. A most important form of capital that economic actors had was not, therefore, financial (money) but *relational* capital, that store of personal ties, connections, and mutual aid that came through interactions with other economic actors established over time and in the face of the vagaries of the planned economy.[26]

As the Soviet system fell apart, particularistic exchange and soft budget constraints changed character and developed. As the Soviet system began to fragment, the flow of goods to enterprises did not become commercialized—based on monetary, market exchange—but took place in the form of barter through the networks of particularistic exchange that had always supplemented the plan. Trading through barter and/or without regard to the monetary value of goods traded meant that production that was not profitable was still possible; since they were able to maintain production, enterprise directors were able to keep their positions and prestige and continue to control the resources that a factory had. Particularistic exchange was thus necessary for much of Russian industry to keep up at least a semblance of economic activity and a means by which the sections of the *nomenklatura*, the Soviet elite, could protect the resources and hence the power that they controlled because of their administrative positions in the economy. Economic managers could also derive personal economic gain even as the rest of the economy declined. Goods and resources could be transferred between elite members at low, fictitious prices, and the state could be deceived and not paid its due in the form of taxes. This form of economic activity and the wealth derived from it was not profit seeking as in capitalist economies where profit is produced through producing to meet demand and maximized by being efficient in the use of labor and resources. It was rent-seeking, taking wealth from economic activity by extracting it from the public purse or by manipulating distortions in the economy caused by policy. Moreover, particularistic exchange was a barrier to the acquisition of power by those outside of elite networks. Particularistic exchange devalues resources not held by members of networks since they cannot be converted into other goods or services. In Russia, this meant that the resources held by the mass of the population and the state were devalued. The chief resource held by the population at large was cash money, and the chief means that any state has of accumulating resources is taxation and the gathering of money. However, money had no great power while particularistic exchange prevailed since access to economic resources flowed not from the possession of money but from connections.

Post-Soviet Policies

Relative backwardness would have been bad enough on its own, but its combination with the antireform social structure of post-Soviet society based on particularistic exchange meant that simply flooding Russia with investment was not going to resolve the country's problems. The policy response chosen—radical economic reform or "shock therapy"—aimed to deal with the system of economic exchange and to alter the balance of power between antireform interests, the state, and the government. It would do this by using the market to change society, breaking up existing blocks of economic power and replacing them with new social forces loyal to the government, and because in a market economy the power of the state is great because of its control over money. Interest rates, taxation, and exchange rates are controlled to a great extent by the government and state, and hence the state has immense influence over what people do—what they consume and where and how they will invest and work. The state is also a major consumer of goods and services when it manages a market economy that generates taxes.

Reform did not deal with relative backwardness directly, therefore, but aimed to change the nature of Russian economic society and power within it as a condition for further modernization. This focus on changing society led to charges that reform was "revolutionary," neo-Bolshevik, and antidemocratic.[27] There is some truth in these charges; reform was justified in a high-handed fashion and was dismissive of alternatives. At the same time, however, there were few other realistic and practical alternatives to radical reform. Socially, there was no consensus on what change should be, and there was no political group with a clear alternative platform to radical reform. Radical reform was what international financial institutions and governments recommended so that it looked like the shortest route to investment from overseas. It was also highly expedient politically. Reform promised to alter the balance of power in the economy in favor of the Russian central state, to do so in a short time, and to turn the economy around—to bottom out the recession that would accompany economic change and begin recovery—within the electoral cycle. It even provided solutions to Russian President Boris Yeltsin's personnel problems since radical economic reform had a team of proponents who were prepared to take up the reins of government.[28]

Reform did not deliver a complete restructuring of Russian society; rather, the economy fragmented. The national economic space was fractured as regions went their own way economically, creating unique systems of economic administration, sometimes with the collusion of central authorities and sometimes in opposition to them. Central economic policy and administration were also divided among competing ideological and bureaucratic groups. These developed informal relations, sometimes corrupt, sometimes of convenience, and sometimes both, with business interests. All strained to secure Yeltsin's ear and some comparative advantage for themselves. The economy was fractured as different forms of property holding emerged and as struggles over property created shifting patterns of ownership, something that continues to this day.[29] New forms of legal and illegal entrepreneurship emerged and also engaged in contests over property and access to markets; lines between criminality and honest economic activity blurred as economic administration floundered and fragmented.[30] The result was crisis, not only the transitional recession caused by adjusting from one economic system that everyone expected but also an ongoing fiscal crisis of the Russian state. Partly this was a crisis of taxation collection (analyzed in more detail in chapter 3). But it was also a crisis caused by the incompatibility of the competing interests produced by the fragmentation of the economy. It was this crisis that produced the August 1998 devaluation and debt crisis, and it was at this problem that Vladimir Putin took aim when he succeeded Yeltsin.

We cannot hope to describe all the interests that emerged in the Russian economy at this time. What we can do is look at them as different sectors of the economy: the nontradables sector, the internationalized sector, and made up of both of these, the state-supporting sector.[31] The nontradables sector is that sector of the economy that produces goods and services that are not salable in international markets either because they are selling in markets that are naturally local (local retailing, many services, the public sector, and much of construction) or because they are not competitive in international markets. As can be seen from our discussion, Russia had a larger nontradables sector than would be usual for advanced industrial economy because of Soviet economic backwardness. Not only were services, construction, and so on nontradable, but so was much of industrial production since it was "negative value added." Inevitably, the size of the internationalized sector—that part of the economy that can produce goods that are salable on international markets and/or that generate actual or potential profits that make it attractive to foreign investment so that it becomes part of the international investment system—was smaller in Russia. This natural smallness of the internationalized sector was exaggerated since Soviet foreign trade was centrally and politically controlled, and there were only very small inflows of foreign investment into the Russian economy at the end of the Soviet period.[32] Many producers who were potentially profitable on world markets or who might have secured foreign investment did not know that they could compete in international markets[33] and, as a result would act as though they were a part of the nontradable sector. The only areas clearly able to compete were those where international prices were already known because export markets existed—as they did for oil, gas, and metals.

The state-supporting sector overlaps the other two sectors and is made up of those parts of the economy over which the state maintains some control and/or from which it can take resources that can be deployed to finance public services and used to meet state functions of warfare, welfare, and the maintenance of social order. The size of this sector fluctuates over time. It had been great when Soviet leaders could control prices and wages and use coercion freely in the economy; Soviet leaders had artificially grown the sector's size. Over time, however, it shrank and was very small at the end of the Soviet period as the breakdown of political order and the prevalence of particularistic exchange weakened the state's ability to raise resources in the economy. This sector of the economy was also small because of the weakness of the Russian government at the onset of reform in the face of the vast relational capital that was held by managers (see also chapter 3).

Post-Soviet economic policy has been about dealing with these three sectors of the economy since tackling them involved confronting the antireform bias of Soviet social structure and economic exchange and overcoming the relative economic backwardness that Russia inherited. The sectors changed and developed in response to reform, and much of the struggle over the economy and the nature of Russia's political economy has been over the relationship between these sectors and their respective sizes. The steps in this process were the struggle over radical economic reform and the crisis of the state that followed it, the reassertion of state economic power in the 2000s, and the renewed reform effort and response to the international economic crisis that overlapped from 2007 on.

Radical Economic Reform and Crisis: The 1990s

Reform Plans

Radical economic reform was aimed at altering the system of economic exchange and the balance of power between antireform interests and the state. To do this, it sought to alter the system of economic exchange and hence realign social structure and the relative powers of the state and economic elites groups. The new Russian government did not have the administrative capacity to make these changes through direct interaction with every part of the Russian economy. Although political change had come at the apex of the political system, it had not changed regional and local government particularly. In some regions of Russia, power rested in the hands of the bureaucrats and economic managers who knew only the Soviet system and who were used to using that system to their advantage. These officials were not sympathetic to Yeltsin or understanding of reform so that the administrative system that Yeltsin inherited was not one that could be used to support reform. Economic reformers argued the Soviet system of public administration did not need to be used to implement change. Radical economic reform, "shock therapy," promised that the legacies of the Soviet era could be tackled through economic policy without building up a new administrative system to implement economic reform. Compliance with government policy depended on persuading people that the government had a "credible commitment" to reform, that it was dedicated to reform and would pursue it no matter what, and that evading the implementation of reform would lead only to the pursuit of more reformist policies to keep reform on track. Once people were convinced of the credibility of reform, Soviet legacies would be diluted as reform provided incentives to act differently and empowered the state and new economic groups relative to the old *nomenklatura*.

Reform, as conceived by Yegor Gaidar (the intellectual leader of the reform economists who became minister for finance and deputy prime minister in 1991 and then acting prime minister for the last six months of 1992 before entering government again briefly from late 1993 to early 1994) and his team, would take place in two stages.[34] The first stage (January 1992 to early 1993) was supposed to achieve macroeconomic stabilization, that is, financial and monetary stabilization: it would involve controlling inflation and stabilizing the ruble and the budget deficit by liberalizing prices and commercializing economic activity as subsidies were cut and state spending was reduced. The second stage, which was to last from early 1993 to 1995, would consolidate the financial and monetary stabilization and see the restructuring of property rights as mass privatization would pass the bulk of industry and commercial activity into private hands.

The key to success was the successful completion of the first stage, when policies to effect price liberalization and financial stabilization were supposed to be mutually reinforcing. The reasoning went as follows. Central government would end subsidies to industry and consumption by liberalizing prices. Without subsidies, enterprises would be dependent on private investment and credit to cover their economic activity. Acquiring private investment would require transparency in corporate governance, which would be detrimental to the semilegal control of enterprises by the *nomenklatura*, and a commercial response to market opportunities. Where managers did not respond to the market or open up their books to outsiders, they would push their enterprises to the brink of bankruptcy and would be pushed out of office by workers whose livelihoods would be threatened. The ending of subsidies and price liberalization would create accurate information about costs and demands so that there would be ample information about how to commercialize economic activity for managers. It would also create the incentive of profit. Money as a means of accounting and measuring success and as a common unit of exchange would be re-created across Russia. The need to commercialize and ability to make profit would also ensure a flow of goods to consumers. As demand would be satisfied, prices would be brought down after an initial rise in prices caused by too much money pursuing a few goods. Inflation would thus be controlled, and money would become a stable store of value.

Cutting subsidies and freeing prices and trade would thus create a vicious circle. They would create an incentive—profit—to change behavior and a threat—loss of control over enterprises—to those who might ignore this incentive. As this circle was completed and behavior, or management, changed, particularistic exchange would be broken down and replaced by common, monetized exchange, which the state could tax and regulate through its control of credit emissions from the Central Bank and through taxation policy and interest rates.

The completion of this vicious circle would be helped by the entry of Russia into global markets. Controlling inflation by cutting the state budget and liberalizing prices would help facilitate the introduction of foreign capital into Russia and the expansion of trade by expediting the creation of a convertible and stable ruble. Trade, in the form of imports to Russia, would help break down particularistic exchange by introducing market prices to Russia in the form of a ready-made price system used to trade goods with the rest of the world. Competition with importers would force the restructuring of production to ensure competitiveness and prevent monopolies from raising prices once they were freed by providing more consumer choice. Without a major restructuring effort and commercialization to facilitate access to resources for modernization, Russian industry could not compete with foreign industries that might enter Russia or sell their products to it. Russian industry at the end of the Soviet period was outdated technologically and made goods of low quality that were unsalable on world markets and concentrated in monopolies. Trade would thus support the commercialization of economic activity by setting Russian market prices at levels comparable to those on world markets and forcing competition on to Russian industry, and any enterprise that might hope to access foreign capital would have to restructure and open up its management to the detriment of elite power.[35]

Stage 1 of reform was supposed to create the conditions, therefore, in which the nontradable sector of the economy would shrink and the internationalized sector would grow. It would also increase the size of the economic sector that supported the state through tax payments. By destroying particularistic exchange, removing soft budget constraints, and restoring value to money, it would balance out the power of the *nomenklatura* by destroying part of it and by creating new economic actors who would have an interest in promoting and supporting the market rather than the Soviet old-boy network. This would help secure both the Yeltsin regime and the power of the central state. Yeltsin would have the support of new actors in the economy and of a population able to purchase goods and with greater economic freedoms. The state— with Yeltsin at its head—would be empowered over old elites since it would be able to raise resources by taxing economic activity that would now be transparent, that is, measured in money and taking place in the open market. Its control of money would enable it to shape economic activity—and hence the balance of power in society—through fiscal policy. The state, by setting interest rates to control access to credit, by controlling the amount of money going into the economy from state-controlled printing presses, and by setting tax rates and customs tariffs, would control the amount of money that people and firms could spend and on what. Since money and market exchange would be national, it would be able to do this across the whole of Russia.[36]

Reform Outcomes

The success of reform depended on convincing Russian society that cutting subsidies and achieving macroeconomic stabilization was inevitable because the government would be implacable in pursuing stabilization. This proved impossible to achieve. Consequently, none of the things that stabilization was supposed to secure came to pass: the connection between money and economic exchange remained weak, new economic agents did emerge but not at the expense of old ones whose economic power was based on relational capital, economic and social structures continued to be dominated by the nontradable sector, and the state-supporting sector of the economy remained small.

The reasons for reform's failure were both political and economic. Politically, it was impossible to maintain the government's credible commitment to economic reform. The executive branch of the Russian state was divided over reform, with parts of Yeltsin's presidential administration and the vice president, Alexander Rutskoi, working against the reformers in the government—of which Yeltsin was the head as prime minister—under Gaidar. The legislature, the Congress of People's Deputies and Supreme Soviet, soon locked in battle with Yeltsin over a postcommunist constitutional settlement, agitated against economic reform, and weakened the control of radical economic reformers over the government and over monetary policy. Regional governments likewise refused to press reform home, preferring to keep control over their local economies and maintain relationships with local economic managers that had been built up under the planned economy.

Economically, the task was simply too big, and Soviet legacies were too entrenched. Where radical reform had met some success in Eastern Europe after 1989, the planned economy had been less entrenched; political expediency had meant either that it had not been fully introduced or that it had broken down. Either way, there was more private and international economic activity in countries like Poland before radical reform was introduced; there were therefore social groups and international economic relations that supported reform. Such supports did not exist in Russia; reform met only with resistance.

Politically, the result of this was that Yeltsin backtracked on reform, moving from a reformist government to a loose coalition government in which representatives of old economic elites balanced reformists in an unhappy consensus government. Clashes at the meeting of the Congress of People's Deputies parliamentary sessions in April 1992 forced Yeltsin to compromise over the government and appoint ministers with backgrounds in Soviet industry. In June 1992, Yeltsin was forced by the Congress to step aside as prime minister. Although he secured Gaidar's appointment as his replacement, it was only as acting prime minister. Finally, in December 1992, the Congress refused to ratify Gaidar's appointment, and he was replaced by Viktor Chernomyrdin, one of the ministers with a background in Soviet industry who had been brought into government in the compromises in April 1992.[37] Yeltsin's personal power was guaranteed by these personnel changes, enabling him to defeat his parliamentary rivals and install a constitution guaranteeing presidential political supremacy. But the changes and the general political chaos that came from Yeltsin's struggle with the legislature meant that it was impossible for the government to persuade anyone that its commitment to reform was credible. Changes to government and opposition meant that reform was chipped away at and slowed. The consensus government that Yeltsin built to support his rule did not press reform forward particularly, nor did it roll reform back. Once reform momentum was lost, it was impossible to regain. Even after Yeltsin emerged victorious in the struggle with the legislature over the constitution, he did not use his power for any positive end but tried to maintain the consensus that had secured victory in the first place. Figure 2.2 shows this. It summarizes indices of economic transition produced by the European Bank for Reconstruction and Development.[38] The bank scores economic transition on a scale of 1 to 4, where 1 equals no reforms undertaken and 4 equals complete economic reform in the direction of a market economy. Across the four sets of measures scored in Figure 2.2, there is progress—that is, policies for reform are initiated—at the start of the postcommunist period in Russia. Policy then does not progress, however, but gets locked in place as the political will to progress it declines. After the success at initially introducing reform (some of which happens anyway as the old

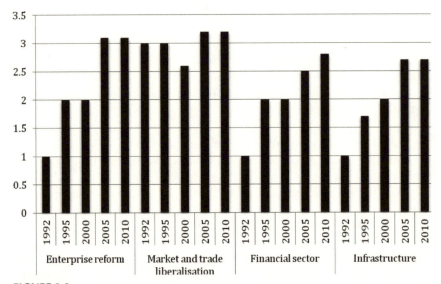

FIGURE 2.2
The Plateaus of Reform. *Source:* **Calculated from data in European Bank for Reconstruction and Development, "Data Base: Structural Indicators," 2001, http:// goo.gl/erjwX.**

system collapses), the reform indicators stay static between 1995 and 2000. Comparatively, and unlike some of its old Eastern European clients, Russia became stuck in a situation of "partial reform."[39]

Economically, the result of reform failure was that policy only dented but did not defeat the networks of relational capital that had developed under the Soviet system. Firms traded with one another on credit (often using fictitious prices), bartered with one another, skimped on wage payments or made them in kind, and avoided paying their energy and tax bills, often with official connivance. These were survival mechanisms for old elites that enabled them to keep their old relational capital in play and politically effective. They served to undermine the push to commercialize economic activity and created what came to be known as the "virtual economy."[40] In this virtual economy, business kept going without exposing itself to competition and ignoring whether it was possible for it to make changes; do without subsidies; become more efficient in the use of labor, tools, and finance; and compete on world markets. Instead, not paying taxes, energy bills, and wages created rent (essentially unearned and undeserved profits); the state (which should have gotten the taxes), private households (wage earners), and the energy firms and society (which owned them still for part of this period and which might have been able to sell energy on world markets for a good profit or at least to have taxed such sales) took the loss (the virtual economy is also discussed in chapter 3).

Subsidies re-created in this fashion were huge. By the end of 1993, overdue payments of wages, taxes, and interfirm debt were equivalent to over 15 percent of GDP.[41] Such subsidies and the behaviors that induced them were not a simple reaction to the onset of reform either: they endured. As table 2.1 shows, wage arrears grew right through the period to the crisis year of 1998. The state did not manage to retrieve its fiscal position either: government balances remained significantly in deficit as firms and regions avoided tax payments or paid in ways that defrauded the state (largely by paying in kind and overestimating the worth of the goods paid in as taxes). As reform was stymied, the transitional depression continued. Instead of economic reform quickly forcing the bottoming out of the depression, GDP and industrial production shrank year by year; the only year of growth was in 1997, but this was far from constituting a recovery. Investment—needed to reverse the relative backwardness inherited from the Soviet Union—contracted rather than grew; instead of attracting investment, Russia witnessed vast amounts of capital flight.[42] Russia maintained its old, Soviet pattern of trade, exporting energy and raw materials (see table 2.1).[43] While this generated a trade surplus, it did not work through the economy to help its modernization. Part of the trade surplus was converted into subsidies; the gas monopoly, Gazprom, was one of the largest subsidizers of industrial

TABLE 2.1
Selected Economic Indicators, 1992–1998

	1992	1993	1994	1995	1996	1997	1998
Gross domestic product (GDP, %)	-14.5	-8.7	-12.6	-4.2	-3.5	0.8	-4.6
General government balance (% GDP)	-18.8	-7.3	-10.4	-6.0	-8.9	-7.9	-8.0
Industrial production (%)	-18.2	-14.2	-20.9	-3.0	-4.0	1.9	-5.2
Fixed investments (%)	-40.0	-12.0	-27.0	-13.0	-18.0	-5.0	-6.7
Trade surplus (U.S.$ billions)	10.6	15.4	17.9	20.4	26.9	19.8	14.4
Metals, metal products, fuels, and precious stones (% of total exports)	68.5	69.9	71.6	68.0	71.1	71.8	69.7
Wage arrears (U.S.$ millions, end of year)	69	614	1,183	2,884	6,221	6,657	8,240
Income inequality (Gini coefficient)	37.1	46.1	44.6	47.1	48.3	—	—

Sources: Calculated from Bank of Finland Institute for Economies in Transition, *Russian Economy—The Month in Review* 6 (2000): 1, 3; European Bank for Reconstruction and Development, *Transition Report 1995: Investment and Enterprise Development* (London: European Bank for Reconstruction and Development, 1995), 205; European Bank for Reconstruction and Development, *Transition Report 1999: Ten Years of Transition* (London: European Bank for Reconstruction and Development, 1999), 260–61; European Bank for Reconstruction and Development, *Transition Report 2001: Energy in Transition* (London: European Bank for Reconstruction and Development, 2001), 189; Organization for Economic Cooperation and Development, *Russian Federation* (Paris: Organization for Economic Cooperation and Development, 1997), 257; Vladimir Tikhomirov, *The Political Economy of Post-Soviet Russia* (Basingstoke: Macmillan, 2000), 23; and Goskomstat, *Rossiiskii statisticheskii ezhegodnik* (Moscow: Goskomstat, 2000), 582–83.

production and was owed over U.S.$10 billion by the middle of 1996 alone; liquidity, as Shleifer and Treisman put it, "was injected into illiquid parts of the economy not in the form of money but in the form of fuel."[44] This subsidy was offset by the energy sector's export earnings and by the state's granting it some autonomy and export privileges. Part of this export revenue never came back to Russia but stayed offshore as capital flight.

Resistance to reform and its erosion as a credible policy meant that the nontradable sector of the Russian economy did not shrink. The state-supporting sector did not grow because the subsidies that maintained the nontradable sector did not shrink; some of that sector could have become profitable and funded the state but did not, as it could not or would not escape from the networks of relational capital developed in the Soviet era. The internationalized sector did not grow—it did become more privatized, as we shall see—because reform did not occur and because the economy was more or less impenetrable to outsiders. The failure to change economic exchange meant that as initial rounds of privatization occurred, the people best placed to exploit them were existing managers. The degree of insider takeovers during privatization was thus very high and management turnover very low.[45] Insider control rebuffed foreign capital that would have balanced out the power that managers had because of their possession of relational capital. This cut large swaths of Russian industry off from investment and technological inflows that might have relieved its relative backwardness. Foreign involvement in the Russian economy was limited to a few service sectors that had been chronically underdeveloped in the Soviet economy and the energy industry; it was, in the words of one commentator, "enclave investment," cut off from and not influencing the rest of the economy.[46]

Since neither the structure of the economy nor the system of economic exchange changed, the balance of power between the state and economic interests remained largely untouched. The immediate effect of this was, as the figures for government balances in table 2.1 show, a permanent fiscal crisis for the Russian state. How the Russian state dealt with this led to changes in the internationalized sector of the economy and, eventually, helped create the August 1998 crisis. Since the state could not generate tax revenues or savings, it dealt with its budget problems in two ways. First, it began to transfer control over strategic firms to private interests in the banking sector. These banks had cash surpluses because they financed foreign trade deals and engaged in currency speculation. They were, therefore, a part of the internationalized sector of the economy. A "loans-for-shares" deal announced in 1995 linked them to some of the main export revenue–earning sectors of the Russian economy (oil and metals companies in particular) and to some other profitable sectors, such as telecommunications. Under the loans-for-shares deal, the banks loaned money to the government for a specified period of time and took over the management of these strategic firms. The banks were supposed to finance the reform of the firms and restructure them during their period of management so that they could be national industrial champions, revenue centers, and models of economic reform. At the end of this period, the firm would be auctioned off. The original loan would be repaid and any profit split between government and bank. In practice, what this meant was that banks lent the government very small amounts of money in comparison to the worth of the firms that they then managed. At the end of the loan period, the banks controlled the auctions and sold to themselves or subsidiary firms for far less than the worth of the firm. The profits were huge: Menatep, for example, gained control over Yukos for U.S.$350 million; Yukos's initial stock market capitalization in 1997 was U.S.$9 billion.[47] The effect of this was to privatize firms that had been state supporting and to put their revenues in the hands of a few bankers.

Second, the government borrowed directly from the banks as it entered the short-term bond market. The sale of bonds began in late 1994 and by the spring of 1997 equaled 12 percent of GDP.[48] As with the loans-for-shares scheme, this was very profitable for the banks. Interest rates for the bonds were very high to encourage lenders to roll over debt into fresh bond issues. The speed and extent of the growth of the short-term bond markets eventually exceeded the capacity of domestic Russian banks to fund loans to government in this way. At the end of 1996, the market for government short-term debt was opened to foreign lenders who would work through Russian banks to buy government bonds.

The loans-for-shares scheme and the emergence of a government debt market changed the internationalized sector of the economy, linking banks to production in sectors that could compete in the global economy and linking them to international financial markets without particularly expanding it. These developments saw the emergence of financial industrial groups (FIGs)[49] and of the oligarchic economy, that is, the concentration of economic power in the hands of a group of financiers who had a considerable media presence and political clout.[50] The power of these oligarchs was considerable over economic production given the size and strategic role of the firms that they had come to control.[51] However, this growth of the internationalized sector did not translate into greater support for the state despite the connivance of the government in its creation. Borrowing on the bond market was expensive and had to roll over debt from one loan period to the next. Tax revenues did not improve, even after reforms in the mid-1990s to try to force up revenues (see chapter 3 for more details). Not only did firms in the nontradable sector operating in the virtual economy not pay taxes and seek to get subsidies, but so too did FIGs, which sought to increase profits through tax avoidance, nonpayment of bills, and so on. Part of the profitable internationalized sector, in other words, tried to pass itself off as part of the virtual economy/nontradable sector to increase the amounts of profit that it could make from the state.

This had two effects. First, it meant that the state remained weak. In essence, the state-supporting sector of the economy was just a regime-supporting sector; that is, it provided only enough income to help Yeltsin and his immediate political coterie stay in power. The rest of the state—the armed and security forces, the welfare systems, and so on—were left to fend as best they could. As a result, they decayed, with obvious social and other effects. For example, life expectancy fell (see also chapter 5), and military performance in the wars in Chechnya was poor. The collapse of social protection under conditions of financial crisis, coupled with the extraordinary profits made by FIGs through deception, bonds, and loans-for-shares deals, underlay the deep gulf that grew up in Russia in the 1990s between rich and poor. Table 2.1 shows this in its last row, which records the growth of income inequality in the 1990s through a standardized measure (a Gini coefficient). The higher this coefficient is on a scale of 1 to 100, the greater the gap between the top and bottom income groups. Some change was to be expected, as Soviet income policies ended with reform, but the growth of inequality (in 1988 the Soviet Union had a low Gini coefficient of 23.8) was much more rapid and higher in Russia than in other postsocialist states undergoing reform in Eastern Europe at the same time.[52]

Second, the collapse of state financing eventually became inevitable. There were efforts at improving the financial position of the government after Yeltsin's reelection as president in 1996, but to no avail. Disputes over property between oligarchs spilled over into government; parliament, which at this time had a Communist Party plurality, objected to reform measures; a dip in oil prices dried up essential revenue; and international lenders, who now underpinned government borrowing on the short-term bond market, began to withdraw their money as the 1997 Asian crisis spread to Russia. The result, in August 1998, was a crash. The government debt market collapsed, and the defense of the ruble rapidly became unsustainable. The ruble had to be allowed to float, leading to a rapid devaluation, and a moratorium on debt repayments was announced.[53]

From Bust to (Oil) Boom: The 2000s

The August 1998 crisis showed that the dual demands of the virtual economy and of the oligarchs at the summit of the internationalized sector could not be reconciled: something had to give financially and duly did. Over the next few years, the balance of power in the economy changed, and economic growth restarted. These changes were in some ways surprising: Russia was a partially reformed economic system, and such systems were supposed to be resistant to further change because of the power of economically successful winner groups like the oligarchs who dominated the internationalized sector of the Russian economy.[54] The oligarchs, divided into competing factions and compromised by their association with the failures of the 1990s, were unable to stop the state from consolidating its power. Oligarchic power turned out to be a straw man; when pressed, they protected themselves and did not work in concert as a group.[55] Their power collapsed. First, those with media interests were disenfranchised. The rest were then disciplined and warned to stay out of politics. The power of the oligarchs proved to be great only in the absence of strong political power.

Putin was able to change the balance of power in the economy because a major outcome of the August 1998 crisis was political rather than economic. The crisis strained the relationship between Yeltsin and the economic and regional elites who had supported him and led to intense political competition over who would control the succession to Yeltsin.[56] To preserve his power and to protect his chance of handpicking a successor, Yeltsin had to fall back on his constitutional powers rather than rely on balancing the interests of the various factions that surrounded him. These constitutional powers had previously protected Yeltsin but had not really been used to produce any grand, positive political outcomes. Now they were used to secure, eventually, Vladimir Putin's ascension as prime minister and hence to the post of acting president when Yeltsin resigned on New Year's Eve 1999.

Economically, the immediate effects of the crisis were panic and bank runs, but this soon passed. The influence of a financial crisis in an economy that is not heavily dependent on a well-developed system of financial intermediation—banks, credit markets, personal loans, and so on—is limited.[57] Russia's firms and families did not on the whole have debts since markets for company and personal credit were small; the banks had made their money through currency speculation, loans for shares, and the government bond market, not through long-term lending to small firms or credit cards and mortgage loans. The collapse of the government bond market meant losses (some of which were passed over to foreign lenders) and some bank closures, but the apex of the internationalized sector of the economy survived: if you control a few billion dollars of oil reserves that you brought for a few hundred million dollars, you can take a hit on the financial markets. In political terms, the economy recovered very quickly, and this helped the consolidation of Putin's power. Devaluation of the ruble meant that imports contracted and domestic industry became competitive without having to reform. The transitional recession meant that there was spare industrial capacity that could meet increased domestic demand as people brought local rather than imported goods. Investment, which would have been hard to come by because of the financial crisis, was thus not needed to stimulate increased output. As table 2.2 shows, August

TABLE 2.2
Selected Economic Indicators, 1999–2010

	1999	2000	2001	2002	2003	2004	2005	2006	2007	2008	2009	2010
Government balance (% gross domestic product [GDP])	−0.9	1.9	3.0	0.9	1.3	4.5	8.1	8.4	6.0	4.9	−6.2	−5.3
GDP (% change, real terms)	6.4	10.0	5.1	4.7	7.4	7.2	6.4	8.2	8.5	5.2	−7.9	4.4
Industrial output (% change)	11.0	8.7	4.9	3.1	8.9	8.0	5.1	6.3	6.3	2.1	−10.8	
Private consumption (% change GDP)	−2.9	7.3	9.5	8.5	7.5	12.1	11.8	11.4	13.7	10.7	−8.1	
Public consumption (% change GDP)	3.1	2.0	−0.8	2.6	2.2	2.1	1.3	2.4	3.4	2.9	1.9	
Metals, metal products, fuels and precious stones (% of total exports)	72.7	75.5	81.4	76.9	75.3	78.0	81.6	82.2	80.8	91.0	90.3	
Income inequality (Gini coefficient)			39.6	35.7			37.5		43.6	42.2		

Sources: Calculated from European Bank for Reconstruction and Development, "Data Base: Macro Economic Indicators," 2011, http://goo.gl/Nv5HB; Rosstat, *Rossiya v tsifrakh: 2004* (Moscow: Rosstat, 2004), 405; Rosstat, *Rossiya v tsifrakh: 2007* (Moscow: Rosstat, 2007), 463; Rosstat, *Rossiya v tsifrakh: 2010* (Moscow: Rosstat, 2010), 528; and World Bank, "Indicators: Russian Federation," 2011, http://goo.gl/H2qAc.

1998 was not the precursor of a further transitional dip but rather marked the moment that the Russian economy began to grow; GDP and industrial output expanded in 1999, and the fiscal deficit shrank to a post-Soviet low before entering a period of surpluses that lasted until the international crisis impacted Russia in late 2008. Private consumption dipped in 1999 as the crisis hit household budgets but soon rose again—and rose dramatically. The state's stronger fiscal position also enabled it to expand its spending, albeit cautiously so as not to be inflationary, so that public consumption rose.

The first thing that we should note about this change in economic circumstances was that it was coincidental with the increased power in the Kremlin under Putin; it did not follow on from that change in political power. Changing political fortunes did not cause economic change; if anything, the opposite is the case since Putin's popularity—on which much of his ability to rule rested—was (and is and probably will be) very much related to economic fortune, in particular to the wealth that high oil prices produced.[58] Putin's administrations made some effort at economic reform, but again it was not followed through. As figure 2.2 shows, reform indicators improved between 2000 and 2005 but reached a plateau again and did not shift upward from 2005 to 2010. Overall, governance in the economy did not improve, and economic reform was often compromised by the poverty of public administration and because of political risk; when reform looked likely to provoke a public backlash, an oil-rich administration backed away from it. The 2005 monetization of welfare benefits is a case in point. Some welfare payments were paid in kind as a legacy of Soviet social policy to groups like veterans; these groups received things like free transport, medicine, and health care. Plans to replace the benefits in kind with money payments largely failed since poor public administration meant that much of the reform could not be implemented, certain key provisions of the policy were delayed after protest, and regional governments were unable to administer the policy.[59]

Building up power within the Kremlin did not, therefore, translate into the development of the state as an engine for economic management and change. Putin's achievement was in a narrow political field of regime consolidation rather than in the larger field of state building. There was, of course, some spillover between the processes of regime consolidation and state building since success in consolidating power in the Kremlin unified decision making and gave Putin more control over the economy than Yeltsin had possessed. Putin was ruthless at ensuring that the state-supporting sector of the economy expanded through changes in revenue raising (see chapter 3) and via direct control over parts of the internationalized sector of the economy. The most famous example of the latter was the takeover of the Yukos oil firm,[60] but this was just the apex of an extension of state supervision over major firms during this period. This secured the state's revenue position and bound part of the economic elite closer to the presidency. But this is not the same thing as developing state capacity.[61] Russia's scores on the World Bank's governance scores for Russia barely changed at all after a brief improvement at the end of the Yeltsin period (for a graphical representation of this, see figure 9.1 in chapter 9).

Since reform of the economy and political system did not drive growth, Russia had to rely on good fortune coupled with some fiscal prudence. As we have already seen, after the crisis of 1998, growth was initially driven by the devaluation of the ruble; subsequently, much of the growth that occurred was due to the boom in hydrocarbon prices. Some measure of this can be seen in figure 2.3, which tracks the development of oil prices and per capita GDP in Russia; there is a close relationship between the two. It is not the case, of course, that changes in oil prices are the sole factor affecting GDP, and even where oil prices are important, they will be mediated by and through other things. However, the very close relationship between the two is illustrative of the degree to which Russian growth was dependent on oil prices and on the expansion of oil production, which until the early 2000s had been stagnant in Russia. Russia had two oil booms in the 2000s. The first was brought about by the merciless exploitation of rents by their private owners in 2000–2004. The export value of oil, gas, and metals nearly doubled in dollar terms between 1998 and 2002. This was due partly to increased prices and partly to increased

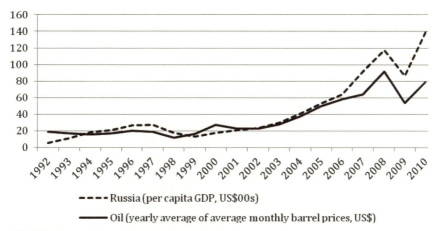

- - - - Russia (per capita GDP, US$00s)

———— Oil (yearly average of average monthly barrel prices, US$)

FIGURE 2.3
Oil Prices and Russian Gross Domestic Product. *Sources:* Calculated from data in Index Mundi, "Crude Oil (Petroleum) Monthly Price," 2011, http://goo.gl/XzSTu, and European Bank for Reconstruction and Development, "Data Base: Macro Economic Indicators," 2011, http://goo.gl/Nv5HB.

export volumes, as economic actors cashed in on assets acquired under Yeltsin. Oil exports rose between 2000 and 2002, and six major private oil firms accounted for nearly all these additional exports; state-owned firms barely expanded production. This expansion of oil exports accounted for about a quarter of Russia's growth in 2001–2004.[62] Russia had a kind of resource windfall, therefore, even before the better-known spike in energy prices between 2005 and 2008 leading to the second oil boom. Again, the limited range of Russia's exports and dependency on energy and metals for the bulk of its exports can be seen in table 2.2: they never accounted for less than 70 percent of exports in this period and were often much more (see also chapter 7).

Growth was thus spectacular, but its base, as the Organization for Economic Cooperation and Development noted, rested more on "temporary factors" than on deep-seated structural change.[63] The institutional bases of development remained weak, in particular the development of the Russian financial system, where the state began to squeeze out private banks but did not resolve the problem of the availability of credit to Russian business. Foreign investment was frequently *not* foreign but came from tax havens to which Russian money had been directed in order to avoid taxes. The foreign investment and borrowing that did occur went to the large enterprises in export sectors (energy and metals) and/or was spent not on modernization but on asset acquisition and mergers by Russian firms, acquisitions that were frequently overseas. There was some expansion of the service and construction sectors, but overall the economy did not diversify or modernize, and the parameters of the nontradable and internationalized economies remained much the same. Russia's competitiveness did not improve either generally or in comparison with other emerging market economies.[64] As the international financial crisis began to hit Russia in late 2008, labor and capital productivity were only 26 percent that of the United States in five sectors (retail banking, housing construction, retailing, electricity generation, and steel production).[65]

Since the economy did not change to become more diversified from energy dependency, how did it survive given that much of it was noncompetitive? The answer, again, is subsidies, which Russia could, thanks to the energy booms, now afford. Again, the source of these subsidies was energy. Domestic energy prices remained below international market prices so that the subsidies to industry remained in place. This perpetuated a key plank of what had been the virtual economy under Yeltsin, transferring value from the energy sectors to the rest of the economy and in particular to the highly energy-inefficient industrial economy. Under Yeltsin, this had led to demonetization, the nonpayment of taxes and wages, or their payment in kind. These were now paid in money, thanks in part to tax reform and also because of the remonetization caused by the 1998 crisis and the greater wealth created by the energy booms. Both booms provided means to transfer value from the energy sectors to the rest of the economy so that it continued to be a hybrid between the "normal" market and the virtual economy.[66]

Subsidies were also indirect, routed through other parts of the state. The Central Bank of Russia intervened in currency markets to try to protect Russian industry from imports and maintain competitiveness. This intervention slowed the appreciation of the ruble. Appreciation was still significant and fast, so the bank was constantly chasing a moving and costly target. However, the bank could deal with this thanks to the massive revenues earned from oil and gas sales. This massive intervention helped maintain some industrial competitiveness by leaving the ruble undervalued by about 10 to 20 percent.[67] This was, in effect, another subsidy to Russian producers—another transfer of value from energy sectors made through the state—but it was only partially successful since the volume of imports grew at a greater rate than domestic production so that there was, excluding oil and gas, a growing trade deficit.[68] In many ways, Putin was getting the worst of both worlds, using the Central Bank to subsidize domestic-oriented industry from oil revenues but still seeing its uncompetitive nature as imports grew using oil money and as this money funded the growth of nontradable sectors in construction and services. Still, intervention helped to maintain some growth in domestic industrial output even if this growth was primarily directed to satisfying domestic demand and did not lead to parts of industry leaving the nontradable for the internationalized economic sector.

The internationalized sector did not lose out totally from this situation. The revenues generated by record global energy prices and the availability of cheap credit in the United States and Europe meant that it was cheap for Russia's major businesses to borrow in foreign currency: on average, the ruble cost of dollar loans was 1 percent between 2003 and mid-2007. There was therefore a flurry of borrowing by Russia's major firms, such as the aluminum concern Rusal, and by many state-owned firms, including the oil company Rosneft and the gas giant Gazprom. This borrowing was done partly to generate investment revenue for development in Russia in the absence of a developed domestic banking sector and partly to fund purchases outside Russia as firms bought both upstream and downstream and developed as global players in metals and energy. The borrowing on global markets suited the Russian government since it created investment and suited the firms involved since it spread their assets and sometimes their ownership beyond Russia, thus freeing them from some of the risk to economic actors inherent in Russia (see chapter 4). The very low rates at which borrowing took place represented a subsidy from energy production to the borrowers. External borrowing by industry, including state-owned firms and corporations, reached $307 billion in June 2008, and the financial sector borrowed another $200 billion by June 2008—all told some 40 percent of GDP.[69]

In Place of a Conclusion: Crisis Again, but Reform?

It was this borrowing that was to become a problem as economic crisis spread from the West to Russia in 2007–2008. The Russian government was well aware of its general economic vulnerability before the crisis hit. As part of planning for the presidential succession, Putin outlined how the economy was to be developed over the course of 2008–2020 using a combination of foreign investment and the strategic spending of reserves built up from energy revenues.[70] This type of thinking then fed into the rhetoric on "moderniza-tion" that became the signature tune of Putin's successor, Dmitri Medvedev. By modernization, Medvedev meant diversification away from dependency on energy as the motor of economic growth and technological renewal. In other words, Medvedev's and Putin's intentions were directed at dealing with the same problems that have beset all Russian leaders since the gains made in the first wave of Soviet industrialization lost their luster: they wanted to end relative backwardness. However, the problem remained (and remains): who is to move to end backwardness, and who leads reform? Although the economy grew up until the global economic crisis, it did not create a large set of new economic actors able or willing to lead change. The antireform social structure that was a legacy of the Soviet system and that had mutated into the virtual economy of the 1990s was not as visible as it had once been but was still present in the close connections between economic and political elites. These connections could save a firm or condemn it, as Sakwa shows in chapter 4. They created uncertainty over property rights so that invest-ment remained low and capital flight high—with obvious implications for overcoming relative backwardness. The question that was permanently posed by Russia's economic problems remained the same: would economic policy initiatives alone be enough to deal with these problems, to create an environ-ment in which modernization could happen? If the answer to this question is no, who is to launch what kind of change, how extensive is it to be, and who, politically and economically, will bear the cost, and will they tolerate it?

The initial model of modernization that Putin proposed in 2008 sought change through the agency of the state, through the creation of national development projects and the creation of new national industrial champions in high-tech areas such as nanotechnology. This idea has carried through under Medvedev into projects such as the Skolkovo Foundation development outside Moscow.[71] Before the crisis and the end of Russia's growth spurt, this type of solution could be presented as being adequate to Russia's needs. It looked to solve the problems of the Russian economy—not diversified enough, too reliant on oil, too backward, and in need of new export sectors that would generate revenues for the state from new internationalized economic sectors in case oil and gas prices slip—and to do so in a way that was nonconfrontational. New sectors of the economy would grow and supplant the old gradually while the already internationalized sectors of the economy spread through their foreign borrowings and acquisitions. Change would not, therefore, be disruptive and could be contained within the political and economic arrangements that had made Russia stable under Putin after the crisis years of Yeltsin.

The crisis, even if it did not produce any fresh solutions, ended this path to change. The crisis hit Russia from three angles: first, there was spillover from the international financial crisis; second, global energy prices fell; and, third, confidence in Russia fell because of the war with Georgia, which led to capital flight and tightened lending to Russia. Together, these lowered Russia's growth (see table 2.2), hit its budget, and raised the costs of state and private firm borrowing. In many ways, the governmental response was in line with the responses made by governments elsewhere to the crisis in 2008–2009: it increased its spending in order to try to alleviate the crisis and provide credit in the economy. It was helped in this by its reserve funds built up from oil wealth so that it was not pushed as far into deficit as would otherwise have been the case given the fall in tax revenues as energy prices fell. The form that this relief took reflected the peculiarities of Russia's economy. Whereas much effort in liberal capitalist economies was concentrated on replacing (or stabilizing) the banks as lenders, Russian policy supported, stabilized, and preserved the politically sensitive areas of the economy and reduced their exposure to foreign influences. Initially, this focused on alleviating pressure on those elements of the Russian economy that had borrowed heavily in foreign currency. This credit was no longer cheap, as falling oil prices and the fallout of the Georgian war put pressure on the ruble and threatened to raise the costs of debt repayment. As the ruble began to slide with falling energy prices and as foreign capital fled Russia or simply dried up, the costs of repaying loans rose and the possibility of rolling them over decreased. The government stepped in to relieve the pressure on these firms. It did so, first, by delaying the collapse in value of the ruble so as to slow the rate at which the cost of loan repayments grew. This was little more than a wait-and-see policy created by a belief that the fall in energy prices would be short lived and that the negative economic effects of the Georgian war would dissipate and by a misplaced confidence that had led Medvedev, Putin, and the government to see crisis initially as an American problem.

This head-in-the-sand position could not last, however, as it soon began to drain the state's reserves and threaten the state's ability to mediate between the domestic and the global economy. A variety of anticrisis measures were therefore introduced throughout 2008 and into 2009. Again, the chief focus of this was to relieve the pressure on the major firms—some state owned—that had foreign loans. Generally, therefore, companies at the apex of the economy benefited most from the anticrisis measures, the relationship of the internationalized sectors of the Russian economy to the global economy was maintained, and government control over them was expanded. The government essentially took over their debts, directly and indirectly, by providing government credit guarantees and interest rate subsidies, stalling tax payments, and setting preferential export and import tariffs. The chief beneficiaries of these policies were energy firms, metals producers and other rent-generating firms, and those whose closure would have the greatest social impact because of the dominance of local economies (one-company towns).[72] This minimized the damage to the elites and to those areas of the country where an economic downturn would have sparked protest while keeping the government at the center of economic management. The cost fell both on households, as devaluation eventually decreased real wages, and on firms that lacked access to the government's largesse. Some of these briefly reverted to the practices of barter that had kept them "solvent" in the 1990s.

The anticrisis measures that were adopted thus supported elite interests rather than fostering the diversification of the economy through the protection of small and medium-size enterprises. In general, these smaller firms benefited only partially and at secondhand from the anticrisis measures. Thus, when the crisis began to abate at the end of 2009, recovery was not based on any change in economic activity but was led, once more, by the oil sector and driven by fresh rises in energy prices in 2009 and after (figure 2.3). The prospects of any change from this reliance on oil were also probably reduced by the anticrisis measures. Although the anticrisis measures staved off the collapse of Russia's banks, they were nevertheless weakened, and their borrowing power—and hence their ability to channel money into the wider economy—was reduced. The large firms bailed out by the government have been able to roll their debts over and extend their credit thanks to the support of the government, but Russian banks were unable so to do.[73] As a result, lending to firms by Russian banks was small in the aftermath of the crisis, and the banks' position was weakened and made more dependent on the state.

The crisis did not, therefore, mark a break with the past: in the words of one group of Russian analysts, "the opportunities that the crisis offered for modernization were wasted."[74] Russia was cushioned by its wealth and saved by a stabilization of oil prices that kept them above the range (initially U.S.$60 to U.S.$70 per barrel and, more recently, U.S.$100 to U.S.$120 per barrel) at which its budget was forecast to break even. In the end, the anticrisis measures amounted to another transfer of social wealth generated by the energy boom to the apex of the economy, with little appreciable gain in terms of dealing with the problems that had exposed Russia to the crisis in the first place. The reliance on oil was deep. The total budget deficit caused by the crisis and the measures adopted to deal with it was modest, about 6.4 percent of GDP, but the non-oil deficit was more than twice this as a percentage of GDP and far in excess of estimates of what would be sustainable from oil revenues over the longer term.[75] The transformative effects of this spending, however, were weak because of its concentration on minimizing the exposure of large firms; many of the anticrisis measures have been described as ineffective and were introduced only after the crisis had passed. As one Russian analyst has put it, the "government continues the game as before. . . . There is no guarantee that the allocated money will be used to develop advanced technologies and expand production, rather than to cover losses or new currency and financial speculation."[76]

Crisis and the government's response to it has raised questions over whether reform should be made broader and should include some breaking down of political power generally and over the economy specifically.[77] Medvedev responded to these questions in 2011 by ordering the removal of state representatives from the boards of major firms and calling for the reorganization of the state's development agencies, control of corruption, and the improvement of public administration in order to facilitate a better investment climate.[78] Following the December 2011 elections and the protests that followed, Putin, now candidate for reelection to the presidency, joined with calls for reforms in politics to support economic diversification. Declarations of intent are, however, a long way from results, as we have seen repeatedly in this chapter, especially when the range of problems to be confronted is so great.

Notes

1. For such, see Alec Nove, *An Economic History of the USSR*, rev. ed. (London: Penguin, 1993); János Kornai, *The Socialist System: The Political Economy of Socialism* (Oxford: Clarendon Press, 1992); and Philip Hanson, *The Rise and Fall of the Soviet Economy: An Economic History of the USSR 1945–1991* (London: Longman, 2003).

2. Many commentaries on Russia will be cited below. For summaries of the debates on reform policy, see Gérard Roland, *Transition and Economics: Politics, Markets, and Firms* (Cambridge, MA: MIT Press, 2000); Martin Myant and Jan Drahokoupil, *Transition Economies: Political Economy in Russia, Eastern Europe, and Central Asia* (London: Wiley, 2011); and Gerard Turley and Peter J. Luke, *Transition Economics: Two Decades On* (London: Routledge, 2010).

3. Joseph Stalin, "O zadachakh khozyaistvennikov: Rech' na pervoi Vsesoyuznoi konferentsii rabotnikov sotsialisticheskoi promyshlennosti, 4 fevralya 1931g," in *Voprosy Leninizma*, by Joseph Stalin, 355–63 (Moscow: Gospolitizdat, 1952), 362.

4. There is a large literature on these issues dating back to the 1920s. For summaries, see Michael Ellman, *Socialist Planning*, 2nd ed. (Cambridge: Cambridge University Press, 1989); Peter Rutland, *The Myth of the Plan: Lessons of Soviet Planning Experience* (London: Hutchinson, 1985); and Kornai, *The Socialist System*. An excellent fictional explanation of the problems and their outcomes can be found in Francis Spufford, *Red Plenty* (London: Faber & Faber, 2010).

5. Ed Hewitt, *Reforming the Soviet Economy: Equality versus Efficiency* (Washington, DC: Brookings Institution, 1988), 185.

6. Stephen Whitefield, *Industrial Power and the Soviet State* (Oxford: Clarendon Press, 1993).

7. Kornai, *The Socialist System*, 160, 163.

8. Kornai, *The Socialist System*, 166–68, 175.

9. Hewitt, *Reforming the Soviet Economy*, 89–90.

10. Stephen Kotkin, *Armageddon Averted: The Soviet Collapse 1970–2000* (Oxford: Oxford University Press, 2001).

11. Linda J. Cook, *The Soviet Social Contract and Why It Failed: Welfare Policy and Workers' Politics from Brezhnev to Gorbachev* (Cambridge, MA: Harvard University Press, 1994).

12. Thane Gustafson, *Crisis amid Plenty: The Politics of Soviet Energy under Brezhnev and Gorbachev* (Princeton, NJ: Princeton University Press, 1989), 36.

13. Paul R. Gregory, *The Political Economy of Stalinism: Evidence from the Soviet Secret Archives* (Cambridge: Cambridge University Press, 2004), 271.

14. Kornai, *The Socialist System*, 298–300.

15. Susan Collins and Dani Rodrik, *Eastern Europe and the Soviet Union in the World Economy* (Washington, DC: Institute for International Economics, 1992), 51.

16. D. Kuzin, "Rossiiskaya ekonomika na mirovoi rynke: problema konkurentosobnosti," *Obshchestvo i Ekonomika* 3 (1993): 33.

17. Roland McKinnon, *The Order of Economic Liberalization*, 2nd ed. (Baltimore: Johns Hopkins University Press, 1993); Clifford Gaddy and Barry Ickes, "Russia's Virtual Economy," *Foreign Affairs* 77, no. 5 (1998): 53–67.

18. Anders Åslund, *Gorbachev's Struggle for Economic Reform*, 2nd ed. (London: Pinter, 1989), 17.

19. Goskomstat SSSR, *SSSR v tsifrakh v 1987 godu* (Moscow: Goskomstat, 1987), 32.

20. Goskomstat, *Rossiiskii statisticheskii ezhegodnik* (Moscow: Goskomstat, 2000), 630.

21. Erik Hoffman and Roy Laird, *The Politics of Economic Modernization in the Soviet Union* (Ithaca, NY: Cornell University Press, 1982).

22. Matthew Wyman, *Public Opinion in Postcommunist Russia* (Basingstoke: Macmillan, 1997), 211.

23. David Woodruff, *Money Unmade: Barter and the Fate of Russian Capitalism* (Ithaca, NY: Cornell University Press, 1999).

24. János Kornai, "The Soft Budget Constraint," *Kyklos* 39, no. 1 (1986): 3–30, and Kornai, *The Socialist System*, 140–44.

25. On the politicoadministrative roots of particularistic exchange in the Soviet Union, see Michael E. Urban, "Conceptualizing Political Power in the USSR: Pat-

terns of Binding and Bonding," *Studies in Comparative Communism* 18, no. 4 (1985): 207–26, and Neil Robinson, *Russia: A State of Uncertainty* (London: Routledge, 2002).

26. Clifford Gaddy and Barry Ickes, *Russia's Virtual Economy* (Washington, DC: Brookings Institution, 2002), 55–58.

27. See, for example, Peter Reddaway and Dmitri Glinsky, *The Tragedy of Russia's Reforms: Market Bolshevism against Democracy* (Washington, DC: United States Institute for Peace Press, 2001).

28. Neil Robinson, "The Presidency: The Politics of Institutional Chaos," in *Institutions and Political Change in Russia*, ed. Neil Robinson, 11–40 (Basingstoke: Macmillan, 2000).

29. See Andrew Barnes, *Owning Russia: The Struggle over Factories, Farms, and Power* (Ithaca, NY: Cornell University Press, 2006), and chapter 4 in this volume.

30. Vadim Volkov, *Violent Entrepreneurs: The Use of Force in the Making of Russian Capitalism* (Ithaca, NY: Cornell University Press, 2002).

31. For a discussion of similar terms in relation to interests in capitalist economies, see Geoffrey Garrett and Peter Lange, "Internationalization, Institutions and Political Change," in *Internationalization and Domestic Politics*, ed. Robert O. Keohane and Helen V. Milner, 48–75 (Cambridge: Cambridge University Press, 1996).

32. Neil Robinson, "Path Dependency, Global Economy and Post-Communist Change," in *Reforging the Weakest Link: Global Political Economy and Post-Soviet Change in Russia, Ukraine and Belarus*, ed. Neil Robinson, 106–26 (Aldershot: Ashgate, 2004).

33. Matthew Evangelista, "Stalin's Revenge: Institutional Barriers to Internationalization in the Soviet Union," in Keohane and Milner, *Internationalization and Domestic Politics*, 159–85.

34. The basic reform strategy adopted in Russia was laid out in speeches made by Yeltsin in October 1991 and January 1992 (*Sovetskaya Rossiya*, October 29, 1991, and *Rossiiskaya gazeta*, January 17, 1992) in the memorandum on economic reform written by Gaidar and Georgii Matyukhin (then head of the Russian Central Bank) in *Nezavisimaya gazeta*, March 3, 1992, and in Russian Government, "Medium-Term Programme of the Economic Reforms of the Russian Government," *Russian Economic Trends* 1, no. 3 (1992): 43–69.

35. Neil Robinson, "The Global Economy, Reform and Crisis in Russia," *Review of International Political Economy* 6, no. 4 (1999): 531–64.

36. Woodruff, *Money Unmade*, 12–13.

37. Chernomyrdin represented the energy industry, having worked for nearly his entire career in the Soviet gas industry. He became the Soviet minister for gas in 1985 and from this position was a founder and the first chairman of Gazprom, the state-owned enterprise and gas monopolist that replaced the old Ministry of Gas. Victor Chernomyrdin, *Так govoril Chernomyrdin: O sebe, o zhizni, o Rossii* (Moscow: Eksmo, 2011).

38. European Bank for Reconstruction and Development, "Data Base: Structural Indicators," 2011, http://goo.gl/erjwX.

39. Joel S. Hellman, "Winners Take All: The Politics of Partial Reform in Postcommunist Transitions," *World Politics* 50, no. 2 (1998): 203–34.

40. Gaddy and Ickes, "Russia's Virtual Economy"; Gaddy and Ickes, *Russia's Virtual Economy*.

41. Vladimir Tikhomirov, *The Political Economy of Post-Soviet Russia* (Basingstoke: Macmillan, 2000), 22–23.

42. Vladimir Tikhomirov, "Capital Flight from Post-Soviet Russia," *Europe-Asia Studies* 49, no. 4 (1997): 591–615.

43. See also the figures in I. N. Ustinov, *Mezhdunarodniye ekonomicheskie otnosheniya Rossii: Entsiklopediya statisticheskaya* (Moscow: Ekonomika, 2004), 125–79.

44. Andrei Shleifer and Daniel Treisman, *Without a Map: Political Tactics and Economic Reform in Russia* (Cambridge, MA: MIT Press, 2000), 76.

45. Igor Filototchev, Mike Wright, and Michael Bleaney, "Privatization, Insider Control and Managerial Entrenchment in Russia," *Economics of Transition* 7, no. 2 (1999): 481–504; on the policies of privatization, see Barnes, *Owning Russia*.

46. Andrei Kuznetsov, *Foreign Investment in Contemporary Russia: Managing Capital Entry* (Basingstoke: Macmillan, 1994).

47. Richard Sakwa, *The Quality of Freedom: Khodorkovsky, Putin, and the Yukos Affair* (Oxford: Oxford University Press, 2009), 44–45; for more details on the program generally, see Barnes, *Owning Russia*, 100–115.

48. European Bank for Reconstruction and Development, *Transition Report 1997: Enterprise Performance and Growth* (London: European Bank for Reconstruction and Development, 1997), 197.

49. Juliet Johnson, "Russia's Emerging Financial Groups," *Post-Soviet Affairs* 13, no. 4 (1998): 333–65; Y. S. Pappe and Y. S. Galukhina, *Rossiiskii krupnii biznes: Pervie 15 let. Ekonomicheskie khroniki 1993–2008* (Moscow: Izdatelskii dom GU VShE, 2009), 39–52.

50. Hans-Hennig Schröder, "El'tsin and the Oligarchs: The Role of Financial Growth in Russian Politics between 1993 and 1998," *Europe-Asia Studies* 51, no. 6 (1999): 957–88.

51. Sergei Guriev and Andrei Rachinsky, "The Role of Oligarchs in Russian Capitalism," *Journal of Economic Perspectives* 19, no. 1 (2005): 131–50.

52. World Bank, "Indicators: Russian Federation," 2011, http://goo.gl/H2qAc; Neil Robinson, "The Myth of Equilibrium: Winner Power, Fiscal Crisis and Russian Economic Reform," *Communist and Post-Communist Studies* 34, no. 4 (2001): 429.

53. There is a large literature on the 1998 crisis and its causes; for a sample, see Tatiana Fic and Omar F. Saqib, "Political Instability and the August 1998 Ruble Crisis," *German Institute for Economic Research Discussion Papers* 626 (2006); Martin Gilman, *No Precedent, No Plan: Inside Russia's 1998 Default* (Cambridge, MA: MIT Press, 2010); Andrei Illarionov, "Mify i uroki Avgustskogo krizisa," *Voprosy ekonomiki* 10 and 11 (1999): 4–19 and 24–48; Thierry Malleret, Natalia Orlova, and Vladimir Romanov, "What Loaded and Triggered the Russian Crisis?," *Post-Soviet Affairs* 15, no. 2 (1999): 107–29; Neil Robinson, "So What Changed? The 1998 Economic Crisis in Russia and Russia's Economic and Political Development," *Demokratizatsiya: A Journal of Post-Soviet Democratization* 15, no. 2 (2007): 245–59; Peter Rutland, "The August 1998 Crash: Causes and Consequences," in *Business and the State in Contemporary Russia*, ed. P. Rutland, 173–86 (Boulder, CO: Westview, 2001); M. L. Shakkum, *Ekonomika Rossii ot krizisa k stabil'nosti k ustoichivomu rostu* (Moscow: Globus, 1999);

and Vladimir Tikhomirov, "The Second Collapse of the Soviet Economy: Myths and Realities of Russian Reform." *Europe-Asia Studies* 52, no. 2 (2000): 207–35.

54. Hellman, "Winners Take All."

55. Robinson, "The Myth of Equilibrium."

56. For a description of the political turmoil of this period, see Timothy J. Colton, *Yeltsin: A Life* (New York: Basic Books, 2008), chap. 16.

57. Neil Robinson, "August 1998 and the Development of Russia's Post-Communist Political Economy," *Review of International Political Economy* 16, no. 3 (2009): 433–55.

58. Daniel Treisman, "Presidential Popularity in a Hybrid Regime: Russia under Yeltsin and Putin," *American Journal of Political Science* 55, no. 3 (2011): 590–609.

59. Cameron Ross, *Local Politics and Democratization in Russia* (London: Routledge, 2008), 116–18; I. Sinitsina, *Experience in Implementing Social Benefits Monetization Reform in Russia: Literature Review* (Warsaw: Case Network Studies & Analyses, 2009).

60. Sakwa, *The Quality of Freedom*, and also chapter 4 in this volume.

61. For an extended analysis, see Brian D. Taylor, *State Building in Putin's Russia: Policing and Coercion after Communism* (Cambridge: Cambridge University Press, 2011), 289–315.

62. Rudiger Ahrend, "Russia's Post-Crisis Growth: Its Sources and Prospects for Continuation," *Europe–Asia Studies* 58, no. 1 (2006): 14–15.

63. Organization for Economic Cooperation and Development, *Russian Federation* (Paris: Organization for Economic Cooperation and Development, 2009), 21.

64. Julian Cooper, "Of BRICS and Brains: Comparing Russia, China, India and Other Populous Emerging Economies," *Eurasian Geography and Economics* 47, no. 3 (2006): 255–84; Julian Cooper, "Can Russia Compete in the Global Economy?," *Eurasian Geography and Economics* 47, no. 4 (2006): 407–26; Raj M. Desai and Itzhak Goldberg, eds., *Can Russia Compete?* (Washington, DC: Brookings Institution, 2008).

65. See McKinsey Global Institute, "Effektivnaya Rossiya: Proizvoditel'nost' kak fundament rosta," 2009, http://goo.gl/9qgIq.

66. Eteri Kvintradze, "Russia's Output Collapse and Recovery: Evidence from the Post-Soviet Transition," *IMF Working Paper* 10/89 (2010).

67. Depending on the methodology used to calculate value, see International Monetary Fund, *Russian Federation: 2007 Article IV Consultation—Staff Report: Staff Statement and Public Information Notice on the Executive Board Discussion* (Washington DC: International Monetary Fund, 2007), 6.

68. Organization for Economic Cooperation and Development, *Russian Federation*, 28.

69. Richard Connolly, "Financial Vulnerabilities in Russia," *Russian Analytical Digest* 65 (2009): 4.

70. Vladimir Putin, "Speech at Expanded Meeting of the State Council on Russia's Development Strategy through to 2020," *Johnson's Russia List* 29 (February 11, 2008).

71. This is supposed to be Russia's version of Silicon Valley, bringing together advanced academic scientific research with high-tech companies, financial services, and business administration programs. This combination is supposed to maximize the commercialization of Russian scientific expertise and act as a magnet for inward investment and technology transfer (see Skolkovo, "The Official Website of the

Skolkovo Foundation," 2011, http://goo.gl/GRuOj). It is also supposed to be a model for other areas to follow.

72. See the list of beneficiaries in Gosudarstvenii universitet—Vysshaya shkola ekonomiki (GU–VSE), Mezhvedomstvenii analyticheskii tsentr, "Otsenka antikrizisnikh mer po podderzhke real'nogo sektora rossiiskoi ekonomiki," *Voprosy ekonomiki* 5 (2009): 21–46.

73. World Bank, *Russian Economic Report* 21 (2010): 11.

74. N. K. Akindova, S. V. Alekashenko, and E. G. Yasin, *Scenarios and Challenges of Macroeconomic Policy: Report at XII International Conference on Economic and Social Development, Moscow, April 5–7, 2011* (Moscow: Higher School of Economics Publishing House, 2011), 5.

75. Akindova et al., *Scenarios and Challenges of Macroeconomic Policy*, 13.

76. S. Dzarasov, "The Russian Crisis: Sources and Lessons," *Problems of Economic Transition* 52, no. 5 (2009): 66.

77. Institute for Contemporary Development, *Rossiya XXI veka: Obraz zhelaemogo zavtra* (Moscow: Ekon-Inform, 2010); V. L. Inozemtsev, ed., *Demokratiya i modernizatsiya: K diskusii o vyzovakh XXI veka* (Moscow: Evropa, 2010).

78. See, for example, his speech at a meeting of the Commission on the Modernization and Technological Development of the Russian Economy in Magnitogorsk in March 2011, in Dmitri Medvedev, "Zasedanie Komissii po modernizatsii i tekhnologicheskomu razvitiyu ekonomiki Rossii. 30 marta 2011 goda," 2011, http://kremlin.ru/transcripts/10777.

3

Revenue Imperatives

State over Market in Postcommunist Russia

Gerald M. Easter

A RECURRING THEME IN THE STUDY of the state is that power inevitably finds wealth. What power does to access wealth once it is found, however, is not inevitable. The history of the means by which power acquires wealth—plunder, tribute, rents, and taxation—is the history of the rise of the modern state. The particular means by which power acquires wealth has larger institutional implications for state–society relations. This general observation can be seen in postcommunist state building. In the postcommunist transitions, power was forced to devise new means of accessing wealth, which in turn influenced the subsequent institutional reconfiguration of state and society. Power and wealth relations were sorted out through battles waged in postcommunist tax systems. Here we observe two distinct patterns in Eastern Europe by which power gained access to wealth—taking and trading.

Revenue Imperatives: Taking versus Trading in the Russian State

The differences between accessing wealth by taking or trading are probably obvious. Taking is simply that; it is the impulse to take something from someone else because you can. Taking implies preponderance in power resources, particularly coercion, which enables one to gain access to wealth without having to bargain. The most recognizable forms of taking are plunder and tribute; it represents the ideal typical early modern state conceptualized in Tilly's protection racket model.[1] The main incentive for giving up at least part of one's wealth is that to do otherwise risks physical harm to person or property. It is possible that taking comes instinctually; trading, however, has to be learned. Trading is an alternative means of gaining access to wealth, which may become a more attractive option when the distribution of power resources is more evenly balanced, the costs of using power resources are higher than the economic resources returned, and/or the need to access a particular source of wealth is more frequent. Power still gets wealth but not on its own terms. With trading, wealth is given up as part of an exchange with power; something is received in return—physical security, public goods, social status, or political rights, for example.

Among postcommunist states, Russia represents an example of power and wealth relations based on taking. Extraction by taking is hardly unprecedented in Russian history, where those who control coercive resources have also long controlled economic resources. Instead of a division of coercive and economic resources between state and society, as occurred in some early modern European states, there was a concentration of these power resources in the Russia realm. The state claimed ownership over the most valuable assets in the economy and, as a result, determined the criteria for conferring elite status in society. In the early history of Russian state building, Muscovite princes used force to establish a rent-seeking monopoly on the trade in furs and other forest commodities; in the process, they crushed merchant-run Novgorod and its "trading"-based political institutions. Imperial Russian tsars subsisted on the agricultural resources of an estate economy, whose lords owed their elite status to state service and royal whim. Soviet Russia's Bolshevik bosses briefly employed a "trading"-based extraction strategy of sorts with the peasantry, imposing an agricultural tax on wealthier peasants and allowing for self-taxation in the villages. In exchange, peasant villages were left to run their own affairs. But this arrangement soon gave way in a flourish of coercion. The communist regime's command-administrative system represented a new form of "taking" for the industrial age in which the state forcibly restructured its revenue base into large-scale productive units whose economic wealth could be directly extracted.

The collapse of the communist regime created a new opportunity in Russia for building a system of revenue extraction based on "trading." The neoliberal-inspired rush toward market capitalism was supposed to unleash society's suppressed natural economic instincts. In principle, the postcommunist state would be forced to bargain, or "trade," for tax revenue from a newly arisen set of legally protected, autonomous private economic actors. Of course, this is not what occurred in the 1990s in Russia. By 1998, the state lay in fiscal collapse, and the old inclination for revenue by "taking" was revived. This chapter examines the inherent tensions between "trading" and "taking" in the building of a new postcommunist system of tax collection. It is organized into three parts: 1) the initial attempt and failure to build a system of extraction based on trading, 2) the unleashing of state coercion to return to a system of extraction based on taking, and 3) the effort to reconcile trading and taking in Russia's concessions economy. The larger implications for state–society relations are briefly considered in the conclusion.

Failure of Extraction by Trading under Yeltsin

The dismantling of the command economy and introduction of neoliberal reform marked yet another experiment by the Russian state with a system of revenue extraction based on trading. As in the 1920s, the state withdrew from direct management of the economy and instead sought to subsist by taxing the income of autonomous actors. In late 1991, the Russian government, led by Yegor Gaidar's team of neoliberal market reformers, launched a program of radical economic reform. At this moment, the postcommunist Russia was on the edge of fiscal crisis.

As part of the plan to stabilize state finances, acting Prime Minister Gaidar insisted that "changes in the tax system were most necessary so as not to reduce income to the budget."[2] In late December, the framework for a new tax system, designed for a market economy, was established.[3] The new system was supposed to fundamentally transform revenue extraction by shifting the tax burden: from production to consumption, from the public sector to the private sector, from corporations to households, and from large businesses to smaller ones. The main policy features included a valued-added tax (VAT) and excise taxes, replacing the old turnover tax on enterprises; a corporate income tax (CIT), replacing the profits tax on enterprises; and a personal income tax (PIT) on households.[4] It was modeled after the tax systems of the advanced market economies. Tax rates were high but consistent with the rates throughout Europe. The new tax system fit the transition awkwardly. It was capitalist design built with postcommunist material.

According to Gaidar's revenue strategy, the state would have to wait for the emergence of the market. There was little consideration of any deliberately devised exchange of public goods and services for a share of private wealth. Instead, the assumption seemed simply to be that neoliberal reforms would create new sources of privately generated wealth, which in the near future would become the main source of tax collection. Investment in the public sector would be drastically cut so as to free up investment capital to invigorate the private sector and to starve to death the bureaucratic remnants of the old command economy. In the meantime, to maintain basic levels of essential services and social welfare, the postcommunist state would remain fiscally dependent on the reliable revenues sources of the old regime—lucrative commodity exports, especially from the energy sector. Beyond this, Russia's new government of market reformers did not give much consideration to cultivating societal compliance with the new tax system. In terms of compliance strategies, the conditions that influence taxpayer behavior—exchange, fairness, and cost/risk—all registered negatively: the state did not offer a sufficient exchange for tax payments, the tax burden was distributed unevenly, and the costs of compliance were quite high, while the risk was low.

First, the state drastically curtailed its delivery of public services and goods, which had long subsidized households. Public health deteriorated, education went unfunded, and infrastructure fell into disrepair. In addition, as budget revenues dwindled, public sector employees were repeatedly paid their wages late or not at all. Instead of an exchange for public goods, the popular perception was that tax collections were diverted into the private pockets of tax officials. The government only reinforced this view when it tried to give tax collectors a material incentive to find more income by allowing its revenue agents to keep a share of the taxes they collected in a kind of bureaucratic tax farming scheme.

Second, a sense of fairness in the distribution of the tax burden was lacking. The widespread perception among taxpayers was that fellow citizens were not paying taxes and were not being caught either. Frequent statements to the press by government officials of widespread tax evasion only confirmed this notion. The list of politically favored delinquent large taxpayers was regularly updated in the mass media. The head of the Ministry of Internal Affairs (MVD), in 1998, estimated that as many as 60 million taxpayers (more than 90 percent) were involved in some way in the shadow economy.[5] Tax officialdom's own internally conducted surveys of the public revealed that taxpayers both distrusted the state to provide public goods and distrusted fellow taxpayers to pay their taxes.[6]

Finally, the costs of compliance ran high. The unrestrained competition among federal, regional, and local state administrations to collect revenue undermined any sense of order or routine to the tax collection process. Even if new small and medium-size businesses wanted to comply with their tax obligations, it often meant financial ruin with so many state agents claiming a share of the same income sources. Reporting income ran the risk of further scrutiny of tax administrators. The general uncertainty about rates and competing revenue claims prompted many corporations and regions to withhold their tax payments to the central government. The risk of punishment, meanwhile, was low. The state's underdeveloped administrative capacity for monitoring and enforcement reduced the probability of detection. The tax administration had only a distorted and incomplete picture of the income of small businesses and households.[7] With high costs and low risk, noncompliance became the norm throughout society.

In the 1990s, the Russian state offered society very little by which a tax system based on trading could develop. Not surprisingly, the reaction of society was to ignore, avoid, and evade the state's revenue claims. Not only did neoliberal market reforms fail to cultivate new sources of revenue, but by mid-decade the existing revenue base began to contract. At the outset of the transition, the Russia state remained fiscally dependent on large manufacturing and commodity exports in general and the energy sector in particular. But soon even these usually reliable sources of income could not meet the most basic fiscal needs. The state's extractive practices led to the demonetarization of the revenue base. Russia's transitional economy became a "virtual economy" (see chapter 1) headed not toward market capitalism but toward post-Soviet industrial feudalism.[8]

First, in the mid-1990s, the overall decline in enterprise profits coincided with the Central Bank's newfound resolve to maintain a tight monetary policy, resulting in less capital available to the corporate sector.[9] To keep the economy going, interindustrial transactions increasingly took the form of barter. In July 1992, only 10 percent of industrial transactions involved the exchange of goods and services instead of cash, but in January 1997, barter-type exchanges accounted for 45 percent of industrial transactions.[10] Non-monetary means of economic exchange inventively appeared to cover other forms of payment—promissory notes, IOUs, regional script, wage substitutes, and ration coupons.[11] The transitional economy became a "virtual economy" in which enterprises retreated from the market into Soviet-like accounting networks of mutual subsidies and debt swapping.[12] The virtual economy was in turn sustained by a system of virtual revenue extraction.

The use of barter may have begun as a survival strategy for cash-poor and hard-pressed enterprises, but the economy's rapid transmogrification into post-Soviet industrial feudalism was directly driven by the transitional tax regime.[13] The state's multiple revenue claimants and rapacious practices caused many firms to fall behind on their tax bills, a circumstance compounded by the punitively high penalties that kicked in almost immediately. Once a firm was officially declared to be in arrears, the tax administration had the authority to confiscate all income directly from its bank account, except for a portion set aside for wages. As a result, enterprises moved outside the banking sector to carry out transactions, using offshore foreign currency accounts, promissory notes, and barter. The large public enterprises facilitated the disappearance of cash from the management of state finances. Adapting to the Central Bank's tight monetary policy, the government, in 1994, enabled public firms to satisfy their outstanding debts to suppliers by issuing a special treasury coupon that the supplier could redeem either in a future cash payoff or by canceling past-due taxes.[14] This offsetting of budgetary expenses and incomes was supposed to make the government's ledgers appear to be in order, but an imprudent precedent had been set. Once it was acceptable to satisfy the central state's revenue claims through tax offsets, big businesses took advantage, using nonmonetary means of payment to fulfill tax obligations to the state center.

State fiscal policy was unintentionally causing the demonetarization of the revenue base. Large corporations actually had an incentive to accumulate tax arrears, penalties and all, instead of paying on time and in cash, knowing that the Chernomyrdin government would authorize further debt swapping and barter schemes that would clear their tax debts without touching their cash assets. Tax arrears to the central state budget increased notably as a percentage of gross domestic product (GDP)—in 1995, 2 percent; in 1997, 4 percent; and in 1998, 6 percent.[15] In 1997 alone, the number of firms classified as "large debtors" grew from 1,100 to over 3,300.[16] And nonmonetary tax payments grew in accordance to meet the rise in tax arrears: in December 1995, nonmonetary payments made up 25 percent of the total tax take for the central state budget; in December 1996, the figure climbed to 50 percent, and in December 1997, the figure was close to 65 percent. Meanwhile, regional political leaders used similar schemes to finance the local public sector. Regional leaders shared the same incentive as local enterprises to hang on to their cash assets, thereby keeping them in the region instead of the Moscow treasury. Of the revenues collected on their territory, regional leaders sent the central budget more nonmonetary payments and kept more cash income for themselves.

Second, the revenue base was whittled down further by the numerous special deals, which big business finagled to reduce their tax burdens as part of the state-elite revenue bargain. The capital-rich energy sector was especially active. In 1995, LUKoil was able to secure over $1 billion in tax deferments.[17] According to the Ministry of Finance, in 1995, special tax exemptions cost the budget roughly U.S.$6 billion in lost revenue; in 1996, the cost of such exemptions was estimated to have grown to U.S.$30 billion.[18] By 1998, the amount of revenue lost through tax privileges was close to one-third of the total taxes collected for the consolidated budget and more than two-thirds of the total taxes collected for the federal budget.[19] Sometimes these deals were done formally in negotiation with state actors, but sometimes they were done informally and unilaterally.

Third, as the state became ever more desperate for revenue, taxpayers concocted ever more elaborate avoidance and evasion schemes. Most common was to try to hide at least some portion of income from tax collectors. Businesses routinely kept separate books, prepared specially for tax inspectors. In addition, the larger corporations concealed income by setting up a network of territorially dispersed "shell" companies that the decentralized tax administration could not keep track of. In this way, income moved "offshore" to avoid higher rates. Offshore sometimes meant offshore, to a tax haven like Cyprus, but it also meant downriver, to a tax rate-cutting region like Kalmykia. To hide income from the visible official economy, businesses made use of a pervasive shadow cash economy. A tax police department head estimated that the shadow economy was sustained by as many as 3,000 money-laundering operations.[20]

The richest corporations and regions, on which the state budget was fiscally dependent, were the most flagrant tax evaders. In 1996, unpaid taxes topped U.S.$20 billion, or 5 percent of GDP, with just 73 large corporations accounting for over 45 percent of the tax debt to the central state budget. Meanwhile, in 1996, only six of eighty-nine regions met their designated tax obligations to the central budget, and only thirteen additional regions managed to send in more than 80 percent of their designated tax obligations. More than half the regions failed to collect 70 percent of their designated tax obligations to the central state budget.[21] The wealthier donor regions, in particular, lagged behind in tax collection. At the end of 1997, the donor regions topped the list of regions with the highest tax debt to the federal budget. Nearly one-third of all tax-delinquent firms were located on the territories of these ten regions.

The state's extractive practices chased many taxpayers into the shadow economy. The estimates of the shadow economy as a percentage of GDP varied depending on who was doing the estimating. The state statistical agency put the number between 20 and 30 percent, the tax administration between 30 and 40 percent, and the law enforcement agencies between 40 and 60 percent. To independent observers, the 40 percent figure seemed about right. As the informal shadow economy in society expanded, the formal revenue base of the state was diminished. The transitional tax system increasingly reflected mutually reinforcing antagonism between state and society. Society increasingly did not recognize the legitimacy of the state's revenue claims.

Resort to Extraction by Taking under Putin

The Russian state's resort to revenue extraction by "taking" was not initially successful. As the state fell deeper into the abyss of fiscal crisis in the late 1990s, the Yeltsin administration raised the threat of coercion against the largest corporate tax delinquents but could not strike sufficient fear to reverse the revenue decline. After the 1998 fiscal collapse, however, the means of revenue extraction increasingly reflected the central state's preference for coercion. In the mid-2000s, a former tax police chief who insisted that "people must learn to be afraid of us" led the government. Coercion was subjected not to institutional constraint but to political disposition. The political decision to keep coercion on a loose leash was visibly apparent in four areas of tax collection: 1) refortified and more aggressive tax administration, 2) enhanced revenue role for law enforcement agencies, 3) criminalization of tax avoidance, and 4) weakening of legal-institutional checks on revenue agents.

First, the tax administration underwent an internal restructuring to strengthen extractive capacity, especially in relation to the large corporations that had previously been protected by political patrons. Tax administrative capacity was enhanced by the strategic redeployment of bureaucratic and human resources to align with the narrow revenue base. The most effective organizational innovation was the creation of sector-based, interregional departments, enabling the tax inspectorate to monitor more closely the economic activities of large taxpayers. These special departments set up offices on the premises of big corporations, and inspectors monitored transactions daily.[22] In 2001, the tax administration created three special interregional departments: oil, natural gas, and alcohol and tobacco. Interregional Department No. 1 included LUKoil, Rosneft, and Slavneft as clients/targets, while Interregional Department No. 2 focused on Gazprom. According to the head of the Federal Tax Service, after the formation of Interregional Department No. 2, tax receipts from Gazprom to the state budget increased by more than 13 percent. In 2003, four additional interregional departments were established: electricity and energy, metallurgy, transportation, and telecommunications. Besides organizational reforms, the new business elite was also confronted with a more aggressive tax administration under the leadership of Anatoly Serdyukov, a furniture store businessman and political protégé of the St. Petersburg secret police. As a matter of practice, tax inspectors were instructed to focus attention routinely on manager salaries and to suspect automatically well-paid managers of evasion.[23]

Second, the police played a more prominent role in revenue extraction. The postcommunist state was bequeathed a rich inheritance of coercive resources, but for most of the 1990s, it did not seem to know what to do with them. The security agencies of the new state were subordinated to presidential authority and were not effectively constrained by civilian political or legal institutions. President Yeltsin and the police shared mutual interests in keeping the security forces insulated on the executive side. The police apprehensively watched the new elite consumed by self-destructive political fights and self-enriching capital flight. The ability of the state to govern, meanwhile, grew weaker from enfeebled power and plundered wealth. The policeman's instinct to restore political order was strong, as was his desire to get in on the redistribution of riches.

The 1998 fiscal collapse became the opportunity for security and law enforcement agencies to be more actively involved in tax collection. The tax police was especially well positioned to play a larger part. In 2001, the tax police underwent a change in leadership. Vyacheslav Soltanganov, who had publicly voiced reservations about coercion and compliance, was forced into retirement: "I have worked in the power structures for three decades, so I speak with authority, forceful methods are one of the mechanisms that must be utilized by the state, but not the main mechanism."[24] By contrast, his replacement, Mikhail Fradkov, was a strong advocate of stricter application of coercion to encourage tax compliance.[25] Fradkov proposed a change in existing legislation that would impose mandatory jail terms and confiscation of property for those found guilty of "large-sum" tax crimes. Anything more lenient, he warned, would keep tax evaders in the shadows.

Official figures show the increased role of the police in tax collection. In 1997, the tax police initiated 5,700 criminal cases; in 1999 (one year after the fiscal collapse), the agency initiated 16,500 criminal cases; and, in 2000, the number doubled to 32,000 criminal cases.[26] The target of tax police investigations changed as well; the force was unleashed against the economic elite, who could no longer rely on political patrons to protect them from the central state's revenue agents. The agency launched investigations into the political machines of the powerful regional governors of Tatarstan and Primorskii Krai, leading to criminal charges and arrests.[27] Next up was the commercial banking sector, including the powerful banks authorized to handle tax payments for the treasury. In 2000, the tax police investigated 300 of these banks and uncovered numerous schemes by which bankers and clients colluded to make "fictitious" tax payments to the treasury. In Moscow alone, this campaign led to the initiation of forty criminal cases, one alone in the amount of R17 million in taxes.[28] Finally, the tax police were placed at the front line in the assault on Russia's new energy tycoons that began with the Yukos case. But carrying out this assault required the criminalization of tax avoidance.

Third, the fine line of legal technicality that separates evasion from avoidance was smudged over by police and prosecutors who determined that any violation of tax law, whether of the letter or of the spirit, would bring punishment in equal measure. In the mid-1990s, only two articles of the Criminal Code dealt with tax evasion, but by 2002 the number had increased to fifty-three articles.[29] In the 1990s, law enforcers repeatedly ranted that the fight against tax evasion was undermined by legislative imprecision. Now more compliant legislators rewrote tax legislation, and tax avoidance schemes were declared illegal by less constrained law enforcers. As a warning to the corporate elite, especially in the energy sector, the expanded mandate of law enforcement was broadcast loudly from executive quarters: German Gref, minister of economic development, in December 2003: "Besides the fact that the oil companies acquired huge properties in just a few years, they still use tax optimization schemes worth billions of dollars annually. Our patience has run out." Alexei Kudrin, minister of finance, in January 2004: "We will continue to pursue oil groups for unpaid taxes. The use of measures with retroactive force can not be ruled out." Igor Shuvalov, deputy head, presidential administration, in October 2004: "Everyone who uses tax optimization schemes illegally must be called to account for their actions."[30]

The process of unraveling and criminalizing the myriad tax avoidance schemes of Russia's corporate elite was worked out during the state's long investigation of the Yukos oil company. The state's assault on Yukos was launched in 2003, but the investigation dated back to 2000. The insider knowledge and tactical experience gained from the Yukos campaign was put to use against other large energy-export corporations. One by one, favorite avoidance schemes of the oil companies were outlawed. In 2001, internal tax havens and special tax-exempt cities, created by the Yeltsin administration to garner political support and help out economically distressed regions, were abolished. By registering in a tax haven, oil companies reduced the profit tax rate from 35 to 11 percent. The Ministry of Finance estimated that closing down tax havens increased income by 1.6 percent of GDP to the 2001 state budget.[31] In 2002, the transfer-pricing scheme, in which oil companies paid less tax by selling at reduced prices to their own subsidiaries, was eliminated when the state replaced the sales tax with a fixed-rate tax on production.[32]

Finally, there was supposed to be defined limits on coercion as a means of revenue extraction. The use of coercion in tax collection was proscribed in law and regulated by legal and administrative mechanisms. The system indeed worked as designed much of the time. The problem was that it did not work all the time. Instead of autonomous judges, the Putin presidency showed a preference for centralized bureaucratic checks. Ultimately, the legal and institutional checks intended to safeguard societal capital from state coercion proved vulnerable to political pressure.

It was not always that way. In the 1990s, tax authorities had a harder time getting their way with the legal system. Both the Constitutional Court and the Arbitrazh courts generally protected taxpayers from tax collectors, who exceeded their legal mandate. As of 2000, the tax police, for example, could persuade the prosecutor's office to pursue less than one-quarter of criminal cases sent.[33] In the summer of 2000, the tax police finally took on corporate titans LUKoil and Avtovaz, filing criminal charges for tax evasion and demanding back payments and fines totaling hundreds of millions. But they did not get far: the prosecutor general ordered the case against Avtovaz closed for insufficient evidence, and the Moscow Arbitrazh Court threw out almost every charge against LUKoil, reducing to a pittance the amount of back taxes owed.[34] According to then Director Fradkov, the tax police in 2001 achieved successful prosecution of only twenty-seven criminal cases. He attributed the poor showing to both the ingenuity of evaders and the ambiguity of the law.[35]

But in the early 2000s, the courts appeared to switch sympathies in favor of the state. The change in behavior followed the change in presidents. When President Yeltsin was frustrated by the courts over the resolution of tax disputes, he appealed to the Higher Arbitrazh Court to reexamine court practices in regard to tax evasion and offer some proposals to clarify the law. When the courts disappointed President Putin, he sent a former secret policeman and deputy head of his administration to instruct a meeting of regional judges on how to conduct their work. With the change in presidents, the court turned out to be an ineffective check against the state's more aggressive stance. Indeed, the Constitutional Court readily constructed a legal foundation for revenue taking by coercion.

In 2000, taxpayer challenges to the expanding mandate of the tax police led the Constitutional Court to reaffirm the agency's power: to put firms in double jeopardy by launching investigations independent of the tax administration, to gain access to a wide array of personal financial information, and to conduct surprise searches, surreptitious surveillance, and secret audits on taxpayers.[36] In 2004, the Constitutional Court upheld the power of tax authorities to apply Article 169 of the Civil Code to tax evasion. This article stated that any economic transaction deemed "antisocial" or "immoral" could be declared criminal and the assets received thereof confiscated.[37] In 2005, the Constitutional Court ruled that the three-year statute of limitations on tax evasion crimes, explicitly stated in the Tax Code, did not apply in cases of "deliberate" tax evasion—apparently, ambiguity was not always a bad thing. One district judge summed up nicely the new approach when his verdict openly acknowledged that the actions of a company director on trial for tax evasion "fell within the boundaries of the law" and then handed him an eight-year jail term.[38] At the same time, in the Arbitrazh courts, the trend of favoring taxpayers was reversed. By the tax administration's accounting, the courts in 2000 favored taxpayers in 64 percent of cases decided, but in 2006 the courts sided with tax authorities in 83 percent of the cases.[39]

In Putin's first term, the Russian state reasserted its fiscal interests in the transitional economy and by unleashing coercion reverted back to revenue extraction by taking. While the Yukos case was the best-known example, aggressive tax investigations were also conducted against Sibneft, Avtovaz, and other large corporations by which the state was able to gain more direct access to the wealth they generated. But the Putin administration was not only about coercion and taking. In the 2000s, the Russian government undertook a parallel set of tax reforms that were meant to give taxpayers an "economic" incentive to comply with their revenue obligations. These seemingly contradictory tax policies found expression in the "concessions economy," wherein the state tried to reconcile trading and taking.

Reconciliation of Taking and Trading in the Concessions Economy

The means of extraction employed by the Russian state helped to shape the transitional economy. Coercion served the state's short-term fiscal needs but at the cost of long-term economic development. Russia's economic transition led not to *market* capitalism but instead to *concessions* capitalism.[40] While the contemporary Russian economy is multifaceted, the concept of concessions capitalism puts the emphasis on what distinguishes it from command socialism and market capitalism. The most valued economic resources of the communist state were not fully redistributed to society in the form of private property. Rather, these assets were made into state concessions.[41] Postcommunist Russia's concessions capitalism is a kind of "upstairs-downstairs" economy in which upstairs is found strategic industries in the form of large corporations that remain directly or indirectly subordinated to the state sector, while downstairs is found mass-consumption retail and trade in the form of small and medium-sized enterprises that are organized into a regulated private sector. Under Putin, the upstairs economy was increasingly characterized by extraction by taking, while new efforts were made to establish extraction by trading in the downstairs economy.

This organizational scheme of concessions capitalism first appeared under Yeltsin but was consolidated under Putin. Putin rudely disabused the postcommunist business elite when they pushed to convert the acquisitions made under Yeltsin into private property. The economic resources found upstairs belonged to the state. Compared to Yeltsin's improvised and personalistic approach, Putin fashioned a more corporatist-style arrangement to state–business relations, with the threat of coercion giving the state a distinct advantage in the bargaining process. State concessions are not managed directly by state ministries and agencies, as was the case in the command economy. They are regulated not by enforceable contracts but by the personal discretion of high-level state actors. Concessions are farmed out to politically favored corporate executives who are charged with turning a profit while navigating the pitfalls of global capitalism and fulfilling the obligations of the central state. For those concessionaires who can manage all of the above, the opportunity for personal enrichment is great. And for those who either fall short or, worse yet, aspire for more, their economic holdings are vulnerable to confiscation.

The campaign to reclaim economic resources was announced with a barrage of official bombast. Boris Gryzlov, former militia head turned parliament speaker: "the country's natural resources do not belong to any corporation or particular person, but to all the people of Russia."[42] Evgenii Primakov, former prime minister turned corporate lobbyist: Russia's energy resources "were given by God to all the people." And if there was still a question as to how "all the people" would exercise ownership, it was soon made clear. Sergei Ivanov, former KGB cop turned defense minister: Russia's natural riches "belongs to the state, they are not private property."[43] After a decade of decline, the state sector began to grow again, as indicated by the increase of state-owned shares (from 20 percent in 2003 to 35 percent in 2007) on the Russian stock market.[44]

This reversal was facilitated by the use of coercion as a means of revenue extraction by taking. State investigators leveled tax evasion charges against scores of big businesses, along with whopping bills for back taxes and penalties. The outstanding tax debts were settled only when a state-run enterprise finally acquired a sizable, often controlling stake in the ownership of the targeted firm. In 2005 alone, Gazprom grabbed up 75 percent of oil giant Sibneft; Rosneft captured 99 percent of Yuganskneftegaz, a lucrative subsidiary of Yukos; and Rosoboroneksport, the state arms manufacturer, found itself with 60 percent of Avtovaz, the country's largest car manufacturer.

Meanwhile, the state took a different approach to cultivating tax compliance with the small and medium-size business sector. As the Putin administration was expanding state intervention into the "upstairs" economy, it was restricting state predation on the "downstairs" economy. The small business sector's view of the tax administration is, unsurprisingly, decidedly negative. The business community begged the government for relief from the high tax burden and unrestrained tax collectors. In this regard, a series of tax reforms were enacted in the 2000s intended to give taxpayers in the downstairs economy more positive incentives to comply with tax obligations. These changes involved reducing the rates and checking the collectors.

The most notable reform was the radical flat tax reform, which reduced rates on particular taxes and lowered the tax burden on the economy in general. The centerpiece was the 2001 PIT reform. The new 13 percent flat rate was among the lowest PIT rates in the world and replaced a progressive rate scale of six categories ranging from 12 to 45 percent.[45] Business taxes were also reduced but in a less radical manner. The 2002 CIT reform reduced business taxes from 35 percent for industrial and retail firms and 43 percent for financial firms to a flat 24 percent rate. Moreover, the CIT reform finally made allowances for deduction of business costs from reported income. Reducing VAT rates proved to be more contentious, however. Finance Minister Kudrin took a cautious approach to cutting the main source of income to the state budget despite near constant pressure from corporate lobbies and rival government ministries. In 2004, the VAT was finally reduced from 20 percent to 18 percent, with promises of future cuts depending on world energy prices.[46]

Further tax reforms were aimed at giving incentives specifically to small businesses. In 2003, a new tax arrangement was created to encourage small business activity by establishing a consolidated reduced 15 percent rate. Continuing the trend, the Unified Social Tax rate was cut from 36.5 to 26 percent in 2005. And, after much interministerial debate, the Ministry of Finance finally got its way and, in March 2007, declared a tax amnesty in an effort to bring income back into the country that was secreted abroad. The amnesty allowed self-employed entrepreneurs and individuals to pay a 13 percent tax into a special account set up to minimize interaction with the tax administration on undeclared income received up to five years before December 2006 without incurring penalties or criminal charges.[47] The amnesty was a small success, bringing in more than U.S.$150 million additional revenues to the treasury.

While state coercion was let loose in the upstairs economy, the government sought to restrain the state revenue agents in the downstairs economy. Putin admonished local officialdom's predations on small businessmen as "legalized bribery." In response, the government made a genuine effort to limit bureaucratic coercion and use other means to induce small businesses to come out of the shadow. First, the government passed legislation aimed at lowering the cost of compliance by streamlining the Tax Code and simplifying the administrative process. At the end of the 1990s, the tax code included more than 200 different taxes, claimed by central, regional, and local state authorities. So many taxes had the perverse fiscal effects on tax collection by encouraging competition among the different levels of government for the same revenue source, causing confusion for tax administration officials, and imposing an excessive burden on taxpayers. By 2002, the total number of taxes was reduced to fifty-four, a dramatic decrease of three-quarters of all existing taxes. The pruning continued as road use fees, foreign currency fees, turnover taxes, and sales taxes were abolished. By 2005, the number of taxes contained in the tax code had been cut even further to a total of nineteen among all levels of government.

Next, the central state tried to delimit and regulate the powers of tax inspectors, tax policemen, and regional authorities. In 2005, the MVD, for example, issued a new set of rules for small business investigation that forbade freezing bank accounts, seizing property, and closing down operations. In 2003, Putin surprised even the tax police director when the 50,000-man force was stripped of autonomy. But the initial relief of businessmen was short lived. The tax police was not dismantled, just reorganized: two-thirds were subordinated to the economic crimes division of the MVD, while one-third was reassigned to a new narcotics enforcement agency.

But it is not so easy to maintain differing policies simultaneously upstairs and downstairs. The restraint that the center urged on local agents often went unheeded, especially when shown the example of unchecked coercion by the state center. The small business sector experienced modest growth under Putin. The number of small and medium-size enterprises finally exceeded 1 million in 2005. But the Russian state remained fiscally dependent on the wealth generated by the "upstairs" sectors of the concessions economy.

Conclusions: Taking versus Trading in Postcommunist Russia

The fiscal needs of the state are at the core of the concessions economy. Historically, Russian rulers have long relied on economic commodities that could be directly taxed—forests, land, and minerals. They have not been terribly troubled, past or present, to pursue movable assets through indirect taxation of transactions, preferring instead to concentrate on fixed assets in a way that would yield readily extractable rents. As a result, Russian rulers throughout history have resorted to the threat of coercion and "taking" as the means of revenue extraction rather than bargain with autonomous economic actors in a system of extraction by "trading."

This pattern of revenue extraction has had a profound influence on state and society relations in the past and the present. Postcommunist Russia's concessions economy is defined by several features associated with Putin's tenure, although they existed since the early 1990s. First, in the redistribution of the communist state's economic resources, the line between public and private property was not distinctly delineated. Under Yeltsin, the state was generous in granting economic concessions but was vague about formalizing proprietary claims of private actors and thereby creating a recognized protective boundary. With Putin, the line between private and public not only remained blurred but also shifted to the advantage of the state. Second, the economic elite in Russia is not autonomous but, rather, a state creation. Power and wealth relations may have been a bit fuzzy under Yeltsin, whose impulsive leadership style and frequent absences allowed favored business tycoons to gain influence in state policymaking, but the relationship between power and wealth was made crystal clear under the more resolute and steady Putin. Russia's postcommunist economic elite does not own its wealth: its members are concessionaires. They lack the power resources to assert autonomy; they are too weak either to capture the state or to bargain with it as equals. Third, economic concessions come with obligations of state service, which mainly means revenue. Here, leadership style matters. The politically embattled Yeltsin was lax in forcing the business elite to fulfill its social obligations, but the politically secure Putin coerced the business elite to pay taxes to the state and to bestow gifts on the nation in the form of recovering lost art treasures, funding health clinics, and outfitting sports teams. Not to comply meant to risk losing it all. In these ways, state fiscal imperatives shaped Russia's transition toward a reconfigured political authoritarianism and state monopoly capitalism.

Notes

1. Charles Tilly, "War Making and State Making as Organized Crime," in *Bringing the State Back In*, ed. Peter Evans, Dietrich Rueschemeyer, and Theda Skocpol, 169–91 (Cambridge: Cambridge University Press, 1985).

2. Yegor Gaidar, *Dni porazhenii i pobed* (Moscow: Znanie, 1996), 99.

3. A. I. Tolkushkin, *Istoriia nalogov v Rossii* (Moscow: Iurist, 2001), 297.

4. D. G. Chernik, ed., *Nalogi* (Moscow: Finansy i statistiki, 1998), 49–53.

5. See the interview with former MVD chief Anatoly Kulikov, *Obshchaia gazeta*, July 30, 1998.

6. V. I. Volkovskii, *Nalogovie organy i ekonomicheskaya bezopasnost': Rossii* (Moscow: Fond podderzhki uchenikh "nauchnaya perspektiva," 2002), 68–74.

7. A. V. Perov, *Nalogi i mezhdurodnie soglasheniia Rossii* (Moscow: Iurist, 2000), 157.

8. Richard Ericson, *The Post-Soviet Russian Economic System: An Industrial Feudalism?*, Institute for Economies in Transition Working Paper 8 (Helsinki: Bank of Finland, 2000).

9. International Monetary Fund, "Russian Federation: Recent Economic Developments," *IMF Staff Country Report* 99/100 (1999), 16, fig. 6.

10. Organization for Economic Cooperation and Development, *Russian Federation* (Paris: Organization for Economic Cooperation and Development, 1997), 116, fig. 23.

11. David Woodruff, *Money Unmade: Barter and the Fate of Russian Capitalism* (Ithaca, NY: Cornell University Press, 1999).

12. Clifford Gaddy and Barry Ickes, "Russia's Virtual Economy," *Foreign Affairs* 77, no. 5 (1998): 53–67; Clifford Gaddy and Barry Ickes, *Russia's Virtual Economy* (Washington, DC: Brookings Institution, 2002).

13. Ericson, *The Post-Soviet Russian Economic System*, 9.

14. Brian Aitken, "Falling Tax Compliance and the Rise of the Virtual Budget," *IMF Staff Papers* 48 (Special Issue): 186, 187.

15. International Monetary Fund, "Russian Federation," 60, fig. 13.

16. Vito Tanzi, "Creating Effective Tax Administrations: The Experience of Russia and Georgia," in *Reforming the State: Fiscal and Welfare Reform in Post-Socialist Countries*, ed. János Kornai, Stephan Haggard, and Robert R. Kaufman, 53–74 (Cambridge: Cambridge University Press, 2001), 62, 63.

17. Organization for Economic Cooperation and Development, *Russian Federation* (Paris: Organization for Economic Cooperation and Development, 1995), 46.

18. *Kommersant*, February 20–21, 1997.

19. Goskomstat, *Finansy v Rossii: Statisticheskii sbornik* (Moscow: Goskomstat, 2000), 24.

20. Figure cited in a press conference by Major General Khvorostyan, *Interfax*, March 17, 1998.

21. V. N. Koshkin, "O dopolnitel'nikh nalogakh i sborakh, vvodimykh organami vlasti sub'ektov RF," *Nalogovyi vestnik* 28 (1997): 33–35; Vladimir Tikhomirov, *The Political Economy of Post-Soviet Russia* (Basingstoke: Macmillan, 2000), 66.

22. Interview with G. Bukaev, *Interfax*, March 5, 2002.

23. Mikhail Orlov, head of the State Duma's Expert Council on Taxation, revealed this practice, *Kommersant*, May 6, 2006.

24. *Delovyi liudi*, no. 113 (August 2000). Soltanganov went on to say, "It is very rare in practice that the tax police pursues punishments, such as incarceration. We are a very humane organization." As the "first step" toward increasing compliance, he endorsed a significant lowering of tax rates.

25. *Izvestiya*, July 10, 2001; *Rossiiskaya gazeta*, March 14, 2001.

26. V. F. Soltaganov, *Nalogovaya politsiya: Vchera, segodnia, zavtra* (Moscow: Dashkov, 2000); *Nalogovaya politsiya*, no. 3 (February 2001); *Rossiiskaya gazeta*, March 14, 2002.

27. *Nalogovaya politsiya*, no. 7 (April 2001); *RFE/RL Crime and Corruption Watch*, March 7, 2002.

28. Soltaganov, *Nalogovaya politsiya*, 58, 60.

29. *Rossiiskaya gazeta*, April 14, 1999, and March 14, 2002. The two main articles of the Criminal Code dealing with tax evasion were nos. 198 and 199.

30. *Kommersant*, November 12, 2004.

31. Tax-exempted cities in Russia and the Commonwealth of Independent States were closed down in 2001. The national autonomous republic tax havens (Mordovia, utilized by Yukos; Chukotka, utilized by Sibneft; and Kalmykia, utilized by everybody) were finally shut down in 2004.

32. *Kommersant*, November 12, 2004.

33. Volkovskii, *Nalogovie organy i ekonomicheskaya bezopasnost'*, 104.

34. *Moscow Times*, August 8, 2000. In the Avtovaz case, the giant carmaker was accused of manufacturing 280,000 cars with the same identification number so that no record would exist for the tax administration.

35. *Vedomosti*, March 14, 2002. The Russian chapter of the international nongovernmental organization Society of Taxpayers maintains that the tax police have won fewer than 5 percent of the criminal cases that have actually gone to trial.

36. A. N. Kozyrin, ed., *O federal'nikh organakh nalogovoi politsii: S postateynymi materialami* (Moscow: Statut, 2000), 21, 30, 68–70.

37. Article 169 was successfully used in cases against large oil companies Yukos and Russneft and a collection of Bashkortastan-based financial and energy firms. The Arbitrazh courts did not always accept the tax authorities' attempts to apply this controversial article, although it was used in tax evasion cases prosecuted against targeted

corporate and regional elites. In April 2008, the Higher Arbitrazh Court, in Resolution 22, finally defined a limited range of tax-related behavior to which this article could be applied and instead urged tax authorities to use the Tax Code, not the Civil Code, in tax evasion cases.

38. *Moscow Times*, March 15, 2001.

39. *Kommersant*, February 26, 2007.

40. Concessions are not unfamiliar to capitalist economies. The owner of a sports stadium concedes a space or privilege to a private firm to sell popcorn and soda. The concessionaire profits from the noncompetitive market and in exchange pays off the stadium owner with a fee and share of the profits. The concessionaire does not own the space; it is a paid for privilege subject to contractual agreement. Of course, Russian state concessions are not regulated by the terms of legally enforceable contracts, so the popcorn vendor has more rights than the oil baron.

41. The concessions economy is one of the major recurring structural patterns in Russia; see Stefan Hedlund, *Russian Path Dependence: A People with a Troubled History* (New York: Routledge, 2005).

42. *Moscow Times*, October 30, 2003.

43. *Kommersant*, November 17, 2003.

44. David Woodruff, "The Expansion of State Ownership in Russia: Cause for Concern?," *Development and Transition* 7 (2007): 11–13.

45. Through 1999, the PIT scale included five categories with an upper margin of 35 percent, but a sixth level of 45 percent was added in 2000 for income exceeding R300,000 (U.S.$100,000), though, because of avoidance and privileges, the effective rate on personal income was estimated at 13.5 percent.

46. Prime Minister Kasyanov and Minister of Economic Development and Trade German Gref joined corporate lobbies in calling for more radical VAT reductions. Gref, for example, told the country's top retailers that the VAT rate should be cut to 13 percent; *Moscow Times*, January 22, 2004.

47. *Kommersant*, February 28, 2007.

4

Systemic Stalemate

Reiderstvo *and the Dual State*

Richard Sakwa

BOTH PRESIDENT BORIS YELTSIN AND President Vladimir Putin declared their loyalty to the 1993 constitution, but their commitment to the spirit of constitutionalism is less clear. Structures and rules do not provide a framework for order; instead, political actors and economic entrepreneurs subvert structures and rules and at the same time create new ones to sustain the regime while bypassing the formal constitutional order. The rush to the market in the 1990s entailed a high degree of "institutional nihilism," and this allowed the development of what Dmitry Medvedev called "legal nihilism" in 2008. Thus, two types of domination, or rule, identified by Max Weber as "patrimonial" and "legal-rational," generate two distinctive political orders that in turn have given rise to a "dual state." The neopatrimonial elements generate systemic insecurity about which rules will apply at any particular time, and thus actors have recourse to a range of informal behaviors to reduce risk, but this only generates further systemic insecurity and undermines the consolidation of the formal constitutional rule-bound political order. Formal and informal rules operate at the same time, reproducing dualism at all levels and allowing actors to operate elements of either but undermining the inherent internal logic of both. This has provoked the systemic stalemate in which Russia now finds itself. This is more than the "hybridity" characteristic of regimes in post-Soviet Eurasia but represents a historical conjuncture of extended developmental stasis. Historical experience suggests that such stasis is overcome by either revolution or collapse. However, the distinctive character of Russia's dual state may allow an evolutionary transcendence of the developmental stalemate. The tension remains between the developmental and predatory aspects of the Russian state. The fate of democracy and modernization depends on how this fundamental issue of property rights is resolved.

The Dual State, Systemic Stalemate, and Metacorruption

A dual system has taken shape in Russia in which the formal procedures of the *constitutional state*, together with the political practices of public competition between parties and other representatives of society, are balanced by the shadowy and opaque structures of the *administrative regime*, populated by various factions and operating according to the practices of Byzantine court politics and mafia dons.[1] Since the Yukos affair of 2003, a rough parity has been established between the two systems, and thus Russia today finds itself in a deeply entrenched stalemate. The tension between the two systems is the characteristic feature of Russian politics today; there is a continuing struggle between the two orders to shape the future of the country.

The contrast between an administrative and a constitutional state provides the key to interpreting developments in postcommunist Russia. In Russia, the fundamental legitimacy of the regime is derived from being embedded in a constitutional order to which it constantly proclaims its allegiance. However, in certain cases, as in the Yukos affair and in the Togliattiazot (Toaz) case (the two examples that are discussed in this chapter), elements of a prerogative state have emerged. The divergent fate of the two companies illustrates the tension between the orders. In the case of Yukos, the "raid" on the company was successful, and the company disappeared, whereas Toaz was able to resist the raiders, drawing on the resources of the constitutional state, and remains an independent company in the hands of much of the old management. Thus, the interaction between the constitutional (legal-rational) and administrative (neopatrimonial) states in Russia has become the defining feature of the regime. This dynamic tension precludes assigning Russia simply to the camp of authoritarian states in an essentialist manner, but it also means that Russia cannot be classified simply as a democracy (defined above all as adherence to the rule of law accompanied by political competition conducted on a level playing field). The rule of law in Russia remains fragile and, as the Yukos affair amply demonstrates, is susceptible to manipulation by the political authorities, but no fully fledged prerogative state has emerged. Russia thus remains trapped in the gray area between an administrative and a genuine constitutional state.

Consequent on this, two political systems operate in parallel. There is the system of open public politics, with all the relevant institutions described in the constitution and conducted with pedantic regulation in formal terms.

At this level, parties are formed, elections fought, and parliamentary politics conducted. However, at another level, a second, adjacent and overlapping "parapolitical" world exists based on informal groups, factions, and operating through the framework of the inner court of the presidency. This Byzantine level never openly challenges the leader but seeks to influence his decisions. By permitting the parapolitics of the second system, Putin ensured that the formal side of political life was liable to become little more than "show politics," a spectacle to satisfy the formal demands of the system and the international community but lacking the efficacy that, however limited, is one of the characteristics of modern democracies.[2] By seeking to reduce the inevitable contradictions that accompany public politics into a matter of technocratic management, Putin exacerbated the contradictions between the groups within the regime itself. Putin placed a high value on civil peace and thus opposed a return to the antagonist politics that was typical of the 1990s, but this reinforced the pseudopolitics typical of court systems. The suffocation of public politics intensified factional processes within the regime and corruption in society as a whole.

This situation emerged as Putin's administration claimed to stand above the historic divisions of the modern era and, indeed, purposely sought to reconcile the forces that had torn Russia apart in the twentieth century. The democratic process was managed by a force standing outside democracy, co-opting elements of political society willing to compromise and marginalizing the rest. This was a type of passive revolution that for Antonio Gramsci entailed "an abortive or incomplete transformation of society." This can take a number of forms, including one where an external force provokes change, but this lacks a sufficiently strong domestic constituency and runs into the resistance of entrenched interests. When the forces are equally balanced, a stalemate emerges, giving rise to a situation of "revolution/restoration."[3] We have in Russia a situation where class forces (in particular, the entrenched bureaucracy resisting the challenge of an independent bourgeoisie) are equally balanced, allowing the regime to act with autonomy. The Russian government continued the revolution in property and power begun in the late Gorbachev years but at the same time restored elements of the previous regime. Promoted as the ideology of reconciliation, the inconclusive nature of the system takes the form of the dual state, with all its inherent contradictions and accompanying stalemate.

While Putin's regime insulated itself relatively effectively from political movements and civic associations, it became prey to two processes: the importation into the regime in the form of factionalism of the political pluralism that it suppressed in society and the "economization" of its transactions. This economization at the most basic level took the form of venal corruption, which, as we shall see, eroded the administrative system, but it was also accompanied by metacorruption, where the logic of the market undermined the autonomy of politics. As in other capitalist democracies, citizenship was commercialized and labor commodified. This was the sting in the tail of the depoliticization strategy, but it also reflected a broader process in mature capitalist democracies. The global hegemony of neoliberalism in the early postcommunist years was accompanied by the retreat of the state from earlier levels of social protection and public service, accompanied by what Cox identified as loss in "confidence in the integrity and competency of the political class": "Political corruption is inherent in the transformation of public goods into marketable commodities."[4]

A key expression of this corruption is the politicization of law and legal proceedings. The Yukos affair amply demonstrated the ability of the regime to apply "telephone law," that is, to influence judicial outcomes desired by the regime.[5] The Yukos affair was a classic case of a "prosecution to order" (*zakazannoe delo*) accompanied by the malpractices that became known as "Basmanny justice."[6] Mikhail Khodorkovsky, the former head of Yukos, had his detention hearings in the Basmanny District Court, located next to the offices of the General Prosecutor's Office, but the term has now entered the lexicon to denote administrative interference in judicial proceedings. These were indeed defined as abuses by the Russian public sphere and ultimately remained susceptible to remedy. However imperfect the 1993 constitution may be, it provides the framework for the development of a pluralistic political society and open public sphere, and as long as the system remains dual, there remains a dynamic of renewal. During the Putin presidency (2000–2008), especially in the early years, considerable effort was devoted to strengthening the judiciary as an institution and the legal system as a whole. Measures included the adoption of a new Criminal Procedural Code, shifting the power of detention from prosecutors to the courts; significant wage rises for judges to insulate them from the pressure of bribes; an increase in the number of judges by a quarter; and an extensive program of court building and refurbishment.

The legal-constitutional pillar was reinforced in institutional terms, but the independence of the judiciary was undermined by the continued application of Basmanny justice (metacorruption) and numerous varieties of venal corruption, including the use of "intermediaries" to help fix outcomes. A range of informal practices subverts the world of formal institutions, with the former operating with semiformalized rules of their own, becoming a type of "institution" in their own right.[7] The two pillars of the dual state, consequently, cannot be ascribed simply to the formal and informal worlds. Although the two are analytically distinct, in practice they become mutually constitutive.

In cases of importance to the regime, the dual state allows formal constitutional principles and legal norms to be suspended. Thus, in criticizing shortcomings in the Russian judicial system, we should be aware that we are dealing with a diffuse and contradictory system. When the rule of law comes into contradiction with political expediency, the former tends to suffer. Thus, the system allows highly placed factions to pursue their individual and group interests in a way that overrides institutional safeguards and generally accepted principles of due process to suborn the courts into compliance with their wishes.

The results are clear, including a poor investment climate and widespread corruption. Already in its Corruption Perception Index for 2008, Transparency International placed Russia in joint 147th place with Bangladesh, Kenya, and Syria, its worst position in eight years.[8] Not surprisingly, Medvedev in June 2008 warned, "It [corruption] is a very painful and difficult problem for our country. . . . Corruption as a systemic challenge, as a threat to national security, as a problem which leads to a lack of faith among citizens in the ability of government to bring order and protect them."[9] A head of state could hardly make a more devastating comment, repeated on numerous occasions thereafter, and the various cases of *reiderstvo* reflect the problem that he identified.

Reiderstvo (Raiding)

"Raiding" entails the hostile attack of one corporate entity against another, often accompanied by physical "raids" by armed state organs. A report on the subject by the Center for Political Technologies (CPT) defines raiding as

> The illegal . . . seizure of property. . . . The winning of control in the widest sense by one company by another using both illegal and legal methods; the seizure of shares by provoking business conflicts; . . . a way of redistributing property which in essence is banditry, but which formally conforms to some sort of judicial procedure.[10]

In contemporary Russia, raiding is categorized by various colors: "black raiding" relies primarily on illegal methods, "gray raiding" uses a combination of semilegal and illegal means, and "white raiding" relies on semilegal actions.[11] The authors of the report categorize the attack on Toaz management as an example of the application of a combination of methods by commercial competitors. In raids of whatever color, criminal proceedings are used to force a business competitor to relinquish their stake to the raider, usually at a considerable discount or for no value at all. State agencies and officials are often complicit in such corporate raids, and the integrity of the courts is undermined.

In launching the report, Alexei Makarkin, vice president of the CPT, categorized the raid on Toaz as "one of the most glaring examples of a corporate raid in modern times, alongside Yukos, Arbat-Prestige, Eldorado and East Line."[12] While the Yukos case has wide resonance internationally, the Russian press is full of stories associated with the abuses associated with other cases. The report provides a useful price list: an unlawful court decision in Moscow apparently costs around U.S.$50,000 to U.S.$200,000, while in the regions the prices fall to only U.S.$10,000 to U.S.$20,000. A report by the INDEM Foundation, an expert in the field of corruption, found that government officials and state employees, including police officers, collected around U.S.$240 billion in bribes annually.[13]

A report issued on September 4, 2008, by the National Anti-Corruption Committee and the Phoenix Group, based on interviews with more than 100 businesspeople and lawyers, provided further details on the role of state bodies in achieving hostile takeovers and the going market rate to ensnare business rivals in a criminal investigation. Officials would take about U.S.$30,000, while a favorable court ruling cost U.S.$35,000 more. In this way, raiders paid corrupt officials to help them seize businesses. As Yelena Panfilova, the head of the Russian office of Transparency International and the coauthor of the report, noted, "Fighting raiding is impossible without fighting corruption."[14] According to Kirill Kabanov, head of the anticorruption committee, Russia's officials are the chief corporate raiders, not other companies: "Officials benefit privately from all companies. It depends on the scale of the business. The bigger the business, the higher the rank of the official involved." He stressed that this made it difficult to study the problem and hard to investigate since it involved corrupt influence.[15]

Factionalism and *Reiderstvo*

The dual state as it developed in the Putin years placed a high premium on the concept of "loyalty" and is one of the central pillars of the semi-institutionalized administrative regime. This rather amorphous concept nevertheless plays an important role in the shaping of factions and the development of Russian policy in its entirety. Neither Vladimir Makhlai nor Alexander Makarov at the head of Toaz owed any loyalty to the Putin regime, and their independence riled the power system and opened them up to attack by businesspeople close to the regime. It was precisely this sort of "velvet reprivatization" that Oleg Shvartsman brought into the open in the run-up to the December 2007 Duma election. Shvartsman, the head of Finansgroup, claimed that his U.S.$3.2 billion fund management company handled the financial affairs of "certain political figures," using a variety of instruments including offshore companies, and had close links with people in the presidential administration, and the domestic and foreign intelligence services (FSB and SVR). He claimed that his company had the backing of the state to conduct corporate raids on private companies to force them back into state ownership, what he called the "velvet-reprivatization" of assets initially privatized in the 1990s. The methods used were what Shvartsman termed "voluntary-coercive instruments," applied with the assistance of the Ministry of Internal Affairs (MVD) departments fighting organized and economic crime.[16]

It is misleading to describe these as battles between "clans" since that would suggest permanence and depth to the various groups involved. "Factionalism" is more appropriate. Thomas Graham in the mid-1990s suggested that faction-type structures had emerged as the shaping force of Russian politics in which various economic structures struggled for access to the president and thus to state resources in order "to engineer a political stability that would ensure their hold on power and the country's financial resources."[17] Graham noted that the major aggregative unit in postcommunist Russian politics was not the political party, the interest group or formal political institutions, but personality-based interest constellations vying to influence the president. These included the traditional industrialists represented by Prime Minister Viktor Chernomyrdin; regional leaders and, in particular, the "Moscow group," headed by the city's mayor, Yuri Luzhkov; the "party of war," including Yeltsin's confidant and bodyguard Alexander Korzhakov, which had encouraged Yeltsin to launch full-scale war in Chechnya; and the various "westernizers" who shaped Russia's liberal economic program (table 4.1). The dominance of the "family," a grouping of oligarchs, relatives, and administration officials in Yeltsin's last years, was always unstable and represented little more than a fluid grouping based on immediate interests although sharing in broad terms a commitment to a set of policy preferences (above all, keeping the communists and their allies out of power).

TABLE 4.1
Russia's Factions

Under Yeltsin	*Under Putin*
Industrialists	*Siloviki*
Regional bosses	Democratic statists (divided into developmental and political statists)
Security officials	Liberals
Westernizers	
The "family"	

Factions are far less substantive and enduring than clans. Above all, they lack substantive resources for independent political action. Factions are oriented to the power system, and thus differences between the three conventional metafactions—the *siloviki* (those associated with security structures in one form or another), the democratic statists (which can be further divided into developmental statists, in favor of an active industrial policy and the like, and the political statists, who focus on managing the public sphere), and the liberals—are trumped by overriding loyalty to the administrative regime. Thus, the axis of factional coalescence shifted from the interest, regional, and professional group orientation of the Yeltsin years to a more amorphous policy-oriented basis in the Putin era. There remain strict limits to their autonomy, and each of the factions has to make compromises in order to be able to retain influence within the policy process. Thus, the liberals had to swallow the persecution of Khodorkovsky and his associates, and in return they retain a powerful influence over economic policy. Equally, hard-liners had to put up with the "reset" and improved relations with America, and in return they were able to prevent the effective pluralization of the political system. Defectors are rare, and, as former Prime Minister Mikhail Kasyanov discovered, infractions against the Putinist code of power incur heavy penalties (although, given the balance within the dual state, not typically criminal sanctions or worse forms of repression). Retribution is swift and implacable. Defectors are cast out into the political wilderness, where opposition politics survives in a blasted and sparse environment. Even loyalty is not enough at times of stress, notably during periods of presidential succession every four years (hence the extension of the presidential term to six years from 2012). In the 2011–2012 electoral round, early victims were Yuri Luzhkov, mayor of Moscow until his summary dismissal in September 2010, and Sergei Mironov, the leader of Just Russia, who was ousted as chair of the Federation Council in mid-2011 when he adopted an independent and critical stance. Despite years of loyal service, when they became superfluous to the overriding imperative of regime perpetuation and elite reproduction, the two were unceremoniously jettisoned. The same applies to the billionaire Mikhail Prokhorov (the former head of Norilsk Nickel), whose brief period as leader of the Right Cause (*Pravoe delo*) party came to an ignominious end in September 2011. There were fears that he would become a "new Khodorkovsky," although by that time the regime had learned the dangers of creating political martyrs.

The presidency under Putin and later under Medvedev was careful to maintain its preeminence by standing above factions, and indeed part of its effective power derived from its ability to arbitrate between different elements of the regime. Conflicting groups have to appeal to the supreme arbiter for support. This is a Bonapartist model of politics, but the fundamental question concerns the nature of the groups above which the presidency stands. There is no agreement what these groups represent. The ruling elite is divided into groups engaged in a permanent "war" for access to resources and superprofitable output. Those able to wield the "power" resource are in a particularly strong position, traditionally exercised through the General Prosecutors' Office. All these groups participated in the creation of supermonopolies in the Putin era—energy, shipping, telecommunications, and so on, which were susceptible to factional control. The state is one of the players in this field and always wins any fight. However, when the state itself is fragmented, the outcome is more uncertain. The fragmented political terrain in the context of a stalemated political system allowed "corporate" raids (with the corporation being a combination of state officials and private interests) against Yukos and other companies, such as Toaz.

Yukos as a Case of Raiding

The Yukos "affair" of 2003–2005 for many marked a watershed in Putin's presidency. Dominating the middle part of his rule, the struggle against Khodorkovsky and his associates threw the spotlight on Putin's political style, the groups able to seize the policy agenda, and the tensions in the whole Putinist style of governance. Coming at a time when primary commodity prices were enjoying a boom—and thus the Kremlin was showered with the accompanying bonanza—competition over the appropriation and application of resources intensified. The *silovik* faction took full advantage of this to press forward their attack on one of the most egregiously independent business leaders. These two factors—the struggle against an "overmighty" oligarch and competition over control of rents—exacerbated fissures that are inherent in Russia's political system and intensified the struggles at the heart of the dual state.

In energy policy, the dominant paradigm until the Yukos affair was the liberal one, although it was far from unchallenged, and policy in this area was driven by the struggle between rival groups for influence.[18] Russia's energy policy as a whole continues to lack detailed strategic perspectives and according to Tompson is a confused mass of tactical expediency, reflecting the struggle for economic and political power between the remnants of the old Yeltsin faction (created through the financial sector) and the new Putin elite, whose power in preeminently of administrative origin. This broad split operated in the Yukos affair, accompanied by the structural factor identified by Tompson of a "state characterized by weak regulatory and rule-enforcement capabilities but enjoying a hypertrophied capacity for the use of force"; facing institutional weakness, the authorities fell back on "time-honoured methods of coercion and direct control,"[19] in other words, a raid. The standard interpretation suggests a tension between economic liberals and the so-called *siloviki*, and there is no doubt that these were two of the factions involved, but, as argued above, none would press home its advantage to the point that the regime itself would be destabilized. The Yukos affair was the most vivid manifestation of a faction able to pursue its policy agenda in one sphere, but in the event, the Yukos affair did not signal a wholesale attack by the state on big business. Other factions were able to blunt the scope of the *silovik* attack on the so-called oligarchs but were unable to save Yukos from dismemberment.

Following the defeat of the "criminal oligarchs" Boris Berezovsky and Vladimir Gusinsky in 2001, no substantial opposition remained in society. From 2003, however, Gleb Pavlovsky argues, "The authorities encountered a new systemic opposition within itself, seeking to modify the president's course from within, relying on part of the state's special services under the flag of supporting and strengthening a 'weak' president."[20] The aim of the intrasystemic opposition, according to Pavlovsky, was to achieve a redistribution of property and a change of elites at the national and regional levels, accompanied by the development of a new state ideology that would allow the "new oligarchy" to consolidate power. A new breed of Kremlin "oligarchs" had already been subordinated to representatives of the state and quasi-state corporations, and now they sought to discipline the independent oligarchs. If these new Kremlin oligarchs won, Pavlovsky noted, Putin would become their hostage. The Yukos affair was presented as curbing predatory capitalism and thus gained a degree of popular legitimacy, but it was designed primarily to rebuff an attempt to transcend the passive revolution and by breaking the stalemate of revolution/restoration would have challenged the privileges of the elite that exploited the ambiguities of the situation. The Yukos affair saw the destruction of the nascent bourgeoisie's ability to pursue independent policies, and instead they became a subaltern class. Big business was subordinated politically to the state. The oligarchs were tamed, but the economic magnates (the "state oligarchs") were allowed to expand their business empires and their wealth and thus acted as a counterweight to the *siloviki*.[21] Putin was too wily a politician to become hostage to any one group.

The attack on Khodorkovsky was prompted less by ideological factors than by concerns about power, with property redistribution a consequence rather than a cause.[22] Belkovsky argues that the merger of Yukos with Sibneft, in effect, the incorporation of Sibneft, "would have entailed the beginning of the end of the Russian Federation."[23] The Yukos affair helped catalyze a powerful but dependent distributional coalition. It feasted on the corpse of Yukos but did so only as long as it remained subordinate to the presidency. The independent "oligarch" as a subject of Russian politics disappeared. Instead, dynamic coalitions between business leaders (notably the now dominant class of "state oligarchs") and administrative officials came together to exploit opportunities and opened up a whole new realm for *reiderstvo*. Political loyalty for both groups was the condition for their continued existence. Intensified democratization was not in the immediate interests of any of these dependent coalitions, although in the long term more democracy would allow them to develop as independent actors and to consolidate their property gains. Genuine constitutionalism, accompanied by free elections and an independent judiciary, would constrain the executive and allow the autonomous operation of political institutions and social forces. Institutional rules would gain a life of their own and undermine the "manual" operation by the regime. However, that would be for the future.

Much of Putin's policy agenda got bogged down in the middle part of his presidency by the struggle over ownership questions and in particular the belief that the "oligarchs" represented a threat to the achievement of his goals, and thus there was the need to reassert state prerogatives in the sphere of political economy and economic policymaking.[24] This took the form of the Yukos affair, which deflected attention away from Putin's reformist agenda and exacerbated divisions within the administration. The priority in the middle period of Putin's leadership appeared to be to deny oligarchs influence over the economy, politics, and the media, a concern that appeared marginal to the real issues facing the country. After a long trial, Khodorkovsky was jailed and the Yukos company dismembered; the reformist agenda was blunted and factional conflict in the Kremlin exacerbated. In the new model of political economy that emerged, the state was obsessed with defending its claimed prerogatives against the business elite. It did this by placing its representatives on the boards of leading companies.

Khodorkovsky was convinced that the attack on Yukos was a function of factional struggles. In an interview three months before his arrest, he argued that the struggle between Kremlin factions in anticipation of the March 2004 presidential elections lay behind the assault.[25] He was probably right, and Igor Sechin is usually identified as the main advocate of a forceful solution to the Khodorkovsky "problem," with FSB director Nikolai Patrushev tagging along. Putin's presidency was characterized by tension between *siloviki* and liberals, but in political terms both factions were oriented toward the regime and were its loyal servants, and the Yukos affair was not primarily provoked by this struggle. There were plenty of former security officials in the employ of oligarchs, notably Colonel General Filip Bobkov, once the second-ranking figure in the KGB, who was head of media oligarch Gusinsky's security service. Similarly, former KGB General Alexei Kondaurov was on Khodorkovsky's staff. Both outranked Putin, who had risen no higher than lieutenant colonel in the service.

All accounts agree that Sechin orchestrated the attack on Yukos. One of the main detectives working on the Yukos case, Salavat Karimov, is alleged to have reported to Sechin twice a week on progress on the case. However, Sechin's *silovik* credentials have been questioned,[26] and there remains disagreement over what precisely his faction sought to get out of the prosecution of Khodorkovsky. Their views overlap with those of the democratic statists, calling for greater state involvement in the economy and a more aggressive role of Russian capital abroad, where they joined forces with the industrial lobby. The *siloviki*, like the Yeltsinite oligarchs earlier, fused power and property although now with "business capture" taking the place of "state capture."[27]

The *silovik* preference for a *dirigiste* economic model promoted the gradual deprivatization of the Russian oil industry. From 2001, about 45 percent of the oil sector returned into state hands, most notoriously through the expropriation of Yukos assets. The major beneficiary was Rosneft, which became Russia's largest oil major with a capitalization by 2007 of U.S.$78 billion and with an annual production of 100 million tons. The destruction of Mikhail Gutseriev's Russneft company, the seventh-largest Russian oil producer, in 2007 marked yet another milestone in the consolidation of the sector. The struggle for ownership of the corpse of Russneft between Oleg Deripaska's Basic Element and Sechin's Rosneft was a proxy test of the strength of the two factions concerned: the *siloviki* and the loyal industrialists.[28]

It would be a mistake to see the Yukos case as simply the exercise of monolithic state power to implement certain goals. The Russian political system is far too fluid and open ended for that and divided as we have seen between the aspiration to achieve genuine constitutionality and elements of the administrative regime. These tensions allowed rampant factionalism to develop, and this is well illustrated by the persecution of individuals associated with the Yukos oil company from 2003. The Yukos case in turn consolidated an environment where other cases could be launched, notably against the management of Sovkomflot, Novoship, Volgatanker, Euroset, and many others. It did not, however, make decision making any more transparent or streamlined, as the tortuous discussions to adopt the long-promised Law on Subsoil Resources demonstrates. As Fortescue notes in his study, there are plenty of cases of coherent and transparent decision making in Putin's presidency, but this was not one of them; instead, the whole process was characterized by "bureaucratic infighting, delay, shifts and turns in policy preferences, and bitter debate."[29] All this clearly demonstrated that there was no consensus over the state's role in the economy, and while there was an element of ideological statism at work in the Yukos affair, this was far from the main driver of the affair. If this was the predominant factor in Putin's coalition, then an economic crisis from mid-2008 provided an ideal opportunity for the state to extend its control over the economy, but it did not do so.

The Yukos affair, however, did allow Putin to centralize the collection of energy rents, ensured a stable set of priorities for their disbursement, and allowed the administrative regime to retain control over their distribution. The third task proved the most difficult in the succession since there were many claimants to control the rent-sharing process. As Gaddy notes,

> A successor must understand Putin's concept of "Russia, Inc.," subscribe to it, and be capable of putting it into practice. He cannot allow rent sharing to devolve into personal enrichment to the detriment of state interests. A fratricidal rivalry among the elites could threaten use of the rents for state interests.[30]

Putin was well aware that a free-for-all over the distribution of resources would allow corruption to emerge from the shadows to take over the system: venal corruption would metastasize into metacorruption and become system forming. Putin's vaunted stability would swiftly erode, and the quality of governance would deteriorate further.

This is one of the main reasons why he chose Medvedev as his successor. Despite Medvedev's liberal reputation (which was justified, within the bounds of the operative politics of the Putinist order), it was clear that he would not threaten the distributional coalition (i.e., the distinctive mix of business and officialdom that became the social base of the administrative regime) that had taken shape in the Putin years. However, as we shall see, he did offer the potential for an evolutionary escape from systemic stalemate. Although in the short term this would entail losses to the distributional coalition, in the long run their position would be regularized. A similar problem had exercised Khodorkovsky in the 2000s when he sought to legitimate the property gains that the "oligarchs" had achieved in the 1990s. However, as Medvedev was to find in his first term, the forces of regime consolidation and systemic renewal were evenly balanced, and the developmental stalemate only intensified during his presidency.

Togliattiazot (Toaz)

We noted above that the attack on Toaz is considered an exemplary case of raiding, although it is distinctive in that the raid was fought off—illustrating the capacity of the constitutional wing of the dual state to withstand the predations of the administrative regime. The Toaz group is by far Russia's largest ammonia producer and provides some 7.6 percent of world ammonia production and also manufactures a number of other products. By the mid-2000s, the capitalization of the company was estimated at some U.S.$600 million. Toaz is the last independent chemical enterprise in Russia, making it an attractive target for raiders, the object of a predatory attack by an "organised group . . . in which there are representatives from both the business world and the authorities," as Valerii Draganov, head of the Duma Committee for Economic Policy, Enterprise, and Tourism, noted.[31]

As in the Yukos affair, the attack was focused on individual managers, in this case, on two senior figures, Vladimir Makhlai, the director general of what was to become Toaz since 1985 and its president since 2000, and Alexander Makarov, who joined Toaz in 1993, becoming managing director in 2000. Makhlai, like many managers of the time, was able to build up a controlling portfolio of shares (71 percent). The company had opted for the so-called option 2 in the privatization process, entitling workers to buy 51 percent of voting shares, the bulk of which over time ended up in the hands of managers. Some 20 percent of shares belong to the workers and another 9 percent to the Synttech Group, which is allied with Viktor Vekselberg's Access Industries/Renova Group. As we shall see, Toaz was involved in a number of lawsuits that have been interpreted as part of an alleged "raid" by Vekselberg on the chemical company to seize control of a majority stake.

Criminal cases against Makhlai and Makarov were commenced on June 29, 2005, by Major Sergei Shamin of the Investigation Committee of the MVD. The case concerned the allegation of tax evasion at Toaz through the sale of products abroad at below-market prices (a typical charge in raiding cases). On October 31, 2005, Makhlai and Makarov were charged with tax evasion and fraud in connection with the privatization of a stake in the company. A subsequent ruling of February 1, 2006, charged them with tax evasion, fraud, and money laundering. The federal government issued extradition requests for Makhlai and Makarov, who by this time had fled, on February 7, 2008.

The leadership of Togliattiazot was the victim of a classic instance of raiding, part of a consistent pattern of attacks against prime companies in contemporary Russia. From late 2005, the company was the target of numerous "inspections," often the cover for hostile actions, with the company the subject of numerous audits by various state agencies and law enforcement bodies. Following a raid on August 26, 2005, by agents of the MVD's Economic Security Department, this culminated with a full-scale raid on the company's premises on September 7 by armed men in camouflage uniforms. They were accompanied by Shamin, who apparently was often to be seen in the company of Vekselberg (who was allegedly the mastermind behind the first stage of the "raid" on Togliattiazot). The management of Togliattiazot, notably Makhlai and Makarov, were astonished to discover that they had been placed on an international wanted list on the grounds, inter alia, that they had been selling ammonia at a discount to reduce taxes.

The Togliattiazot case was accompanied by another feature typical of the Yukos and other raids, namely, the direct attack on the independence of the judiciary. In this case, in March 2006, Nadezhda Kostyuchenko, a judge of the Samara Region Arbitration Court, was dismissed from her post ahead of time by the qualification board. She took her case to the European Court of Human Rights (ECHR) in Strasbourg, complaining that she was sacked as a result of her decisions in the Togliattiazot case, notably in declaring invalid proceedings concerning a disputed 6.1 percent of shares in the 1996 deal. This case, as well as that of Judge Elena Valyavina, who was also pressured over her decisions in the Togliattiazot case (see below), was described by the head of the CPT, Igor Bunin, as "one of the biggest scandals of recent time."

The Yukos affair emboldened predatory raiders: if the state could carry out what was in effect a massive raid against one of the world's largest oil companies, then why should they not try their hand? This precipitated what was feared to be a new wave of "redistribution of property." This certainly is the way that the attack on Togliattiazot was seen. The head of the company's trade union, Ol'ga Sevost'yanova, noted that "it is no secret to any of the Togliattiazot workers that successful companies such as our factory are a tasty morsel for all manner of oligarchs. They are trying to ruin and clean out our factory and pocket the money they get out of it." The report went on to identify Vekselberg as the alleged guilty party in this case.[32] The plant's workers gathered in the central square of Samara in defense of their plant.[33] The solidarity of workers and management against external raiders was also evident in other cases, notably during the attack on the MAIR group of companies headed by Viktor Makushin in southern Russia. It was precisely the lack of such solidarity that allowed Yukos in the end to be picked off so easily.

It is alleged that the combined civil and criminal proceedings against senior Toaz officials were masterminded by Vekselberg, the head of the Renova Group and the fourth-richest man in Russia. With an estimated wealth of some U.S.$10 billion, he was implicated in the attack on the British management of TNK-BP in 2008.[34] Vekselberg has a reputation for conducting hostile takeovers, including the alleged use of illegitimate means and the bribery of state officials.[35] In the Toaz case, it is alleged that Vekselberg operated in conjunction with Nikolai Levitsky, the head of the Synttech Group, one of the Renova Group's affiliated companies. In 2005, Synttech acquired a 9.14 percent stake in Toaz, and it was from that time that the troubles for Makhlai and Makarov started. Vekselberg remained in the background since it is argued that the open involvement of such a high-profile figure would have cast doubt on the stability of Russia's economic development. The authorities had long been favorably disposed toward Vekselberg, and thus the Kremlin feared "being tainted by the negative image of 'raider Vekselberg.'"[36] Just as it appears the political green light was given for the attack on TNK-BP in early 2008, so too it appears that the assault on Toaz had been condoned at the highest political levels. Vekselberg is one of the select handful of Russian magnates considered a "state oligarch," a person who has close links with the administration. It is extremely unlikely that such a long-running and public attack on a major strategic enterprise could have continued for so long without political support at both the regional and the national level, although Vekselberg's precise role remains unclear.[37]

In summary, the hostile takeover used the classic weapons in the armory of "raiding." These included the acquisition of a minority stake that is then used to disrupt the work of the existing management; the launching of civil proceedings against the company, combined with the commencement of criminal proceedings against senior management (with a typical web of subsidiary allegations encompassing innumerable associated companies and individuals, reminiscent in form—although certainly not in substance—with the great "affairs" of the Stalinist purges of the 1930s), in this case Makhlai and Makarov; and various commercial approaches by groups connected in one way or another with the raider. One of these companies in this case is Tringal, a minority shareholder with a 2.06 percent stake in Toaz, which launched civil proceedings for recovery of alleged loss of dividends because of the underpricing of ammonia sales in 2005.[38] In addition, media outlets are mobilized to traduce the characters of the victims of the attack. This was certainly apparent in the unremittingly hostile coverage in early 2008 of Robert Dudley, chief executive officer of TNK-BP at the time (who later went on to head BP following the Gulf of Mexico disaster of April 2010) and was also much in evidence against Makhlai and Makarov with criticism of the way that they ran the company, including the accusation on NTV, broadcast on May 5, 2007, on the eve of the Russia–European Union summit in Samara, that they had allowed the Transammiak pipeline to fall into disrepair when in fact this was far from the case.[39] The allegation appears intended to disrupt the summit by suggesting that Samara was unsafe, possibly even "another Chernobyl," which would have thoroughly discredited the managers of the plant (May 18, 2007). Images of rusty pipes were absurd since the line runs underground all the way, except at points of entry and exit.

A further angle is the plan for Toaz to be taken over by a state-friendly company, Sibur, a St. Petersburg–registered holding company 51 percent owned by Gazprom and controlling twenty-nine petrochemical enterprises. In December 2006, the company established Sibur-Mineral Fertilizers (Sibur-

Minela'nye Udobrenie, MU), whose main shareholder was Gazprom, and three of the seven board seats were held by Gazprom (through its 100 percent subsidiary Mezhregiongaz) (*Kommersant*, February 13, 2007). Mezhregiongaz was headed by Kiril Seleznev (the son of Gennady Seleznev, the former communist speaker of the State Duma), who was also a member of Gazprom's executive board. There are claims that he was the key figure in Gazprom's attempt to get hold of Toaz, although he was not a member of the Sibur-MU board. Since gas is the main raw material of the plant, comprising 80 percent of production costs, a close link with Gazprom made business sense, especially since there had been repeated conflicts between Toaz and Gazprom over the quantity of supplies and prices.[40] Gazprom in the 2000s became one of the main instruments of Kremlin policy, and thus the advances by Sibur on its behalf firmly fall within the general strategy of the Kremlin in the Putin years to create state-dominated "national champions."

By coming under the aegis of a state-affiliated company, Makhlai could have solved his personal problems, although it is not clear that this would have been in the best interests of Toaz as a whole since financial resources would no doubt have been directed elsewhere and not for the development of the business itself. In the event, while Makhlai was ready to give up a blocking share (49 percent) to Sibur, he was not ready to give it a controlling share, and discussions ended inconclusively. This prepared the ground for a renewed attack by other raiders. Later in 2007, Seleznev confirmed that Gazprom was still interested in acquiring Toaz but not through Sibur Holdings but rather through another giant chemicals company called Evrokhim. Gazprom had long wanted to enter directly into the nitrogen chemical fertilizer market, and this appeared to be a way of doing so.[41]

The attempted takeover of Toaz by Gazprom affiliates represented, in the view of one commentator, an "attack from the rear." The frontal attack since 2005 by Renova and its associates had failed largely because of the extraordinary solidarity shown between management and workers. The company had shown a high degree of "social responsibility," of the sort encouraged by president Putin. But the "stability and self-sufficiency of OAO Togliattiazot keep irritating Moscow-based business sharks," and thus it became subject to waves of attacks.[42] Gazprom and its affiliates was an ideal candidate since its public image was that of a benign company defending popular interests. It would be harder for Toaz to maintain a united front against Gazprom than against "Vekselberg, the oligarch."[43]

There is another feature of the Toaz case that firmly places it in the category of politically motivated attacks where one commercial entity comes under attack from another, typically allied with state officials, namely, the prosecution of subordinates. The cases of Svetlana Bakhmina and Vasily Aleksanyan demonstrate how associates of a company under attack (Yukos) are threatened, with attempts to intimidate them to force confessions and the like. In this case, the person who came under attack was Toaz's press secretary, Igor Bashunov. The Toaz Press Service had challenged the various charges against the company's leadership and in particular had questioned the version put out by the MVD Investigative Commission's Press Service. On July 19, 2006, Bashunov was summoned unexpectedly to be questioned as a witness, even though he had joined the company only in December 2005 and had thus not been connected with the alleged crimes, which had taken place before his employment with the company. Despite this, Shamin opened a criminal case against him on September 11, 2006, charging him with refusal to give testimony. He was asked about the circumstances attending the sale and purchase of Toaz shares in 1996–1997, various contracts for the export of ammonia between 2002 and 2004, and the whereabouts of Makhlai and Makarov. Bashunov refused to testify on the grounds that Article 51 of the RF Constitution entitles witnesses to refuse to testify against themselves, but the investigator insisted that the questions related to Makhlai and Makarov. However, the tone and content suggest that from the first, Bashunov was being questioned more as a suspect than as a witness, especially since the case had been opened against unidentified persons to whom more could be added. Bashunov appealed against the opening of the case against him to various instances, insisting that his behavior had not damaged the interests of the state and neither had it been intended in any way to impede the course of justice.

As in so many other cases, the behavior of Bashunov's lawyer, Zamoshkin, also became a matter of dispute with the prosecutors. Zamoshkin's actions as counsel for Bashunov were defended by the Presidium of the Moscow Bar, of which he was a member, and its regional professional body, the Moscow Advocates' Chamber. The case against Bashunov dragged on because no judge was willing to take on the case since it was well known that the case had been sanctioned by a deputy prosecutor general (Grin), and thus it was clear that the state was involved. In the end, a judge of first instance in the Presnensky district (A. P. Dobrosel'skaya) agreed on September 26, 2008, that the limitation period for the case had expired and terminated the case. Overall, Toaz was able to resist the various attacks, and while Makhlai is now retired, Makarov remained an active director of the company.

Reiderstvo and the New "Redevelopmental State"

In the sections above, we have briefly described two cases of *reiderstvo* against Yukos and Toaz, but the list could be extended indefinitely. The

Yukos case was used as an instrument to forge a new model of political economy in Russia. It is not clear what this model should be called, with various terms used to describe the strengthening role of state and semistate companies in the economy. The basic drift was toward the creation of a state corporatist system in which the state does not renationalize the commanding heights of the economy but rather achieves a degree of *deprivatization* by placing its representatives in the boardrooms of leading companies, above all in the energy sector.

The combination of *dirigisme* and market forces prompted a policy based on deprivatization: avoiding wholesale nationalization but bringing important sectors of the economy into alignment with the strategic goals of the government. This created a number of parastatal economic entities who could advance the government's goals. It also created a dangerous fusion of political and economic power. It is within this nexus that "state oligarchs" thrived. Independent business figures like Khodorkovsky have been cowed (and in his case incarcerated), but those who remain are careful to coordinate their actions with the state in a mutually beneficial but highly corrupting relationship. All oligarchs may now be equal in terms of political exclusion, but some are clearly more equal than others, and, as the TNK-BP struggle demonstrated, the new oligarch system in many ways is a bigger threat for foreign firms (and indeed domestic ones, as the Toaz case demonstrates) than corruption.

The most vivid manifestation of deprivatization was the appointment of senior officials of the presidential administration to key boardroom positions, as the Kremlin imposed direct supervision over Russia's strategic companies. The dual state at this time took the concrete form of a system of dual control over state-controlled enterprises. Not only were the professional directors nominated by the administration, but the government then appointed political officials on to the boards of these companies to ensure that its policy preferences were pursued, suggesting a lack of trust in the chief executives of these companies.[44] Senior officials of the presidential administration were appointed to boardroom positions in addition to their official positions. By the end of 2004, seven boardroom appointees supervised nine state companies with assets worth U.S.$222 billion, or 40 percent of Russian gross domestic product.

State corporations emerged as an alternative to genuine privatization or full nationalization. Misgivings about the creation of state corporations, accompanied by factional tensions, delayed the approval of Sergei Chemezov's plan in 2005, the first out of the block, to create a state corporation (Russian technologies) on the basis of the state unitary enterprise Rosvooruzhenie. The plan to create a Nanotechnology Corporation (Rosnanotekh), sponsored by

Sergei Ivanov and the head of the Kurchatov Institute, Mikhail Kovalchuk, also encountered stiff resistance. State corporations entailed the creation of a new type of paraeconomic enterprise (the counterpart of Putin's other experiments with paraconstitutionalism and parapolitics) removed from government control, and the institutional framework whereby the state would regulate these alienated assets was not at all clear. State corporations are to fulfill the goals set out in their founding charters, and each has a supervisory council, staffed in large part by presidential nominees. In the end, seven state corporations were created, as were a number of quasi corporations. The scale of the new development was unprecedented, with some U.S.$20 billion transferred to the state corporations in late 2007 alone as starting capital.

According to Philip Hanson, the increased role of the state in these sectors fostered the creation of a "dual economy" with different rules applying to the different sectors.[45] Market forces would operate freely in the private sector, whereas in the state-controlled (but not necessarily state-owned) strategic development–oriented part of the economy, more *dirigiste* rules would apply. Such intense bureaucratic interventionism would not be disastrous for the Russian economy, but it would probably depress economic growth rates. With large reserves of petrodollars, the state consolidated its hold over profitable sectors of the economy, while the economic consequences were unlikely to be positive since state-owned companies in Russia have not been noted for their efficiency. Soon after leaving his post as head of the presidential administration to manage the "national projects," Dmitry Medvedev insisted that state ownership and management had "far from exhausted their potential."[46] Later, as presidential candidate, he warned against the excessive development of state corporations, and in 2011 he was finally able to reverse the appointment of government officials to the boards of state companies.

Contradictions of the Dual State

The election of a new president is usually the occasion not only for personnel but also for policy renewal, and this was the case with Medvedev's election as president on March 2 and his assumption of the office on May 8, 2008. His presidency starkly exposed the contradictions of the dual state and the developmental stalemate in which Russia found itself as two political orders clashed. The stalemate was exacerbated because Medvedev was Putin's handpicked successor. The aim was to ensure continuity in the succession and to find someone who would continue to implement "Putin's plan." Medvedev was not a mere cipher for Putin, and he clearly had views of his own, but at the same time hopes for a liberal "thaw" were misplaced. Medvedev's election did not represent a revolutionary break with Putin's Russia, but it did provide the opportunity for a modest rebalancing of the system away from the prerogative toward the constitutional state, accompanied by constraints on the struggle of distributional coalitions that had used raids to achieve property redistribution.

In his Civic Forum speech on January 22, 2008, Medvedev called for the struggle against corruption to become a "national program," noting that "legal nihilism" took the form of "corruption in the power bodies." He returned to this idea in his January 29 speech to the Association of Russian Lawyers, of which he was chair of the board of trustees, when he called on his fellow lawyers to take a higher profile in society and to battle "legal nihilism." He clearly had two evils in mind: corruption in the traditional venal sense, characterized by the abuse of public office for private gain, and metacorruption, where the judicial process is undermined by political interference, which is known in Russia as "telephone law" and which had been most prominently in evidence during the Yukos case, which itself had given rise to the term "Basmanny justice."[47]

In a keynote speech to the Fifth Krasnoyarsk Economic Forum on February 15, 2008, Medvedev outlined not only his economic program but also his broad view of the challenges facing Russia.[48] He focused on an unwieldy bureaucracy, corruption, and lack of respect for the law as the main challenges facing Russia. In a decisive tone, he insisted that "freedom is better than lack of freedom—this principle should be at the core of our politics. I mean freedom in all of its manifestations—personal freedom, economic freedom and, finally, freedom of expression." He repeated earlier promises to ensure personal freedoms and an independent and free press. He repeatedly returned to the theme about "the need to ensure the independence of the legal system from the executive and legislative branches of power" and once again condemned the country's "legal nihilism" and to "humanize" the country's judicial system. He promised to reduce red tape and the number of bureaucrats and stated that he was against the practice of placing state officials on the boards of major corporations. The state would continue to play a role, however, but state appointees "should be replaced by truly independent directors, which the state would hire to implement its plans." Medvedev's plans for economic modernization focused on the four "I's": institutions, infrastructure, innovation, and investment.

On May 20, 2008, Medvedev addressed a high-level meeting in the Kremlin devoted to improving the judicial system. He argued that "our main objective is to achieve independence for the judicial system." He openly admitted the problem: "As we all know, when justice fails it often does so because of pressure of various kinds, such as surreptitious phone calls and money—there is no point beating about the bush."[49] This was a bold admission and recognition that "telephone law" had subverted the delivery of justice. Thus, the creation of an independent judiciary was back at the top of the agenda, as it had been in Putin's early years before it had run into the opposition of the judicial community. The new justice minister, Alexander Konovalov, however, announced the creation of a working group to prepare the changes.[50]

The eradication of corruption would be a long-term matter. One of the first cases came to a head in the first weeks of Medvedev's presidency. On May 12, 2008, the head of the Supreme Arbitration Court, Anton Ivanov, filed a request to have Lyudmila Maikova, the chairwoman of the Federal Arbitration Court in the Moscow District and thus the top judge in the field, suspended from her duties for "damaging the authority of the judicial branch and the reputation of the judiciary." Ivanov charged that Maikova, who had presided over a number of legal disputes involving the city administration, received help from City Hall in 2004 to swap her own apartment for two others and to buy another from a developer at less than market price.[51] Maikova had reputedly issued controversial rulings favorable to the tax authorities in high-profile business cases. Ivanov argued that Maikova had violated "ethical norms" by accepting cut-price apartments. Maikova's dismissal had to be approved by a commission of other judges. In his blog, Robert Amsterdam suggested that Maikova was being made a scapegoat for a controversial ruling, notably in the Yukos affair, where she argued that Fargoil had been created as a vehicle for Yukos to avoid paying taxes.[52]

However ambivalent, this signaled that the existing distributional coalitions were no longer sacrosanct, and the shift took place under the cover of a campaign against corruption. On the political front, in its first major judgment in its new home in St. Petersburg on May 27, 2008, the Constitutional Court dismissed the lawsuit against Manana Aslamazyan, the former head of the now defunct Educated Media Foundation, which had been funded by Khodorkovsky's Open Russia, who was accused of smuggling foreign currency. The Boev affair in the early months of Medvedev's presidency demonstrated the way that law had been instrumentalized in the Putin years. Legal action was taken against the media commentator Vladimir Solovev, a reporter for the Serebryannyi Dozhd' radio station, who had declared that "there are no independent courts in Russia—there are courts dependent on Boev."[53] As if to prove his point, the case against him was brought by Valeri Boev, an adviser on personnel appointments in the former Putin administration, in particular dealing with the appointment of judges. Boev dropped the claim after three other judges declared that they were ready to testify against him.[54]

Soon after, Yelena Valyavina, since October 2005 first deputy chair of the Supreme Arbitration Court, testified in court that Boev had threatened to damage her career in 2005 if she refused to reverse a ruling handed down on November 22, 2005, against the Federal Property Fund involving shares in Togliattiazot. If she did not accede to his request, Boev warned her, "Elena Yurievna, you still have to be re-appointed."[55] In her evidence to the Dorogomilovsky District Court on May 12, 2008, she noted that she ran into Boev on a number of occasions when she took up her post since as the deputy presiding judge she was responsible for cooperation with the Supreme Qualifications Board. In her judgment on the contentious case of Togliattiazot shares (a case that other judges tried to avoid), she ruled in favor of suspending provisional measures associated with the ban on holding general meetings. On requesting the case file, a call came from Boev, and then he came for a meeting. She was astonished at the way that the conversation turned out, anticipating a discussion of personnel issues. Instead, Boev "spoke at length about state interests, adding that I was probably failing to understand them correctly." She reminded him that she was the judge in the case and "that he had no right to give me instructions." He was asking her to annul her determination in this case. She told him that she was ready to work as an ordinary judge if she was not reappointed for another six-year term as a presiding judge.

Boev continued to try to exert pressure on the court by visiting senior members, although outsiders of course should not be involved in judicial decisions except when asked in an expert capacity. It is unlikely that Boev was acting on his own initiative, suggesting that his superiors in the presidential administration prompted his actions. Valyavina's declaration was considered "unprecedented." As one lawyer noted, "For the first time at such a high level we heard how the presidential administration through its officials try to influence high judicial proceedings." With the new leadership in place, the scale of political interference in judicial matters could at last be brought to light.

A former judge of the Samara Region Arbitration Court, Nadezhda Kostuchenko, was dismissed from her post by the qualification board of judges in March 2006 after being accused of making "illegal" judgments in the Toaz case (see above). She had adjudicated that steps taken to confiscate the 6.1 percent of Toaz shares would be illegal, as the stock no longer belonged to the defendant. There were persistent press reports that prior to the hearing, she had been pressured by the chair of the court not to return a judgment in favor of Toaz.[56] As we noted above, Kostuchenko appealed against her dismissal to the ECHR.

These were not the only scandals about political interference in judicial matters. The chair of the Moscow City Court is Olga Yegorova, who was urgently appointed to this post at the time of the hearings in the Gusinsky Media-Most (NTV) case in 2000. Under Yegorova, the Moscow City Court became known as "Moscow City Stamp" (Mosgorstamp) because of the eagerness with which it rubber-stamped the decisions of the General Prosecutors' Office.[57] This became a matter of considerable controversy after a Khamovniki court worker asserted that the judge in the second Yukos trial, Viktor Danilkin, had modified his judgment under pressure from above. The court's press secretary and aide to the presiding judge, Natalya Vasileva, announced on February 14, 2011, that the judge had not written the verdict himself, as prescribed by law, but had been influenced by unnamed figures in the Moscow City Court.[58] In Moscow, the total number of acquittals is less than one-third of 1 percent, with 33,919 convictions and only 102 acquittals in 2004, one acquittal for every 330 convictions.[59] Under her leadership, over 80 judges were forced to leave their jobs.[60] The pressure to achieve convictions remains intense.

Yegorova forced the dismissal of an independent judge, Olga Kudeshkina, involved in the trial of the owners of the "Three Whales" ("Tri Kita") furniture store in Moscow.[61] In 2003, Kudeshkina informed the media that Yegorova had put pressure on her when examining the case of Pavel Zaitsev, an MVD investigator who had been working on the Three Whales furniture-smuggling case. Zaitsev was accused of exceeding his authority, suggesting that he was threatening some highly placed individuals. Kudeshkina was dismissed from the Moscow City Court in May 2004, charged with "discrediting the judiciary" because of her critical comments. Ironically, Kudeshkina is married to a former KGB officer, and the owners of the furniture store had close links with the security services. Kudeshkina's various appeals were rejected within Russia, and in 2006 she took the case to the ECHR. Her complaint under Article 10 ECHR was declared admissible on February 28, 2008.

The head of the Supreme Arbitrazh Court is Anton Ivanov, a former university classmate and close friend of Medvedev. In late 2006, Ivanov shocked a meeting of judges when he declared that the Federal Tax Service (FSN) was pressuring judges. The FSN in that year managed to get judges dismissed who had been dealing with the tax affairs against TNK-BP.[62] The "Just Russia" State Duma deputy Gennady Gudkov argued that the corruption of the judicial system had provoked the sharp rise in the number of convictions in recent years, with cases often started as part of business conflicts and "often a symptom of raiding and competitive struggles, achieved with the help of the corrupt law enforcement apparatus." The selective and politically inspired use of law in the Putin era was confirmed by Medvedev's recognition of "legal nihilism." On May 20, 2008, Medvedev called for an independent court system when he addressed a meeting with senior judges and legal officials in the Kremlin: "[Unjust] decisions, as we all know, do happen and come as a result of different kinds of pressure, like telephone calls and—it cannot be denied—offers of money."[63] The struggle against the "nightmaring" of business became the keynote of his presidency, but as the second Yukos trial, the Hermitage Capital case, and many more illustrated, the stalemate in Russian politics was too profound to be resolved by the efforts of one man, even the president, especially when he was locked in a system of tandem rule with the former leader, Putin, under whose leadership the stalemate had developed.

Conclusion

The Yukos and Toaz cases reflect the wilfulness of the Russian political scene and the scope for entrepreneurs to manipulate the law with official connivance to advance their interests. Predatory raiders take advantage of the duality of the Russian state, but that very duality allows a company such as Toaz to withstand the raiders. The duality of the state is in evidence in judicial and legislative attempts to define and inhibit corporate raids. These attempts were much in evidence at the time of the transition of power from Putin to Medvedev in 2008. The Kostyuchenko and Valyavina cases at least opened the lid on pressure against judges, but other cases rumbled on, demonstrating the pressures against lawyers in instances when factional conflict was under way. Medvedev in May of that year gave specific instructions to devise a package of antiraid measures, including amendments to laws and analysis of the work of regional authorities and law enforcement agencies in this sphere.[64] So far, there is no convincing evidence that the situation has improved. The dual state may have changed the way that it operates, with recognition of the arbitrariness of the administrative regime, but the system remains locked in a stalemate the outcome of which remains unclear.

Notes

1. Richard Sakwa, *The Crisis of Russian Democracy: The Dual State, Factionalism and the Medvedev Succession* (Cambridge: Cambridge University Press, 2011).
2. Russia is not the only country to suffer from this syndrome, but it is clearly an extreme case. For a comparable instance in which the comparison is drawn through the concept of "Putinism for the West," see Paolo Flores D'Arcais, "Anatomy of Berlusconismo," *New Left Review* 68: 137–39.
3. Antonio Gramsci, "'Notes on Italian History," in *Selections from the Prison Notebooks of Antonio Gramsci*, ed. and trans. Quintin Hoare and Geoffrey Nowell Smith (London: Lawrence & Wishart, 1971), 116; Robert W. Cox, "Civil Society at the Turn

of the Millennium: Prospects for an Alternative World Order," *Review of International Studies* 25, no. 1 (1999): 3–28.

4. Cox, "Civil Society at the Turn of the Millennium," 12

5. Alena Ledeneva, "Telephone Justice in Russia," *Post-Soviet Affairs* 24, no. 4 (2008): 324–50.

6. Basmannoe pravosudie, *Basmannoe pravosudie: Uroki samooborony: Posobie dlya advokatov* (Moscow: Publichnaya reputatsiya, 2003).

7. Douglass North, *Institutions, Institutional Change and Economic Performance* (Cambridge, Cambridge University Press, 1990).

8. Transparency International, "CPI Table 2008," 2008, http://goo.gl/JxMpc.

9. *Moscow Times*, September 23, 2008.

10. Center for Political Technologies, *Reiderstvo kak sotsial'no-ekonomicheskii i politicheskii fenomenon sovremennoi Rossii: Otchet o kachestvennom sotsiologicheskom issledovanii* (Moscow: Tsentr politicheskikh tekhnologii, 2008).

11. Center for Political Technologies, *Reiderstvo kak sotsial'no-ekonomicheskii i politicheskii fenomenon sovremennoi Rossii*, 13–14.

12. *Samarskie izvestiye*, May 21, 2008.

13. *Moscow Times*, November 8, 2006.

14. *Moscow Times*, September 8, 2008.

15. http://www.khodorkovsky.info/authority/136638.html.

16. *Kommersant*, November 30, 2007.

17. *Nezavisimaya gazeta*, November 23, 1995.

18. Peter Rutland, "Oil, Politics and Foreign Policy," in *The Political Economy of Russian Oil*, ed. David Lane, 163–88 (Lanham, MD: Rowman & Littlefield, 1999).

19. William Tompson, "A Frozen Venezuela? The Resource Curse and Russian Politics," in *Russia's Oil and Natural Gas: Bonanza or Curse?*, ed. Michael Ellman (London: Anthem Press, 2006), 208.

20. Gleb Pavlovsky, "Brat—3," *Ekspert: Luchshie materialy* 2 (2007): 63–67 (originally published in *Ekspert* 32 [September 1, 2003]: 63).

21. Vladimir Shlapentokh, "Wealth versus Political Power: The Russian Case," *Communist and Post-Communist Studies* 37, no. 2 (2004): 135–60.

22. Richard Sakwa, *The Quality of Freedom: Khodorkovsky, Putin, and the Yukos Affair* (Oxford: Oxford University Press, 2009).

23. Stanislav Belkovsky, *Imperiya Vladimira Putina* (Moscow: Algoritm, 2008), 15.

24. William Tompson, "Putin and the 'Oligarchs': A Two-Sided Commitment Problem," in *Leading Russia: Putin in Perspective*, ed. Alex Pravda, 179–202 (Oxford: Oxford University Press, 2005); William Tompson "Putting Yukos in Perspective," *Post-Soviet Affairs* 21, no. 2 (2005): 159–82.

25. United Financial Group, *Morning Comment*, July 7, 2003, cited in Philip Hanson, "The Turn to Statism in Russian Economic Policy," *The International Spectator* 42 (2007): 1029–42.

26. Bettina Renz, "Putin's Militocracy? An Alternative Interpretation of *Siloviki* in Contemporary Russian Politics," *Europe-Asia Studies* 58, no. 6 (2006): 909.

27. Timothy Frye, "Capture or Exchange? Business Lobbying in Russia," *Europe-Asia Studies* 54, no. 7 (2002): 1017–36.

28. *Novaya gazeta*, September 10, 2007.

29. Stephen Fortescue, "The Russian Law on Subsurface Resources: A Policy Marathon," *Post-Soviet Affairs* 25, no. 2 (2009): 160. See also Yuko Adachi, "Subsoil Law Reform in Russia under the Putin Administration," *Europe-Asia Studies* 61, no. 8 (2009): 1393–414. Adachi identifies a three-way struggle between the Kremlin's changing policy priorities, bureaucratic infighting, and the interests of state-controlled mineral-extracting companies.

30. Clifford Gaddy, "Statement of Clifford G. Gaddy, Senior Fellow The Brookings Institution, Committee on House Financial Services Subcommittee on Domestic and International Monetary Policy, Trade and Technology, 17 October 2007," *Johnson's Russia List* 219.

31. *Samarskie izvestiye*, April 25, 2006.

32. *Parlamentskaya gazeta*, November 18, 2005.

33. *Nezavisimaya gazeta*, November 18, 2005.

34. E. Kitashov, "Byt' li russkomu Bkhopalu?," in *Chelovek i zakon*, ed. Anton Samoilenkov, 42–53 (Moscow: Chelovek i zakon, 2007); *Parlamentskaya gazeta*, July 3, 2007.

35. *World Business*, April 27, 2007.

36. *Khronograph* [Togliatti], February 26, 2007.

37. This certainly is the predominant view of press commentary on the case.

38. Cases before the Samara Regional Arbitrazh Court, May 14, 2007, and May 16, 2007.

39. The program "Osobo opasen" was presented by Sergei Avdienko and broadcast on May 5, 2007.

40. *Kommersant* [Samara], February 9, 2007.

41. *Kommersant*, June 20, 2007.

42. *Khronograph*, February 26, 2007.

43. *Khronograph*, February 26, 2007.

44. Li-Chen Sim, *The Rise and Fall of Privatization in the Russian Oil Industry* (Basingstoke: Palgrave Macmillan, 2008), 118.

45. Philip Hanson, "The Russian Economic Puzzle: Going Forwards, Backwards or Sideways?," *International Affairs* 83, no. 5 (2007): 869–89.

46. *Ekspert*, April 4, 2005.

47. *Nezavisimaya gazeta*, January 20, 2008.

48. Dmitry Medvedev, "Vystuplenie na V Krasnoyarskom ekonomicheskom forume 'Rossiya 2008–2020: Upravlenie rostom,'" 2008, http://goo.gl/1VmIz.

49. Dmitry Medvedev, "Opening Address at a Meeting to Discuss Improving the Judicial System," 2008, http://goo.gl/39UYt.

50. *Moscow Times*, May 21, 2008.

51. *Moscow Times*, June 6, 2008.

52. http://www.robertamsterdam.com/2008/05/maikova_as_scapegoat.htm.

53. *Kommersant*, May 13, 2008

54. *Moscow Times*, June 5, 2008.

55. *Vremya novostei*, May 21, 2008.

56. Interfax, June 24, 2008.

57. *St. Petersburg Times*, December 28, 2004.

58. Natal'ya Vasil'eva, "'Prigovor byl privezen iz Mosgorsuda, ya tochno znayu': Otkrovennoe intervyu o dele Yukosa pomoshchnika sud'i Khamovnicheskogo suda," 2011, http://goo.gl/D9awy.

59. *Moscow Times*, December 10, 2004.

60. *The Times*, March 19, 2005.

61. *The Times*, March 19, 2005.

62. *Kommersant*, May 13, 2008.

63. Newsru.com, May 20, 2008.

64. *Parlamentskaya gazeta*, May 22, 2008; *Nezavisimaya gazeta*, May 23, 2008.

5

The Political Economy of Russia's Demographic Crisis

States and Markets, Migrants and Mothers

Linda J. Cook

S INCE THE EARLY 1990s, the population of the Russian Federation has undergone a precipitous decline, with a fall in both overall numbers and
life expectancy that has rarely been seen in peacetime and never before in a
developed industrial state. From 1993 to 2005, the number of deaths exceeded
births by 11.2 million, and the population was continuing to decline by more
than 700,000 per year.[1] In 2008, the United Nations projected a decline in
Russia's population from 142 million in 2007 to 130 million in 2025.[2] Low
birthrates, high levels of middle-aged male mortality, poor reproductive
health, relatively high rates of infant and maternal mortality, and overall
deteriorating health indicators during the postcommunist transition all
contributed. For the first time in 2007, as a delayed effect of persistently low
birthrates, the number of people entering the working-age population failed
to compensate for retirements and premature deaths.[3]

During much of this period, Russia's economy was also contracting—
indeed, some analysts attribute the fertility decline partly to the 1990s economic crisis, deteriorating living standards, and the stresses of transition—
but the end of the 1990s brought a period of strong economic growth that
was sustained until 2008. Economic recovery produced both possibilities and
pressures for addressing the demographic crisis. On the one hand, the government commanded more resources for financing health and social measures as
well as migration policy. On the other hand, demand for labor now exceeded
domestic supply, and the workforce was projected to continue shrinking, by
as much as 17 million, or 24 percent, between 2009 and 2026. In addition,
some of Russia's more remote regions in Siberia and the Russian Far East,

where development had been heavily state subsidized during the Soviet period, experienced massive population exodus.[4]

The effects of demographic decline for economic development, as well as national and territorial security, became major concerns for Russia's government officials. In his annual address to the nation in 2006, then President Putin identified the demographic crisis as "the most acute problem facing our country today."[5] The government gave the crisis top priority, producing in 2007 a "Concept for Demographic Policy through 2025" that mapped out a set of responses in the areas of demographic, health, immigration, labor market, and employment policy.

The demographic crisis, in particular the shrinking working-age population, has large implications for Russia's political economy, affecting the prospects for economic growth and modernization. Labor is already the most deficient production factor in Russia's economy; in 2009, a substantial proportion of employers, including 30 to 50 percent of companies in various sectors, reported shortages of labor.[6] Interregional competition for workers is intensifying, with Siberia and the Far East especially labor deficient. The Russian government's 2006 "Blueprint for Long-Term Development" pointed to the "growing role of human capital as a fundamental factor of development . . . to sustain [Russia's] competitive position in the world economy" and emphasized "concern with the reduction of supply of labor resources in connection with the reduction of the able-bodied adult section of the population and exacerbation of the shortage of skilled personnel."[7] In short, unless the economy finds additional sources of labor over the coming decades, analysts expect stagnation and ongoing decline in economic output outside the energy sector.

As rates of labor force participation for both men and women are comparatively quite high in Russia, there remain two major ways to compensate for the demographic crisis and developing labor shortages: immigration and increased birthrates.[8] Policy efforts have been directed to both, but contradictory political pressures and agendas complicate these efforts. In the area of immigration, stark contradictions are evident between Russia's need for workers and the political, institutional, and societal responses to immigrants. These contradictions are evident in overly restrictive official immigration policies, widespread xenophobic popular attitudes, and demonstrations and physical attacks against immigrants by an extremist minority. In short, political and societal attitudes militate against the policies that Russia needs to increase and rejuvenate its labor force.

The government has also made serious efforts to increase birthrates through pronatalist policies. The pronatalist project relies on financial incentives for mothers and health care providers as well as maternalist employment protections, social subsidies, and a neofamilialist ideology that encourages women to focus on child rearing. Like immigration, pronatalism is contested and complicated in contemporary Russia. It entails new government interventions in labor markets that already suffer from distortions, requiring employers to grant extended leaves and other concessions to women around childbearing. Pronatalist policies provide incentives for women to leave the labor force at least temporarily, interrupting career trajectories of educated workers whose skills are needed. These policies are at best ambiguous for the modernization of Russian society: while most pronatalist policies are based on a contemporary model of family–work reconciliation, that is, making it easier for women to combine the two roles, they have included legislative restrictions on reproductive rights and promotion of neofamilialist and patriarchal ideologies. Finally, most demographers are convinced that pronatalist policies will fail to address the problems of population and labor force declines.

In sum, the Russian government is failing to find viable, effective, or broadly supported responses to its shrinking population and labor force. Both immigration and pronatalist policies are proving internally contradictory and politically contentious. This chapter looks at these contradictions and contentions and analyzes their effects for immigrants, women, labor markets, and Russia's future economic prospects.

The Politics of Immigration

The end of the Cold War proved a watershed event in the expansion of global migration, with especially dramatic effects in Eurasia. Following the collapse of the Soviet Union in 1991, the Russian Federation became a major destination and receiving country for international migration, with entrants from more than 100 countries. The 2002 Russian Federation census found that about 9 percent of permanent residents, about 12.4 million people, were born outside the country, placing Russia second only to the United States as a receiving country for international migrants.[9] The scale, ethnic makeup, and motivations of immigrants shifted over the post-Soviet decades. At first, large numbers of Russian coethnics came as political or involuntary migrants from the post-Soviet states (the "near abroad") fleeing conflicts and nationalist revivals. Later, a more ethnically diverse pool of labor migrants came from both the "near" and the "far" abroad, the latter mainly from the Middle East and Asia. By 2005, an estimated 6 to 7 million immigrants participated in Russia's labor force, constituting a substantial 8 to 10 percent of total employment.[10]

The government's policies also shifted. Initially, returning Russians were welcomed with citizenship rights and resettlement aid, and Russia retained a visa-free regime with most post-Soviet states. Later, officials sought to regulate and restrict growing multiethnic labor immigration, while the expanding Russian market's demand for labor drew large numbers of low-skilled migrants who sometimes entered and often worked illegally. Immigration policy became contentious, featuring debates between those who stressed the demographic and economic benefits of relative openness and those who favored restrictive policies for all except the ethnic Russia diaspora.

Russia is distinct from most migrant-receiving countries in several respects. First, aside from Middle Eastern states, it is the only major nondemocratic and politically illiberal receiving country. Russia's is "an illiberal polity with no ideological impetus for admitting or extending rights to immigrants."[11] Second, population movement was strictly controlled until the 1980s, so the new Russian state had no experience with large-scale immigration and no legislation or regulatory procedures in place when the inflow began. As Oxana Shevel trenchantly observers, the Russia polity of the 1990s therefore had no interests organized around migration issues, and policy developed in response to the events of that chaotic decade.[12] Third, much immigration to Russia has a "postcolonial" nature; that is, Soviet policies created a shared cultural and linguistic space for the large majority of migrants who came from Eurasia.[13] As the number of immigrants as well as the proportion from outside Eurasia (far abroad) has grown, immigration policy has become increasingly restrictive. At the same time, more than other advanced industrial states in Europe and elsewhere, Russia needs immigrants for labor supply and demographic rejuvenation. Table 5.1 shows that without immigration, Russia's working-age population will decline dramatically over the next fifteen years.

Shifting Immigration Patterns in the 1990s

The period of the early 1990s was characterized by large-scale, unregulated immigration, mostly of coethnics. When the Soviet Union collapsed and split into fifteen separate states at the end of 1991, some 25 million ethnic Russians were left outside the Russian Federation. Large numbers of Russian and other

TABLE 5.1
Working-Age Population Change without Immigration in the Russian Federation (millions)

2007–2010	*2011–2015*	*2016–2020*	*2021–2026*	*2007–2026, Cumulative*
−3.9	−5.6	−5.4	−3.2	−18.1

Source: Adapted from Grigory Ioffe and Zhanna Zayonchkovskaya, *Immigration to Russia: Why It Is Inevitable, and How Large It May Have to Be to Provide the Workforce Russia Needs*, NCEEER Working Paper (Seattle: University of Washington, 2010), 33.

Slavic migrants came to Russia, mainly from Ukraine, Moldova, Tajikistan, and the Caucasus, fleeing wars, nationalist revivals, or political and cultural tensions with titular majorities. The Russian government established the Federal Migration Service to manage immigration and coordinate resettlement aid. In 1991, most former Soviet states formed a loose confederation, the Commonwealth of Independent States (CIS), and from 1991 to 2001, all citizens of the CIS had the right to enter the Russian Federation without visas. Although Russia's declining economy offered few employment opportunities during this period and displacement proved painful and often impoverishing, these migrants were officially welcomed, and efforts were made to integrate them into Russian society. Much more restrictive policies were applied to those from the far abroad, that is, outside the former Soviet Union. Small numbers came from Turkey, China, North Korea, Vietnam, Yugoslavia, and other states, though they were not covered by the visa-free regime and generally found it difficult to qualify even for refugee status.[14]

By the mid-1990s, the patterns of immigration had changed. The flow of political migrants declined, and labor migrants became the dominant group. The numbers registered by the Russian State Statistical Administration also fell, though, according to the United Nations, "specialists estimate that the real number of immigrants after 1996 is nearly twice as large as official statistics."[15] Table 5.2 shows the main sources of legal labor migrants from both the near and the far abroad in 2006 (though it is important to keep in mind that official statistics capture only part of immigration). Migrants, mainly men, were "pushed" from sending countries by poverty, the absence of economic opportunities, and the prospect of sending home remittances and were pulled by the demand for low-skilled workers in Russia. Immigrants concentrate in construction, transportation, manufacturing, and agricultural, most but not all working at low skill levels. Two major factors have shaped immigration: self-perpetuating patterns in which immigrant communities formed enclaves that then attracted and aided coethnics and often illegal intermediary firms that organized job placements.

TABLE 5.2
Main Sources of Legal Labor Migrants to the Russian Federation in 2006

Ukraine	16.9%
Uzbekistan	10.4%
Tajikistan	9.7%
China	20.8%
Turkey	10.0%

Source: Adapted from United Nations, *Demographic Policy in Russia: From Reflection to Action* (Moscow: United Nations, 2008), 45, citing Russian Federal Migration Service statistics.

Economic Recovery and Restrictive Migration Policies

In the early 2000s, robust economic recovery pulled in a more diverse pool of labor migrants. Immigrants' educational levels declined, cultural differences with Russian society increased, and many migrants had poor Russian-language skills. The scale of immigration and migrant settlement emerged as major issues for Russian government and society in this period, and the responses of both were conflicted. Some in the Federal Migration Service and many in the business community recognized the value or at least the inevitability of "replacement migration" for its demographic and especially labor market contributions. They pressed for liberal policies, including de facto amnesties for those already working in Russia, and liberal quotas for additional immigrants.

By contrast, most of Russian state's political and administrative elite concentrated on control of immigration and security threats. The thrust of policy changed to stronger regulation and combating illegal immigration. The Federal Migration Service was abolished in 2000, and its functions were transferred to the Ministry of Internal Affairs, marking a turn toward policing and enforcement as priorities in dealing with immigrants. Migration policy became more concerned with anticrime and antiterrorism measures. In 2002, a restrictive citizenship law, "On the Legal Situation of Foreigners," was passed; visa-free travel within the CIS was curtailed; and immigration controls were tightened. The Russian government began bilateral negotiations with neighboring states and on immigration quotas in an effort to manage labor migration.[16] As one analyst summed up the changes, administrative and political considerations took precedence over economic ones.[17]

Russian immigration policy focuses not on borders—it continues to allow limited visa-free entry from some former Soviet states—but rather on entry to the labor market, relying on a system of work permits and quotas. The formal process for establishing immigration quotas is complicated and cumbersome, with excessive administrative barriers, and is technically impossible for many small and medium-size employers. In 2009, about one-third of mostly large employers used the quota system, while the majority employed irregular migrants who lacked official work permits. The number of permits thus falls well below real labor demand, which is high for both skilled and unskilled workers. Regulatory policies in recent years have been shifting and inconsistent, pushing both employers and immigrants into the shadow sector of the economy.[18]

Tensions over immigration have persisted in political circles, played out partly in struggles over the size of immigration quotas. The initial, 2007 CIS quota, supported by immigration authorities, was set at a generous 6 million, effectively allowing an amnesty for many who had previously entered or stayed illegally. With the beginning of the international recession and financial crisis in 2008, work permit quotas were greatly reduced—to 3.4 million in 2008, 2 million in 2009, and 1.3 million in 2010—while an estimated 5 million to 10 million immigrants worked informally (figure 5.1). Russia's semiofficial trade union federation in particular pressed for restrictions. The federation's head, Andrei Shmakov, called for a ban on hiring foreign workers, and they were in fact banned from retail trade and other sectors where they had become a prominent presence (though many devised subterfuges to skirt the ban). Such incidents of official harassment fed the insecurity and social marginalization of immigrant workers as well as the resentment and xenophobia of Russians encouraged by their labor leaders to scapegoat migrants for the economic hardships of the recession.

During this period, immigration policy developed a parallel strand of "compatriot resettlement" as an alternative response to labor market shortages and security concerns. In 2006–2007, while it introduced restrictive

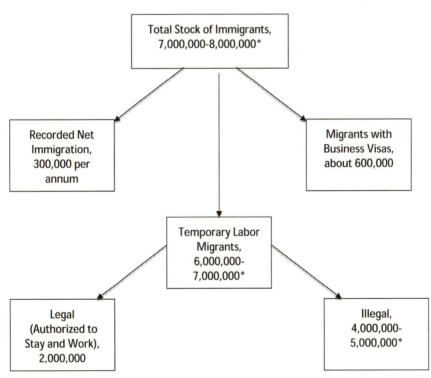

FIGURE 5.1
Legal and Illegal Migration Flows (estimates for 2009; * peak season number). *Source:*
Adapted from Grigory Ioffe and Zhanna Zayonchkovskaya, *Immigration to Russia:*
Why It Is Inevitable, and How Large It May Have to Be to Provide the Workforce
***Russia Needs,* NCEEER Working Paper (Seattle: University of Washington, 2010), 40.**

quotas for CIS migrants, the Russian government established a "program inducing immigration of compatriots" that provided preferential treatment for Russian coethnics in the international diasporas who immigrated over the six-year period to 2012. The program offered aid to individuals and communities, particularly for resettlement in depopulated regions of the Russian Far East, where they would serve as a hedge against feared population pressure from China.[19] Compatriot resettlement, however, has produced disappointing results. The government initially set an ambitious goal of repatriating 300,000 by 2009 but succeeded in attracting only 10,000 to 17,000, even with a rather vague definition of "compatriot." Many of those who did come were settled in remote regions where they could contribute little to economic growth or development.

Negative Societal Attitudes toward Immigrants

Much of Russian society has taken a negative view of most immigration and displayed growing intolerance and xenophobia. In this, it was aided and abetted by the media and parts of the political elite.[20] In representative opinion polls carried out from 2000 to 2011 by the respected Levada Center, more than half of respondents supported implementation of "Russia for Russians" (i.e., Russophone migration or none) as a good idea, at least "within reasonable limits." From 2004, growing majorities agreed that "the Russian government should try to curb the influx of non-resident aliens."[21] Surveys conducted in 2006 showed that majorities of Russian citizens held negative attitudes toward the employment of migrants—a small majority opposed even their employment in trade and services (table 5.3). Majorities also opposed migrants owning property, including apartments and houses. Only 10 percent reported welcoming attitudes. The majority of Russian citizens, in sum, did not accept immigration as a solution to population decline or labor force shortages.

TABLE 5.3
Attitudes toward Immigrants' Employment and Housing Rights

What is your attitude toward the employment of migrants in:

	Positive	Indifferent	Negative	Not Available
Law enforcement	4%	12%	74%	10%
Civic and municipal service	5%	16%	69%	11%
Health, education, and social work	7%	19%	62%	11%
Private business (trades and services)	9%	27%	53%	11%

Source: Adapted from "Tables and Diagrams: Migration and Racism," *Russian Analytical Digest*, no. 7, October 3, 2006, 8, citing Levada Center, representative poll, July 2005, http://www.levada.ru.

Xenophobic and intolerant attitudes toward immigrants are reflected in popular rhetoric and stereotypes. Migrants are commonly framed in popular discourse as sources of crime and potential terrorism and bloodshed. They are also seen as "diseased others," spreading infectious illnesses, despite their positive health selectivity and evidence that many immigrants practice healthier behaviors, such as smoking and drinking less, than their Russian counterparts.[22] Despite antiextremist laws, ultranationalist movements have grown. One of the most prominent, the DPNI (Movement against Illegal Immigration), advocates an anti-immigrant agenda of "Russia for the Russians." Violent, extremist "skinhead" youth periodically attack migrants, maiming and killing randomly, sometimes including children as targets.[23] Hate crimes are seldom prosecuted or punished, and responses from government officials tend to be muted.

Some political elites encourage nationalist and racist sentiment through political discourse. Elite-controlled media typically emphasize ethnic identifiers in reports on crime and security threats. Moscow's longtime former mayor Luzhkov, a notorious immigrant basher, sponsored several forced collective deportations of Caucasian groups from the city. Even more responsible politicians are often slow and evasive in responding to overt racism. According to analysts, societal and elite attitudes are mutually reinforcing, producing in Russia "pervasive institutional and societal manifestations of xenophobia [that] work together to justify restrictive immigration policies."[24]

Consequences

Both state policy and societal attitudes have profound effects on immigrants' integration into Russian labor markets and society. As noted, quotas for work permits set by the state fall far below demand—by millions of workers. Employers and migrants are often unable and/or unwilling to overcome the administrative hurdles to legal employment. As a consequence, a large majority of migrants work informally, perpetuating and expanding the "gray" sector in Russia's economy. Informality is in turn corrosive of the state's capacity to regulate, tax, or even monitor economic activity. Untaxable work and wages undercut the state's income and its ability to invest in modernization, education, and labor force planning. Informality deprives immigrants of legal rights, access to social services, and other protections, forcing them to live a "shadow" existence on the margins of Russian society. Marginality in turn contributes to corruption and the trade of false documents, permits, residences, and so on and contributes to social and political exclusion. The contradictions and unintended consequences of official policy are heavily implicated in creating and perpetuating these problems. In sum, the Russian government "needs to create an environment for legal employment of migrant workers."[25]

The experiences of immigrants to the Russian Federation vary greatly according to their country of origin, ethnicity and confession, legal status, skill level, place of settlement, age, and stereotypes of their group in popular discourse. Generally, Russians and other Slavs have been absorbed most readily and are most likely to become citizens participating legally in labor markets. Muslims from the Caucasus and Central Asia and East Asians, especially Chinese, have confronted the strongest anti-immigrant hostility and suffered the highest incidence of violent hate crimes. Caucasians are targeted because of historical animosities and stereotyped association with perpetrators of the terrorist attacks that have plagued Russia, and Chinese are targeted because of exaggerated fears that they are "creeping invaders" who will eventually come to dominate depopulated regions along the Russian–Chinese border.[26]

Place of residence also matters: both migrant and antimigrant sentiments and activities are more prevalent in large cities, particularly Moscow and St. Petersburg, though immigrants' risk of extreme violence is greater in smaller cities. "Very Russian" regions that have little previous experience with migration have proven especially hostile. By contrast, some development-oriented regional elites have welcomed immigrants and taken proactive measures to integrate them, with some success. The history of the immigrant communities' presence in Russia also affects the experience of newcomers: some groups, such as Armenians, have well-established communities of coethnics with elite and professional strata that provide support for newcomers; others, most notably Tajiks, are comprised mainly of poor recent labor migrants. Proximity and access to nongovernmental organizations and charitable organizations that provide social, medical, legal, and other services is also a factor.

Effects on Labor Markets and Sending Economies

Posttransition immigration has transformed Russian labor markets, particularly those for low-skilled workers. Immigrants have become a critical source of labor for Russia's economy, and their significance is likely to grow over the next ten to fifteen years as Russia's working-age population shrinks and declines as a proportion of the overall population. The transformation has been greatest in major cities, which have served as magnets for migration. One-third of the total number of registered foreign workers, and an estimated one-half of all migrants live in the Moscow region (now referred to as the "inner abroad" for those from the CIS), where they congregate in ethnically segregated enclaves of Asians, Tajiks, Armenians, and others producing highly fragmented urban landscapes.[27] Moscow and St. Petersburg, both centers of Russia's banking and financial services sectors, now conform to the configuration of "global cities," that is, cities characterized by ethnically bifurcated labor markets and income structures.[28] Here, convergence of managerial, financial, administrative, and technical elites produces a concentration of wealth that in turn demands large numbers of low-wage service workers drawn in immigrant flows from poorer peripheral states. Migrants in turn produce networks of communication and support that draw their coethnics into economic niches and residential enclaves. International economic pressures produce these migration flows, which become self-perpetuating. According to Massey, "As the level of out-migration increases, the costs and risks of international movement drop . . . movement is increasingly determined by international wage differentials and labor demand."[29] These patterns are common to developed countries where, as in Russia, the immigration of poor ethnic others provokes hostility, xenophobia, and restrictive policies that cannot be enforced. They result in large urban immigrant communities that are integrated economically but marginalized socially and politically.

Migration to Russia has also had profound effects on the economies and societies of sending countries, providing employment possibilities for excess labor and remittances that contribute to national income as well as the welfare and stratification of families and communities. They in turn produce new patterns of dependence and economic vulnerability for peripheral states. According the Cynthia Buckley, a major scholar of migration, "Eurasia's southern tier, especially Tajikistan and the South Caucasus, are heavily reliant on migrants' remittances for survival."[30]

In sum, migration has contributed to the size of Russia's population. It has also produced a measure of rejuvenation since migrants tend to self-select as young, healthy, and able bodied. However, the scale of immigration is insufficient to produce replacement population growth or satisfy the economy's demands for labor. Experts, extrapolating from current trends, conclude that the Central (i.e., Moscow) District is the only federal district that will be replenished by migration.[31] The prospects of repopulating remote northern and border regions seem especially poor and expensive. Indeed, Russia needs more immigrants in order to repopulate and grow economically, while the limits of "compatriot resettlement" seem to have been reached. Yet the state sets labor immigrant quotas far below the economy's demand for labor, pushing majorities of immigrants into illegal labor markets that escape state regulation, undermine taxation, and contribute to corruption. At the same time, societal xenophobia keeps most immigrants socially marginalized and insecure and unlikely to plan for the long term or develop skills to enhance their economic contributions and welfare.

Pronatalist Policies

Among the Russian government's efforts to address population decline, strong emphasis has been placed on a set of pronatalist policies, that is, policies intended to increase birthrates. The goals of these policies were elaborated in the 2006 Draft National Program for Russia's Demographic Development and the 2007 Presidential Decree "Concept of Demographic Policy for Russia until 2025."[32] According to these documents, the government would direct its efforts first toward stabilizing the population at 140 million to 142 million by 2015 and then toward achieving growth to 145 million by 2025. While these efforts included measures to increase in-migration as well as life expectancy, which diverged sharply from European patterns during the 1990s, the main focus is on increasing fertility from the current 1.3 births per woman to 1.7.[33] The policies adopted to achieve these goals include regulatory interventions that may make labor markets less efficient and remove women with critical skills. At the same time, children born as a result of these policies would not reach entry into the labor force for two decades, doing little to address present and anticipated labor shortages in the medium term.

Pronatalist policies involved a package of maternalist labor policies, family subsidies, and other payments and programs that are designed to increase the numbers of children in a typical Russian household to two, three, or more. In 2006, Russia's government, under the auspices of the National Priority Project "On Health," introduced a high-profile innovation, "maternity capital" (*materinskii kapital*), a financial incentive for a parent with one or more children to give birth to or to adopt another. Such parents (mainly mothers, though single adoptive fathers are also eligible) are promised a one-time payment of R250,000 at their new child's third birthday. This is a substantial sum by the standards of most Russian citizens' incomes, equal to approximately €7,200, or U.S.$10,000. Payment would be made not in cash but as a benefit or subsidy that could be used to pay for the child's education or be contributed to the mother's pension account to compensate for additional time out of the labor force or to purchase housing. Maternity capital was linked to a program of housing and mortgage expansion, with special subsidies for multichild families. The government began registering entitled women in early 2007, issuing more than 130,000 maternity capital certificates by September.[34] The program is designed to continue until the end of 2016, with federal budget expenditures projected at more than R195 billion per year.[35]

Russia's government has also taken measures to improve access and utilization of health care by pregnant women and infants. The Childbirth Certificate Program, introduced in 2006 as part of the broader National Priority Project "On Health," guarantees government payment for obstetric and neonatal medical services. Under this program, regional public health authorities are responsible for issuing childbirth certificates that provide payments of R2,000 at twenty-eight weeks' gestation to a clinic providing obstetric care and R5,000 to a maternity hospital for childbirth. The goals of this policy are to improve care, especially early detection of problems or disease during pregnancy, and to reduce reproductive disorders and infant mortality. The government has also committed itself to build more than twenty new clinics equipped with the latest technologies for perinatal care. More than 2.5 million women and newborns had used the certificate program by 2005. The program has increased access to care, improved outcomes, and given implicit incentives for health care providers to encourage childbearing and discourage abortions.[36]

Soviet-era family supports and subsidies have also been restored and enhanced, with the clear intent of encouraging multichild families. The real value of the Soviet-era package of child and family benefits had fallen steeply during transition.[37] Birth grants were reformed to increase for each successive child, providing a one-time payment of R8,000 for the first child and R25,000 for the third, while the monthly allowance for a child up to eighteen months old was doubled and for a second child quadrupled. The cost to the government of these measures was estimated at R53 billion.[38] Increases are intended to compensate families for longer-term loss of women's income and to alleviate the poverty that disproportionately affected multichild families in the 1990s.

The shortage and cost of places in Russian nurseries and kindergartens, which are essential for allowing mothers to continue participation in the labor force, has also become an issue of high-level political concern. The numbers of preschool and nursery facilities declined dramatically between 1990 and 2003, leaving 1 million preschool children reportedly on waiting lists for places in 2007–2008. President Putin promised to "develop pre-school education and make it truly public . . . in the 1990s . . . many regions saw their networks of kindergartens and nurseries destroyed . . . it is our constitutional duty to ensure that all children have the opportunity to receive free preschool educations."[39] Compensation for preschool child care was introduced, again with an increasing percentage of costs compensated for each successive child: up to 20 percent for the first child, 50 percent for the second child, and 70 percent for additional children.[40] The 2006 federal law "On Education" capped fees for state and municipal child care services, while Moscow placed the onus on regional and municipal governments to provide more facilities.

Housing policy has also been designed with pronatalist goals. The Draft National Program for Russia's Demographic Development proposed a range of government assistance measures for families with children, including a plan to pay off an increasing proportion of the family's mortgage for each successive child: 10 percent for the first child, 30 to 40 percent for the second child, and 100 percent of any unpaid balance for the third child (though restricted to "young" parents up to age thirty-five).[41] These benefits complemented the potential use of maternity capital for housing costs. Problems of poor housing conditions remain serious, however, while only a very small percentage of households have taken mortgages. Analysts claim that subsidies have failed to increase the construction of affordable housing and instead have exacerbated the imbalance between supply and demand and contributed to price increases in some areas.[42]

Maternalist Employment Protections

The government has also intervened in labor markets to reintroduce or reinforce maternalist protections. The Soviet welfare state early built in accommodations for women's employment, including extended maternity leaves, subsidized child care, and family benefits, in order to enable women's dual roles as both workers and mothers.[43] Historically high rates of nearly full female labor force participation in Soviet times declined to approximately 80 percent in 2001, but large majorities of women in their childbearing years continue to work.[44] Legislation in 2006 provided for extended paid maternity leaves for working women, with retention of part of wages and salaries. The minimum monthly maternity leave benefit was set at R1500 for the first child and R3000 for second and subsequent births, with a smaller benefit in cases where the mother had been out of the labor force or unemployed. As in the Soviet era, protections apply mainly to women who are pregnant or caring for very young children, with many receding once children reach three years of age.[45]

Restricting Reproductive Rights

As the discussion so far shows, Russia's pronatalist policies have relied mainly on positive incentives: government and financial support for mothers and families. However, there has also been a restrictive dimension to these policies. From the mid-1950s until 2003, Russia had very liberal laws on abortion, essentially providing access on demand. A gradual tightening of rules began in 2003.[46] Changes in 2004 limited grounds for pregnancy termination in the second trimester. In 2008, requirements for counseling about risks, signed consent from the woman, and other restrictions were introduced, and there is support in both the Duma and the Orthodox Church for a sharply curtailed list of valid medical and social reasons for terminating pregnancies.[47] The Duma has debated but rejected a law requiring husbands' consent.

The abortion rate has in fact declined, partly because of better access to birth control in recent years.[48]

Women, Pronatalism, and Labor Markets: Work–Family Reconciliation or Neofamilialism?

How are pronatalist policies likely to affect women's participation in labor markets? There are conflicting perspectives on this question. On the one hand, the Russian government's approach has much in common with the liberal work and family reconciliation policies that are promoted by the European Union to help balance work and family responsibilities and promote gender equality (as well as to address similar though less severe problems of below-replacement fertility throughout Europe).[49] These policies are designed to increase women's participation in the labor market, numbers of "dual-breadwinner" households, and tax bases. They are based on an ideology and political project that in principle rejects gender discrimination, stresses labor market equality and shared family responsibilities for men and women, and assumes liberal reproductive rights. Such policies are broadly seen as progressive, though women continue to do a very disproportionate share of "care work" in European societies.

By contrast, Russia's pronatalist policy package of extended maternity leaves, benefits for second and third children, and so on have been interpreted as "neofamilialist" policies. The neofamilialist welfare model "aims to support informal care work [for women] and seeks to elevate childbearing, childrearing, and informal domestic labor to parity with formal paid labor."[50] Neofamilialism is based on a set of norms that stress differentiated and biologically determined gender roles, women's primary role in motherhood and family life, and women's primary responsibility to the society and nation to reproduce in the family rather than produce in the economy. From the perspective of gender equality, the concern is that such policies will have the consequence of systematically disadvantaging women in the labor market, reducing their future earnings, and removing some from their career tracks or from the labor force entirely.

Pronatalist policies appear to have had limited impact on Russian labor markets so far. Female employment has remained relatively high and stable; the majority of mothers, even those with young children, remain in the labor force; and women continue to have very few children. Suggested explanations for these limited effects include Soviet legacies of high levels of women's education and labor force participation and intergenerational networks of child care as well as economic need and the inadequacy of family benefits.[51] However, the recent strengthening of maternalist policies, incipient restrictions on reproductive rights, and the emergence of nationalist and patriarchal rhetoric put a traditionalist gloss on family-friendly policies in Russia.[52]

Russia's government claims success for its pronatalist policies. Birthrates have begun to recover, reaching their highest level (since the Soviet collapse) in 2007 and 2008. Already in the spring of 2008, Health and Social Development Minister Tatiana Golikova pointed to the effectiveness of these policies, asserting that Russia was experiencing a "real demographic explosion."[53] Fertility has climbed from 1.3 to nearly 1.5, mainly because of increases in the frequency of second, third, and subsequent children.[54] Officials claim improvements in fertility and quality of medical care for mothers and newborns as results of their natalist and maternalist initiatives.[55]

However, many question the role of government policy in these developments. Demographers argue that *structural demographic factors* are the main determinants of birthrates. The trend toward increased fertility in fact began in 1999, before the introduction of pronatalist policies, and the growth of Russian birthrates from that point probably resulted mainly from increases in the numbers of women of childbearing age who were born during the 1980s, when birthrates in Russia were higher. Russia's "population pyramid"—the bulge in numbers moving into reproductive age at the end of the 1990s—produced expectations of an increasing birthrate in the first decade of the twenty-first century. In fact, the Russian State Statistical Agency (Rosstat) predicted in 2004, before any pronatalist measures, that birthrates would increase until 2016.[56] It is difficult to determine how much growth would have occurred in the absence of policy measures to boost it and so to judge the effects of childbirth incentive measures. Leonid Ryabkovsky, chief researcher at the Russian Academy of Sciences' Institute for Socio-Political Research, takes a typical expert's position in recognizing that pronatalist policies (as well as economic stabilization) may have played some role but arguing that demographic factors were dominant. The same demographic factors lead to pessimism about the sustainability of growth: after 2015, when the smaller cadre of women born during the 1990s reaches reproductive age, the numbers of births are expected to decline. According to most demographers, incentive policies cannot significantly alter this structural reality, and any effects of pronatalism in Russia will inevitably prove transient. Rising educational levels among women also militate against increases in fertility.[57]

Limited available survey evidence also indicates skepticism about the effectiveness of pronatalist policies among the population in general and among educated youth in particular. In a recent survey, young women were asked whether the possibility of receiving maternity capital would affect their decision to become mothers. About 10 percent gave a positive response and almost 90 percent a negative one.[58] More damning, interviews with educated, politically active youth ages eighteen to twenty-six, including some from the nationalistic, pro-Putin *Nashi* youth movement, found that this target population judged virtually the entire package of pronatalist policies to be ineffective and inadequate. Respondents pointed instead to the need for higher living standards and levels of economic well-being as well as more substantial mothers' benefits and support for family values to raise birthrates.[59] While the number interviewed was far too small to be considered representative, the interviews did tap the strata of youth most likely to be receptive to and supportive of the regime's policy approaches.

International experience and comparison also raise doubts about likely effectiveness of pronatalism. Declining birthrates and below-replacement fertility represent much broader trends throughout Europe and the industrialized world, though these trends are exceptionally stark in Russia. A number of countries besides Russia have experienced increases from "lowest-low" fertility during the 1990s in the absence of such pronatalist incentives.[60] Second, while the historical record shows that packages of pronatalist policies have had some limited effects in raising birthrates, no state has approached the level of sustained population growth that Russian officials anticipate. A review of historical experience shows that "there is not a single example from modern history where pro-natal policies have been able to achieve a sustainable demographic reversal. Outside of Russia, few demographers anticipate that depopulation will actually halt over the coming generation."[61] In sum, while government officials claim that pronatalist policies are helping to resolve Russia's demographic crisis, most neutral experts remain convinced that these policies can produce, at best, small and transient effects.

Conclusion

The demographic crisis is having dramatic effects on Russia's political economy, threatening a growing labor shortage that will constrict economic development, modernization, and diversification. The felt imperative to increase birthrates has dictated national policy priorities, leading the government to intervene in health, housing, and labor markets in pursuit of its ambitious pronatalist goals. While they have relied mainly on incentives and European Union–style work–family reconciliation policies in efforts to raise fertility, Russian authorities have also restricted women's reproductive rights and promote neotraditionalist and neofamilialist ideologies intended to confine women's roles in society and economy. The government's willingness to rely on restrictive methods, including curtailed reproductive rights, is also troubling.

Most demographic experts expect these policies to fail, producing at best a modest and temporary increase in birthrates that will solve neither demographic nor labor shortage problems. According to demographers, there has been "no policy-induced reversal of a downward trend in fertility anywhere in the world"[62] or any sustained demographic reversal on the scale projected by the Russian government. Moreover, the demographics of potential mothers in Russia are in decline, and the childbearing practices of higher-fertility groups are changing. Most experts predict that Russia's population decline will continue until mid-century. In sum, whatever policies the state adopts, Russia will almost certainly not see the dramatic growth in fertility sufficient to fill the labor demand gap in Russia or its regions.

Educated young Russian women also report that pronatalist policies have little effect on their childbearing plans. Even if these policies proved more effective, they would risk removing from the current labor force women workers whose skills are in demand while producing a larger entering cohort only two decades from now. In sum, pronatalism at its most effective, even in combination with "compatriot" immigration and some reduction in middle-age mortality, could not begin to compensate for the projected decline in the working-age population.

The politics of immigration have proven even more conflicted: the Russian economy's demand for labor confronts the state's efforts to control population inflow and regulate labor markets as well as xenophobic attitudes in society. In the medium term, the shrinking pool of entrants to Russia's working-age population threatens economic development and modernization, while ethnic-other immigrants appear to be the main available solution. Immigration also has complex and contradictory security implications. Russian authorities fear, though with little apparent reason, spontaneous flooding of Chinese immigrants into depopulated border regions and, for more obvious reasons, terrorist attacks by nationalist and Islamic extremists entering from the near abroad. Finally (though this point is much less emphasized in Russia than elsewhere), Russia's population requires replenishment of young workers to support its social security commitments. There is persistent social and elite resistance to assimilating migrant workers. The consequence of these conflicting pressures and tensions has been "a myriad of poorly-coordinated and contradictory migration policies."[63]

Have immigration policies, then, proven more successful in responding to demographic contraction? Immigration has been the most important factor compensating for net population loss since 1992. During the 1990s, the open visa regime with the CIS and liberal reception policies produced a substantial inflow of legal immigrants, many of them ethnic Russians. Sustained growth in demand for labor after 2000 pulled in immigrants from the near abroad and increasingly also from Asia and the Middle East. Analysts broadly agree that migration is the only possible solution to meet labor market demands.

At the same time, complex and shifting state regulations, combined with the preference of many employers for illegal and informal workers, have pushed many immigrants in the "shadows." Multiple interests profit from the resulting corruption and the vulnerability of illegals to exploitation. In sum, restrictive immigration policies prove largely self-defeating. At the same time, immigration contributes to growing social tensions. Growing urban immigrant communities meet with xenophobic responses from some in Russia's society and political elite. The majority opposes the social integration of migrants that is essential to the long-term goal of sustainable development. According to Buckley and colleagues, "The Russian Federation struggles to balance the economic need for immigrant labor with cultural intolerance toward migrants and security concerns. . . . In-migration is framed as threatening economics, security, and culture . . . drowning out concerns over labor supply, health, and demography."[64]

What of the future? Two prominent demographers have mapped out scenarios for Russia. Assuming that migration is the only way to compensate for the expected deficit in working-age population, they find that even a high-migration scenario would result in labor shortages in much of the country. They predict the following consequences: decline in economic output in most sectors (except energy), further contraction of populated space, growing interregional competition for labor, and growing stress on pensions and other social programs because of the contracting labor force.[65] For immigrants, the near-term future seems likely to be one of work at the bottom of ethnically segregated labor markets in the service economies of "global cities," insecurity and illegality, very limited access to social services, societal and official xenophobia, and the risk of violence. Because these conditions are mitigated by opportunities, absent in sending countries, to work and earn relatively high wages, send remittances to their families, and live in ethnic enclaves with perhaps the support of better-established coethnics or nongovernmental organizations, immigrants are likely to keep coming.

There is one more important theme that runs through this chapter's narrative: the seeming limits of states' power or control in the face of structural demographic, domestic, and global economic forces. The semiauthoritarian Russian state seems unable to influence or incentivize women to stay at home and produce more children or to control the transnational movement of labor across its borders and into its labor markets. Sending states in turn have become dependent on remittances from workers in foreign economies where their governments have no influence over policy. In our story, structural factors trump policy efforts.

Notes

1. Vladimir Putin, "Politika: Poslanie Federal'nomu Sobraniiu Rossiiskoi Federatsii," *Rosskksiaia Gazeta*, April 26, 2005.

2. United Nations, *Demographic Policy in Russia: From Reflection to Action* (Moscow: United Nations, 2008).

3. Grigory Ioffe and Zhanna Zayonchkovskaya, *Immigration to Russia: Why It Is Inevitable, and How Large It May Have to Be to Provide the Workforce Russia Needs*, NCEEER Working Paper (Seattle: University of Washington, 2010).

4. Kazuhiro Kumo, *Demographic Situations and Development Programs in the Russia Far East and Zabaikalye*, Working Paper Series 24 (Tokyo: Hitotsubashi University Russian Research Center, Institute of Economic Research, 2010).

5. Vladimir Putin, "Annual Address to the Federal Assembly, 10 May 2006," 2006, http://goo.gl/xVpR8.

6. Mikhail Kroschenko and Denis Zibarev, *Review of Current Approaches in Monitoring and Assessing Labour Shortages in the Russian Federation and Methods/Procedures in Migration Planning* (Moscow: International Labour Organization, 2010).

7. Ministry of Economic Development and Trade, Russian Federation, "Blueprint for Long-Term Socioeconomic Development of Russian Federation," Ministry of Economic Development and Trade, Russian Federation, June 22, 2008.

8. Some increase could come from declines in the high rates of premature middle-aged male mortality, but this would be both difficult and uncertain. Many middle-aged men are in poor health, many deaths are alcohol-related, and government policies have targeted but not prioritized this population's health problems. Raising the comparatively low pension age is another possible source of labor force increase, but most "younger" pensioners are already employed at least part-time.

9. United Nations, *Demographic Policy in Russia*, 43.

10. Tatiana Yudina, "Labour Migration into Russia: The Response of State and Society," *Current Sociology* 53, no. 4 (2005): 583–606.

11. Caress Schenk, "Open Borders, Closed Minds: Russia's Changing Migration Policies: Liberalization or Xenophobia?," *Demokratizatsiya: The Journal of Post-Soviet Democratization* 18, no. 1 (2010): 104.

12. Oxana Shevel, "Identity, Citizenship, and Tolerance," in *Transnational Migration to New Regional Centers: Policy Challenges, Practice, and Migrant Experience*, ed. Lauren Herzer, Sarah Dixon Klump, and Mary Elizabeth Malinkin, 52–82. Conference Proceedings, Eurasia Migration Papers 2 (Washington, DC: Woodrow Wilson Center International Center for Scholars, 2009).

13. Cynthia J. Buckley, Erin Trouth Hofmann, and Yuka Minagawa, "Does Nativity Matter? Correlates of Immigrant Health by Generation in the Russian Federation," *Demographic Research* 24, no. 32 (2011): 801–24.

14. Yudina, "Labour Migration into Russia"; Shevel, "Identity, Citizenship, and Tolerance"; Timothy Heleniak, "Russia's Population Perils," in *After Putin's Russia: Past Imperfect, Future Uncertain*, ed. Stephen Wegren and Dale Herspring, 133–58 (New York: Rowman & Littlefield, 2010).

15. United Nations, *Demographic Policy in Russia*, 43.

16. Yudina, "Labour Migration into Russia."

17. Vladimir Mukomel, "Immigration and Russian Migration Policy: Debating the Future," *Russian Analytical Digest* 7 (2006): 2–6.

18. Ioffe and Zayonchkovskaya, *Immigration to Russia.*

19. Kumo, *Demographic Situations and Development Programs in the Russia Far East and Zabaikalye.*

20. Timothy Heleniak, "An Overview of Migration in the Post-Soviet Space," in *Migration, Homeland, and Belonging in Eurasia*, ed. Cynthia J. Buckley, Blair A. Ruble, and Erin Trouth Hofmann, 29–68 (Baltimore: Johns Hopkins University Press and Woodrow Wilson Center, 2008); Schenk, "Open Borders, Closed Minds."

21. "Opinion Poll: Nationalism in Contemporary Russia," *Russian Analytical Digest* 93 (2011): 10–12; Yudina, "Labour Migration into Russia."

22. Buckley et al., "Does Nativity Matter?"

23. Returning migrants may also be seen at home as vectors of disease (i.e., HIV, tuberculosis, and hepatitis) or as having "spent their health"—suffered disease or injuries—in exchange for higher wages abroad.

24. Schenk, "Open Borders, Closed Minds," 109.

25. Kroschenko and Zibarev, *Review of Current Approaches in Monitoring and Assessing Labour Shortages in the Russian Federation and Methods/Procedures in Migration Planning,* 5.

26. Mikhail A. Alexseev, "Migration and Ethno-Religious Hate Crimes in Russia: Risk Profiles 2000–2010," paper presented at the 2006 annual meeting of the American Political Science Association, 2006; Moya Flynn, "Reconstructing 'Home/lands' in the Russian Federation: Migrant-Centered Perspectives of Displacement and Resettlement," *Journal of Ethnic and Migration Studies* 33, no. 3 (2007): 461–81.

27. Olga Vendina, "New Migration Destinations," in *Transnational Migration to New Regional Centers: Policy Challenges, Practice, and Migrant Experience*, ed. Lauren Herzer, Sarah Dixon Klump, and Mary Elizabeth Malinkin. Conference Proceedings, Eurasia Migration Papers 2 (Washington, DC: Woodrow Wilson Center International Center for Scholars, 2009), 105. For a map showing the concentrated settlements of ethnic minorities in contemporary Moscow and resulting residential fragmentation of the city, see Yudina, "Labour Migration into Russia," 599.

28. Douglas S. Massey, "International Migration at the Dawn of the Twenty-First Century: The Role of the State," *Population and Development Review* 25, no. 2 (1999): 303–22.

29. Massey, "International Migration at the Dawn of the Twenty-First Century," 306.

30. Cynthia J. Buckley, "Introduction: New Approaches to Migration and Belonging in Eurasia," in Buckley et al., *Migration, Homeland, and Belonging in Eurasia,* 9.

31. Ioffe and Zayonchkovskaya, *Immigration to Russia.*

32. Ukaz Prezidenta Rossiiskoi Federatsii, "Ob utverzhdenii Kontseptsii demograficheskoi politiki Rossiiskoi Federatsii na period do 2025 roda," 2007, http://goo .gl/KVhsV.

33. Tatyana Smolyakova, "140 Million and Not a Soul Less," *Current Digest of the Post-Soviet Press* 58, no. 21 (2006): 4–5.

34. Elena Karmalskaia, "'I Am Concerned about the Quality of Reproduction . . .': Russian State Demographic Policy in the Eyes of Youth Movement Activists in Tver," *Anthropology of East Europe Review* 26, no. 2 (2010): 56–67; Svetlana Misikhina, "Could New Measures to Support Maternity, Increase Fertility, and Encourage Women with Children to Work Be Effective in Russia?," paper presented at the conference "Challenges, Dynamics and Implications of Welfare Reforms: A Dialogue between Post-Soviet and East-Asian Scholars," University of Toronto, 2009; Sergei Zakharov, "Russian Federation: From the First to the Second Demographic Transition," *Demographic Research* 19, no. 24 (2008): 907–72.

35. "Transcript of the Security Council Meeting Devoted to Measures to Implement the Annual Address to the Federal Assembly," June 20, 2006, http://goo.gl/S5JUu.

36. *Kommersant*, October 20, 2005.

37. Zakharov, "Russian Federation."

38. Olga Avdeyeva, "Population Decline, Welfare State Restructuring, and Pro-Natalist Policies in Russia: Evaluation of Policy Response," paper presented at the annual meeting of the American Association for the Advancement of Slavic Studies, 2008.

39. Vladimir Putin, "Beginning of the Session of the Presidential Council for the Implementation of Priority National Projects and Demographic Policy," 2008, http://goo.gl/ffS2p.

40. Misikhina, "Could New Measures to Support Maternity, Increase Fertility, and Encourage Women with Children to Work Be Effective in Russia?"

41. Smolyakova, "140 Million and Not a Soul Less"; Karmalskaia, "'I Am Concerned about the Quality of Reproduction.'"

42. *Vremia novostei'*, September 6, 2006.

43. These policies led some analysts to label communist welfare states as "women friendly"; see Bob Deacon et al., *Global Social Policy: International Organizations and the Future of Welfare* (London: Sage, 1997). At the same time, the state "supported women's 'care' work rather than transforming the domestic division of labor" (see Gillian Pascall and Jane Lewis, "Emerging Gender Regimes and Policies for Gender Equality in a Wider Europe," *Journal of Social Policy* 33, no. 3 [2004]: 373–94), and underdevelopment of the service sector rendered women's dual role as worker and homemaker a heavy "double burden."

44. Tatyana Teplova, "Welfare State Transformation, Childcare, and Women's Work in Russia," *Social Politics: International Studies in Gender, State and Society* 14, no. 3 (2007): 284–322.

45. Alastair McAuley, *Women's Work and Wages in the Soviet Union* (London: Allen and Unwin, 1981).

46. Nicholas Eberstadt, "Russia's Demographic Straightjacket," *SAIS Review* 26, no. 2 (2004): 9–25.

47. Karmalskaia, "'I Am Concerned about the Quality of Reproduction.'"

48. Andrea Chandler, "The Truant Society: Gender, Nationalism and Social Welfare in Russia," unpublished manuscript, 2008.

49. Jane Lewis, "Work/Family Reconciliation, Equal Opportunities and Social Policies: The Interpretation of Policy Trajectories at the EU Level and the Meaning of Gender Equality," *Journal of European Public Policy* 13, no. 3 (2006): 420–37.

50. Teplova, "Welfare State Transformation, Childcare, and Women's Work in Russia," 299.

51. Teplova, "Welfare State Transformation, Childcare, and Women's Work in Russia."

52. Chandler, "The Truant Society."

53. Jonas Bernstein, "Experts Doubt That Russia's Population Decline Can Be Halted," *Eurasia Daily Monitor* 5, no. 8 (2008).

54. "Effekt 'Materninskogo Kapitala'?," *Demoscop Weekly* 447–448 (2010).

55. *Kommersant*, February 4, 2008.

56. Kumo, *Demographic Situations and Development Programs in the Russia Far East and Zabaikalye*. This prediction was later revised to "natural" growth ending at 2011.

57. Zakharov, "Russian Federation"; Kumo, *Demographic Situations and Development Programs in the Russia Far East and Zabaikalye*.

58. Mama i Malysh, "Maternskii kapital," 2011, http://www.2mm.ru/vote/9/result.

59. Karmalskaia, "'I Am Concerned about the Quality of Reproduction.'"

60. Joshua R. Goldstein, Tomas Sobotka, and Aiva Jasilioniene, "The End of Lowest-Low Fertility?," *Population and Development Review* 35, no. 4 (2009): 663–99.

61. Bernstein, "Experts Doubt That Russia's Population Decline Can Be Halted."

62. Ioffe and Zayonchkovskaya, *Immigration to Russia*, 4.

63. Buckley, "Introduction," 15.

64. Buckley et al., "Does Nativity Matter?," 10.

65. Ioffe and Zayonchkovskaya, *Immigration to Russia*.

6

Change in Agriculture

The Development of Russia's Private Farming

Stephen K. Wegren

I N LATE 1990, PRIVATELY OWNED peasant farms (*krest'yanskie* [*fermerskie*] *khozyaistva*) attained legal status with the potential to become one of the most important reforms in Russia's agrarian sector.[1] The 1990s witnessed considerable academic attention to the development of the private farming sector, even as the sector faced considerable obstacles and government policy was inconsistent. By the late 1990s, disappointment began to outweigh optimism, and failures seemed more pronounced than successes, based on the fact that the number of private farms was declining, their contribution to the nation's food supply was insignificant, and their overall economic impact was marginal. Moreover, private farmers' political representation was weak at the federal and regional levels. By the late 1990s, Western analysts grew disinterested, and as a consequence the scholarly literature developed significant gaps.

Today the situation is considerably different. The growth rate of the private farming sector has increased significantly—more so than from large farms or household production—and in recent years prior to the 2010 drought, farmers' grain output allowed Russia to export nearly 20 million tons of grain. Going forward, the private farming sector will be of key importance in helping Russia become a global food supplier and to meet the goals in its Food Security Doctrine.[2]

The contemporary confluence of positive economic, political, and policy factors means that private farming is emerging as a success story in Russia's agrarian reform, a development that warrants further attention because it has escaped the attention of most Western scholars. Recent research has examined the status of private farming and government policy toward it at the national level, arguing that recent success is evident by improving economic performance, the introduction of government-financed assistance programs, and the political mainstreaming of the Association of Peasant Farms and Agricultural Cooperatives in Russia (AKKOR).[3] At the village and household levels, economic differentiation between private farmers and other rural cohorts reflects a significant reorientation in social structure.[4] A focus on private farming is significant and adds to our understanding of post-Soviet Russia in many ways. It is well to remember that it was the intent of reformers in Moscow in the early 1990s to build a private farmer class that would replace the Soviet-era collective farms and that would provide political support in the countryside. During the 1990s, private farmers were progovernment, but reformers' desires were not realized, and private farmers remained economically insignificant. That situation is now changing, as private farmers are becoming important producers of specific food commodities. In particular, private farmers have become significant producers of grain. As Russia emerges as a global food supplier, the government's goal to become the number two grain exporter in the world can be realized only if private farmers continue to experience economic growth. Finally, private farming as a case study is instructive in demonstrating the effects of market-based institutions. This experiment is instructive that financial support combined with a new institutional framework is important. Laissez-faire policies combined with privatization alone are insufficient, as the experience of the 1990s clearly showed.

While it is important to understand national trends in Russia's private farming as a marker of progress in building agrarian capitalism, it may be argued, however, that the real story lies in regional trends. Therefore, this chapter builds on previous analyses by examining regional developments in Russia's private farming sector. Two central questions are addressed: 1) What are regional trajectories that differentiate regions from each other? 2) Is private farming developing in the "right" regions, that is, those that are best suited for agricultural production? The chapter updates our knowledge about private farming at the regional level and begins to fill the holes that have developed in the secondary literature. The remainder of the chapter is organized temporally, with sections on the first decade of private farming (1990–1999), the second decade (2000–2009), and the third decade (from 2010).

The First Decade (1990–1999)

During the 1990s, private peasant farms were interesting to Western analysts because this form of entrepreneurship represented a genuine private sector in rural Russia that had the potential to become significant producers. Up to that time, the "private" sector in Soviet agriculture consisted of household plots, or private plots as they were commonly called (*lichnoye podsobnoye khozyayistvo*). These plots were private in the sense that they were not subject to state planning, but these small plots of land were not privately owned and were used mainly to augment household consumption. In the aggregate, private plots produced significant quantities of certain commodities, but their production was not sufficient to meet urban demand. Reformers in Moscow felt that private peasant farms offered the potential to supplant Soviet-era collective farms as the main food supplier for the nation.

Government Policy

The earliest private farms under Gorbachev were based on land leasing from collective farms because Gorbachev would not consider breaking up the socialized sector and never embraced private landownership. Under Boris Yeltsin, a program of farm privatization was introduced that allowed private farmers to own their land as well as rent additional land if so desired. The farm privatization program distributed land shares to farm members and farm service personnel. The details of farm privatization have been described elsewhere.[5] Following farm privatization, collective and state farms took on new legal status, although many continued to exist and function; they now are called large agricultural enterprises or corporate farms. The main points are that only would-be private farmers received real land (otherwise, very little real land was transferred to individuals) and that a good number of private farms were created out of the farm privatization process—an average of about 10,000 new private farms were registered every month during 1992–1993.

Once created, government policy toward private farms in the 1990s was inconsistent, almost dichotomous. On the one hand, the government proclaimed support for private farms and put considerable stock in their development. For example, Yegor Gaidar maintained a profarmer policy right up to his removal in December 1993. In November 1993, for instance, Gaidar stated that the "priority sector for us [in agriculture] will be the sector of private farms."[6] Under Gaidar, the Russian government allowed the children of private farmers to be exempted from military service and expended hard currency for the purchase of farm machinery for private farmers, and the federal government was supposed to allocate not less than 15 percent of agricultural expenditures to rural investments that would benefit private farmers—the latter condition was never fulfilled.[7] The government also offered paid relocation expenses and free training and agricultural education lessons for new private farmers and offered a generous stipend for urbanites who moved to the countryside to begin private farms. Further, because of the adverse economic conditions in which early private farmers began their operations, the Yeltsin government introduced a support program: the Russian Farmer program.[8] According to this program, new private farmers were exempt from land and income taxes for the first five years of their existence.

Perhaps the most important form of financial support in the Russian Farmer program was subsidized credit to private farmers to buy equipment, livestock, and machinery. Farmers were charged 8 percent interest in 1992 and 25 percent interest in 1993 at a time when the prevailing inflation rate was 2,600 percent in 1992 and 940 percent in 1993.[9] The positive effects of the program were palatable. During 1990–1991, private farm creation averaged only about 2,000 new private farms per month. Once the program began to provide subsidized loans, the registration of almost 10,000 new private farms occurred every month for the next two years (1992–1994). As a result, the number of private farms in Russia increased from 49,000 in January 1992 to over 279,000 at the end of 1994.

On the other hand, government action fell short of its rhetoric, and a litany of obstacles confronted nascent private farmers during the first decade. For example, one Russian scholar noted that "the main factors that are hindering the development of private farming are high prices of agricultural equipment and construction materials, high interest rates for credit, the destruction of channels for food sales, and monopolism in the processing of agricultural products."[10] Other common problems in the 1990s were high start-up costs and limited access to credit, remote locations with fragmented land plots, grossly underequipped farms, insufficient infrastructure, undercapitalized farms, underdeveloped marketing channels, and problems obtaining supplies and inputs.[11] Moreover, a government survey of private farmers concerning state assistance shows that more than 80 percent of farmers reported that they had not received the following advantages from the Russian Farmer program: production subsidies, reduced energy prices, short-term government credit using production as collateral, guaranteed purchase prices, material-technical resources through state leasing programs, or refinancing of debt.[12] The Russian government took few steps to remedy these obstacles or was ineffective in doing so. In sum, the Russian government promised much more than it actually delivered, and after the Russian Farmer program was ended, it would be fair to say that the private farming sector was virtually ignored in terms of national policy initiatives.

Additional Problems in the Private Farming Sector

Other obstacles also existed that affected private farming, one of which was an environment of rampant corruption that surrounded nascent private farmers. During the early 1990s, "the converging interests of criminals, bureaucrats, and local politicians similarly undermined efforts to extend the rights of private ownership. Individual farmers had been permitted their own plots of land, but they found it nearly impossible to obtain credits, machinery, or fertilizer from regional banks and agricultural enterprises, which were controlled by corrupt local officials determined to protect the interests of the large state collective farms."[13] Moreover, food markets were manipulated that caused artificial food shortages in the early 1990s. Thus, market relations and entrepreneurship were constrained by corruption from the start.

Corruption occurred within the private farming sector as well. Although subsidized credit was beneficial to the real farmers who were coping with start-up costs and skyrocketing prices for inputs, many farmers existed in name only and took advantage of free land, cheap credit, and tax advantages to start their fortunes. As the president of AKKOR, V. Bashmachnikov, stated, "We have an awful lot of cunning people who, exploiting the private farmer theme, are accumulating capital and strengthening themselves."[14] As a result, many private farms produced no food at all and did not even have land. The abuses within the Russian Farmer program led then Prime Minister Viktor Chernomyrdin to cancel the Russian Farmer program in the fall of 1993, including access to subsidized credit. After October 1993, the number of private farm bankruptcies began to increase, and the rate of new farm creation fell dramatically.[15]

Even as the federal government offered subsidized credits at negative real interest rates, financial support for private farming was plagued by several problems, the first of which was a decline in inflation-adjusted financial support. Federal budgetary allocations to private farming increased in nominal terms, but because of high inflation, financial support declined after 1992 in real terms. According to reports from AKKOR, in constant rubles, financial support per private farm in 1991 averaged R30,000, the equivalent of R4,500 rubles per farm in 1992, and only R1,000 per farm in 1993.[16] Calculated in dollars, federal support for the private farming sector declined from U.S.\$42.3 million in 1992 to U.S.\$6.9 million in 1995 (not including production subsidies).

A related problem was a shift in the responsibility for providing financial assistance to private farmers. From 1993 on, most of the financial responsibility for assisting private farmers was transferred from federal to regional budgets.[17] Some regions were able to provide adequate support for private farmers— Rostov on-Don, Volgograd, Samara, and Belgorod oblasts and Stavropol' kray and Krasnodar kray were prime examples. With the exception of a few regions, however, most local budgets simply did not have the resources to provide sufficient assistance to private farmers. In 1995, for example, budgetary allocations from regional budgets totaled R140 billion, or R500,000 per private farm—the equivalent of U.S.$100.00 per farm—a level of financial support that was ten to fifteen times less than recommended by government experts.[18] Some regions, such as the Republic of Tartarstan and the Republic of Bashkortostan, did not allocate *any* financial support to private farmers, and several other regions stopped financial assistance during 1995.[19]

Moreover, budgetary allocations indicated only the amount authorized to be spent; in reality, only about one-half to two-thirds of total budgetary assignments were actually distributed. In some cases, financial assistance was used to cover previous loan payments. The distribution of direct production subsidies fared even more poorly, as only 6 percent of the R240 billion assigned in the 1996 federal budget actually reached private farmers. At a time when input prices were rising much faster than farm gate prices, the financial effect was catastrophic for many farmers.[20] One Russian academic reported that whereas "nearly all" private farms were profitable in 1992, by mid-1994 less than 20 percent were profitable, with an average loss of R1.3 million per farm.[21] The obstacles reviewed above go far in explaining why the private farming sector was so weak at the end of the 1990s.

Regional Trends

Overall, at the end of the first decade, there was considerable disappointment in policymaking and academic circles with the private farming movement. The underdeveloped nature of the private farming sector may be measured in three ways, discussed in the following sections.

Food Output

Although the number of private farms increased dramatically during the 1990s, aggregate food production remained rather insignificant. Most private farms were small, and their output was low. In 1999, the year Boris Yeltsin left office, private farmers accounted for only 2.5 percent of the total ruble value of agricultural production in the nation.[22] An environment of undercapitalized and undermechanized farms affected production potential, and once government subsidies ended, farm bankruptcies soared.[23]

Almost two-thirds of farmers engaged in grain production, and they accounted for 7 percent of national grain output in 1999. There was, of course, variance by region. Among regions in European Russia, the largest volume of grain (100,000 tons or more) came from farmers located in Volgograd oblast and Saratov oblast in the Volga federal district, and Krasnodar kray, Stavropol' kray, and Rostov oblast in the Northern Caucasus federal district. Private farmers also produced plant products with intermediary uses such as sugar beet (5 percent of national output) with the Central Black earth district and Northern Caucasus district accounting for more than three-quarters of farmers' output, and farmers produced 13 percent of the nation's sunflower seed, with the North Caucasus federal district producing more than one-half of farmers' total output, with Krasnodar kray and Rostov oblast as the main producers.[24]

In contrast, the animal husbandry sector remained underdeveloped, and private farmers did not produce more than 3 percent of the meat, poultry, or milk in any of the federal districts. The volume of output from private farmers actually trended downward from 1995 to the end of the decade for beef cattle, pigs, sheep and goats, milk, eggs, and wool in each federal district. Furthermore, farmers accounted for minuscule percentages of the commodities produced by private plots for personal consumption nationwide: potatoes 1 percent, vegetables 2.1 percent, and eggs 0.4 percent. These numbers reflect the population's preference for low-risk endeavors, such as privatizing or expanding the household plot instead of dealing with the multitude of problems faced by private farmers. Thus, by the end of the decade, selected plant products for which demand came from processors were farmers' main output.

Popularity of Private Farming

Despite access to subsidized credit, free land to start a private farm, and emancipation from land taxes, private farming did not become very popular in the 1990s. Part of the reason was found in the social origins of private farmers and their start-up difficulties[25] and other problems that were discussed above. Further, Caroline Humphrey writes that "small private farms set up in the early 1990s were not the result of popular pressure. The first private farms were established by officials as showpieces, to demonstrate that reform policy was being followed. . . . This period is now spoken of as the 'privatization campaign' and has passed into history like so many Soviet campaigns before it."[26]

Already by the mid-1990s, the geographical distribution in the number of private farms showed significant regional disparities. Broad stretches of Russian territory had very few private farms: areas in the northwest (Murmansk, Arkangel'sk, Komi, Vologda, Kostroma, and Ivanovo), in the north (including the autonomous okrugs of Nenetsya, Yamalya, Taymyrya, Khantya-Mansya, and Evenkya), and in the northeast (Chukota, Kamchatka, Magadan, and Khabarovsk kray). These areas were generally not suited for agriculture. Northern and far northern areas were sparsely populated during Soviet times, and after the collapse of the Soviet Union, several experienced net out-migration as part of a general pattern out of the north.[27] In contrast, regions located along Russia's southern border and in the southwest (Krasnodar kray, Rostov, and Volgograd) were home to most of Russia's private farms.[28]

One way to measure the popularity of private farming is through the private farm saturation rate, which is defined as the number of private farms per 1,000 persons. This method of measurement can be applied to a federal district, a region, or even a raion. The analysis here focuses on federal districts, and although there was a big jump in farm saturation in nearly every district during 1992–1994, by the end of the first decade only two districts averaged more than two private farms per 1,000 persons—the Northern Caucasus and the Volga—and only one district averaged more than four, as shown in table 6.1. Of the eight districts in the table, five experienced a decline in the number of private farms per 1,000 persons after December 1994, and two remained unchanged. The one exception where the number increased was the Northern Caucasus district; there, the number of farms rose from 4.1 private farms per 1,000 persons in December 1994 to 4.8 farms per 1,000 persons in December 1998.

Landholdings

Private farmers' landholdings in the first decade displayed both positive and negative dimensions. On the positive side, the total area of land registered to private farmers increased dramatically during the 1990s—from 2.5

TABLE 6.1
Number of Private Farms per 1,000 Persons by
Federal District, European Russia, 1991–1999

	1991	*1992*	*1993*	*1994*	*1995*	*1996*	*1997*	*1998*	*1999*
Russian Federation	.33	1.23	1.82	1.88	**1.89**	1.88	1.86	1.84	1.78
Northern	.22	.59	.74	**.77**	.70	.71	.68	.66	.64
Northwest	.28	.90	1.26	1.42	1.45	**1.46**	1.45	1.40	1.32
Central	.19	.71	.96	**1.02**	1.01	1.00	.99	.96	.95
Volga-Vyatka	.21	.68	.96	1.03	**1.05**	1.04	1.06	1.04	1.05
Central Black Earth	.36	1.37	**1.82**	1.64	1.58	1.48	1.44	1.39	1.40
Volga	.38	1.67	**2.23**	2.17	2.12	2.09	2.06	2.03	2.01
Northern Caucasus	.55	2.50	3.87	4.16	4.46	4.74	4.80	**4.81**	4.51
Urals	.32	1.14	1.66	**1.67**	1.60	1.53	1.47	1.43	1.42

Notes: All dates are end of year. The entire population of a region was used in the calculations because either urban or rural individuals could begin a private farm. Bold indicates high point for that region.

Source: Author's calculations using private farm data and population from a variety of sources.

million hectares in 1992 to 14.3 million hectares in 1999. Moreover, farmers' cultivated land also grew, and the most favorable agricultural regions (encompassing the Volga and Northern Caucasus federal districts) experienced the largest gains in cultivated land during 1995–1999, as shown in table 6.2. By the end of the decade, only farmers in these two districts had more than 1 million hectares of cultivated land.

On the negative side, the growth in total area registered to private famers increased more than the growth in cultivated land. The difference between farmers' total land and their cultivated land is reflected in the last two data columns of table 6.2, showing that the average number of cultivated hectares was much smaller than the average size of a private farm in each federal district. Even in the fertile Volga region, only 36 percent of a farmer's landholdings consisted of cultivated land. Nationwide, in 1999, only 42 percent of all farmers' land was cultivated, indicating that a lot of farmers' land expansion could not be used efficiently. Farmers in two federal districts in European Russia (Central and Urals) experienced declines in farmers' cultivated land from 1995 to the end of the decade, and in two other regions (Northern and Northwestern), the increase in cultivated land was extremely modest (table 6.2).

Furthermore, 60 percent of private farmers' land was not owned but leased, the effect of which was twofold: 1) rented land could not be used as collateral to raise capital, and 2) the lack of capital hindered investment in the farm.[29] By decade's end, private farmers held only about 7 percent of the nation's agricultural land, whereas large farming enterprises controlled 82 percent.[30] In comparison, the population used 6 percent of all agricultural land for their household plots. Thus, private farmers made progress during the 1990s, but an overwhelming majority of agricultural land continued to be used by large farms, and instead of supplanting large farms as main food producers, a cynic may be tempted to conclude that farmers had attained a comparable level of insignificance as private plots.

In summary, by the end of the first decade, significant regional differentiation had occurred. The geographical distribution of private farms essentially ran along a north-to-south axis. Vast stretches of northern Russia had few private farms and very little private farmland. Southern areas witnessed more robust development, a belt that ran along the southern border of Russia. Measured in terms of food output, number of private farms, and landholdings, by the end of the first decade private farming had a moderately strong foothold in only two federal districts, and the strongest regions were Volgograd oblast and Saratov oblast in the Volga federal district and Krasnodar kray, Stavropol' kray, and Rostov oblast in the Northern Caucasus federal district.

TABLE 6.2

Private Farms' Cultivated Land by Federal District, European Russia, 1995–1999

	Farmers' Cultivated Land, December 1995 (thousands of hectares)	Farmers' Land as Percentage of All Cultivated Land in District, 1995	Farmers' Cultivated Land, December 1999 (thousands of hectares)	Farmers' Land as Percentage of All Cultivated Land in District, 1999	Average Size, Private Farm, December 1999 (hectares based on total land)	Average Number of Cultivated Hectares per Private Farm in District, December 1999
Russian Federation	5,061	5	6,015	6.8	55	23
Northern	21.3	1.7	27.9	2.5	30	7.6
Northwest	40.3	2.7	46.0	3.6	18	4.4
Central	327.9	2.8	293.6	3.0	29	10.5
Central Black Earth	313.9	3.5	339.5	4.3	63	31
Volga	1,196.3	6.5	1,378.7	8.9	113	41
Northern Caucasus	931.7	7.2	1,367.7	11.7	30	17
Urals	820.9	4.5	810.5	5.2	60	28

Sources: Based on data from Goskomstat, Sel'skokhozyaystvennaya deyatel'nost' krest'yanskikh (fermerskikh) khozyaystv v Rossii (Moscow: Goskomstat, 2000), 61–64; Ministry of Agriculture, Agropromyshlennyi kompleks Rossii (Moscow: Ministry of Agriculture, 2000), 227–28; and author's calculations.

The Second Decade (2000–2009)

The second decade of private farming in Russia witnessed the economic and political fortunes of private farmers improve considerably. After 2000, and especially since mid-decade, governmental programs of financial assistance helped farm income and profitability increase, facilitated a rise in output, and contributed to a growth in farmers' contribution to the national food supply. During the second decade, the growth rate in the private farming sector was more than four times higher than in the agricultural sector as a whole.[31] The emerging success of private farming in its second decade may be measured at the macrolevel by the positive trends occurring in the most favorable agricultural regions. We start first with a brief overview of policy toward private farmers.

Government Policy

On the heels of a disastrous decade for agriculture under Yeltsin—1998 yielded the lowest harvest in fifty years, and the rebound had just started in 1999, when Yeltsin left the political scene—Putin's first term as president was devoted to the recovery of agriculture, in particular large farming enterprises. In other words, Putin was interested in increasing domestic food production and feeding the urban population. He was concerned primarily with the growing volume of food imports, and for this reason he wanted to improve domestic agricultural production and reduce reliance on foreign food. Because private farms produced a small percentage of the nation's food at that time, most policy attention was directed at reviving production on large agricultural enterprises, and various policy initiatives were introduced including debt forgiveness for large farms.[32] Additional assistance early in Putin's first term took the form of import protection policies for several types of food products that applied to all agricultural producers, but because private farmers produced significant quantities for only a limited number of commodities and those commodities tended not to be imported anyway (except for processed sugar), farmers benefited less than large farms from import protection.

The main initiatives relevant to private farming undertaken in Putin's first term were the adoption of a "Program of Support for Small Business" in 2000–2001, the fifth such government program since 1994. This program, however, for the first time included the agroindustrial complex and food processing, although most of this program's goals focused on creating jobs in the industrial sector.[33] A second initiative was revising and updating the 1990 law on peasant farming in 2003, a move that had legal impact but did not include financial assistance, although it did have an economic impact by delineating the difference between private plots and private farms on the basis of the maximum size of a private plot. In doing so, the law distinguished between commercial and subsistence activities, with the latter freed from income tax.

Up to mid-decade, most policy analysis focused on the problems surrounding the integration of private farming into the rural economy and strengthening a sector in which almost 40 percent of private farms were less than ten hectares in size and whose basic economic activity was subsistence.[34] However, in Putin's second term, the government turned its attention to assisting private farmers. Why the turn to private farming? Three hypotheses exist. First, Putin was determined to do anything to reduce food imports. By the end of 2004, the amount of money spent on food imports had grown 87 percent, from $7.4 billion in 2000 to $13.9 billion in 2004, and imports continued to increase to $17.4 billion in 2005.[35] It is within this time period that national security was paramount, reflecting national concerns following the terrorist attack in Beslan in the fall of 2004. A second hypothesis is that Putin was proceeding sequentially. Having assisted large farms—former state and collective farms—he logically turned attention to small forms of farming. A third hypothesis is that Putin began to realize the production limits of large farms. By 2004, large farms produced only 43 percent of the nation's food (measured in ruble value). To reduce imports, he needed to augment production, and private farms were the logical candidates. In any event, by 2005, speeches and articles by Minister of Agriculture Alexei Gordeev reflected, first, the government's intent to direct substantial resources into agriculture and, second, a newfound priority placed on private farming, both of which indicated that a decision had been made at the highest level of government.

In late 2005, the National Program was adopted, with agriculture as one of its four priority sectors; the program took effect in 2006 and ran through 2007. This federal program was the first of a series of financial assistance programs and channeled R47.8 billion into the agricultural sector as a whole.[36] Within the agricultural program, there was a specific section for stimulating the development of small forms of farming, including private farming; this section was allocated a total of R13.75 billion during 2006–2007, not including direct production subsidies. Private farmers were permitted loans of up to eight years with subsidized interest rates.

In July 2007, the national program for the development of agriculture was extended to run from 2008 to 2012 under a new title (State Program for the Development of Agriculture and Regulation of Markets for Agricultural Products, Raw Materials, and Food). The new program envisions expenditures of more than R500 billion from the federal budget and R1.5 trillion from the consolidated budget during this period.[37] Although the 2008–2012 program does not have a specific section devoted to private farming, three of the program's five priorities are relevant to private farmers (the development of sustainable rural communities through regional rural development, the achievement of financial stability for farms, and the development of subbranches of agricultural production). Government data indicate that the bulk of subsidized credits and subsidies go to large farms, but it should be noted that private farmers are eligible for various subsidies that are funded in the program.[38]

In June 2009, a financial program specific to private farmers, titled "The Development of Peasant Farms and Other Small Scale Forms of Farming in the Agro-Industrial Complex during 2009–2011," was adopted by the Ministry of Agriculture. This special program is intended to stimulate the further development of the private farming sector and to "increase the productivity and stability of peasant farms and other small forms of farming."[39] To achieve this goal, the program posits several specific subtasks: 1) developing infrastructure, primary processing, storage, and transportation of agricultural commodities; 2) stimulating innovation on peasant farms and other small forms of farming; 3) increasing the attractiveness of private farming; and 4) facilitating access to financial resources for private farms and other small forms of farming.[40] A primary method of government support is to subsidize interest rates. The total cost of the program is envisioned to be about R8.5 billion.[41]

Further, in August 2009, a special branch project was adopted called "The Development of Family Milk Farms on the Basis of Private Farms during 2009–2011." The goal of this project is to improve the volume of milk production and its quality and to boost rural employment. In 2009, eight regions signed an agreement with the Ministry of Agriculture to create fifty pilot family farms. The farms, grouped in eight to ten farm clusters, engage in the complete production cycle—starting with the production of milk and including its processing and the delivery of processed milk products.[42] The total cost of the program will exceed R12 billion, with funding from a state-owned agricultural bank (Rossel'khozbank), from a state-owned company (Rosagrolizing), and from regional budgets. The implementation of the program is expected to provide employment to 1,500 rural dwellers.[43] In early 2011, the Ministry of Agriculture reported that during the first two years of the program (2009–2010), 310 such milk farms had been constructed or renovated in forty-one regions of Russia, creating 1,627 jobs. The income of each member of the farm was said to be R25,000 to R30,000 per month, or several times that of an ordinary worker on a large farming enterprise.[44]

Regional Trends

Improvement in the economic performance from the private farmer sector in the second decade is discernable at the regional level, and the following sections illustrate several regional trends.

Food Output

At the end of their first decade, private farmers accounted for only 2.5 percent of the total ruble value of agricultural production in Russia. In their second decade, private farmers experienced a rapid growth in the ruble value of their output, reaching 8.5 percent of total output in 2008 before declining a bit to 7.7 percent in 2009. Because the value and volume of output from the agricultural sector as a whole increased during this time, the percentage growth in farmers' contribution represents real economic gain. Most of the growth in earnings occurred in plant production, while animal husbandry remained underdeveloped (about 75 percent of annual farmers' revenue came from plant products).[45]

Even as the private farming sector experienced an aggregate growth in output, the gains were not distributed evenly. During the second decade, a thin stratum of "superwinners" emerged: private farms that had very large landholdings and employed an average of fifty-six workers, with annual earnings that averaged R10.8 million and profits exceeding R2.8 million per farm. The financially strongest 300 private farms throughout Russia are ranked each year, and from this ranking the geographical distribution is evident. Among the strongest 300 private farms during 2006–2007 (the latest data available as this chapter was written), sixty-eight came from Volgograd oblast, followed by forty-one farms in Saratov oblast and thirty-eight in Stavropol' kray.[46] The geographic distribution may be further narrowed: among the top 100 private farms, fifty-eight come from just five regions: four are in the Southern federal district (Stavropol' kray, Rostov oblast, Volgograd oblast, and Krasnodar kray), and one is in the Volga federal district (Saratov oblast).

Improved food production performance by private farmers is seen by the fact that in 1999, farmers produced just 7 percent of the nation's grain; just ten years later, private farmers' contribution rose to 21 percent, or over 20 million tons annually, which is equal to the volume that Russia exported during 2007–2009. Farmers' share of total output rose for sugar beet and sunflower from 5 and 13 percent of output in 1999 to 10 and 29 percent in 2009, respectively. There was an improvement in yields as well: in 1999, farmers' grain yield was 11.2 centners per hectare; in 2008, it reached a high of 21.3 centners per hectare before declining to 20 in 2009. Increases in yield occurred for other plant products as well. In terms of regional contributions, farmers produced 33 percent of the grain produced in the Southern federal district in 2009 and 19 percent in the Volga.

Popularity of Private Farms

In the first decade, the popularity of private farming increased during 1992–1994 but never took off as reformers had originally hoped, as measured by number of private farms per 1,000 persons. In the mid-1990s, only one region had more than four private farms per 1,000 residents (table 6.1). Data from the 2006 agricultural census are used in table 6.3 to update numerical trends.[47] In May 2000, administrative reform reduced the number of federal districts from eleven to seven "superdistricts," meaning that the districts indicated in table 6.3 have a different regional composition than in table 6.1, so direct comparison is difficult. Nonetheless, two broad trends stand out. First, by the middle of the second decade, the geographical concentration of private farms had not changed much from ten years earlier. That is, the areas where private farming was not robust earlier—the northwest, north, and northeast—continued to have few private farms. In European Russia, a few additional areas fell into the category of having fewer than 1,150 private farms: Karelia, Novgorod, Pskov, and Kirov.

Second, there was not much change in private farm saturation, and nationwide the number of farms stabilized at about 1.7 to 1.8 per 1,000 persons, and at the regional level the saturation rate of private farms remained low. As in the first decade, only the Southern federal district has more than 4 private farms per 1,000 persons, and it is the only district to experience an increase in its saturation rate during 2000–2006. Two districts, the Northwestern and Urals, experienced an erosion in their saturation rate: in the Northwestern district, the rate declined from 1.4 to 1.1, and in the Urals district the rate declined from 1.1 to .9.

Beyond the private farm saturation rate is the net change in the number of private farms. The sixth data column in table 6.3 indicates the net change in the number of private farms during 2000–2006, showing a net decline in every federal district except the Southern district in European Russia. This trend comports with farm consolidation that occurred after 2001—the rate of farm closure outstripping the rate of creation, leading to fewer farms with the survivors having more land, a larger average size, and a stronger financial status.[48] The Southern federal district has the most private farms (108,700 in 2006) and is the only district in European Russia to experience a net increase in farm numbers during 2000–2006. With some of the most fertile agricultural land in Russia—Krasnodar kray, Stavropol' kray, and Volgograd and Rostov oblasts—this development is definitely positive.

How private farms are counted affects the calculation of net changes in the number of private farms. In the 2006 agricultural census, the Russian government began to distinguish between private farms and individual entrepreneurs. The two categories are equal in terms of legal rights and responsibilities. Other than that, the distinction seems to lie only in how a person chose to register one's enterprise. The important point is that if individual entrepreneurs are included, a completely different picture emerges, and these

TABLE 6.3
Popularity of Private Farms by Federal District, European Russia, 2000–2006

	December 2000	December 2003	December 2004	December 2005	July 2006	Net Change in Number of Private Farms, 2000–2006	Net Change in Number of Private Farms, Including Individual Entrepreneurs, 2000–2006,	Regional Ranking in Number of Private Farms and Individual Entrepreneurs, 2006
Russian Federation	1.79	**1.83**	1.82	1.80	1.78	–8,600	+23,400	
Central	1.03	1.05	1.05	**1.06**	1.02	–1,398	+1,229	3
Northwest	**1.40**	1.26	1.25	1.23	1.16	–4,123	–3,155	4
Southern	4.35	4.75	**4.78**	4.71	4.77	+9,699	+29,341	1
Volga	1.38	**1.42**	1.40	1.40	1.36	–2,070	+1,817	2
Urals	**1.12**	1.00	1.00	.95	.90	–3,016	–1,930	5

Notes: December dates are end of year. The entire population of a region was used in the calculations because either urban or rural individuals could begin a private farm. Bold indicates high point for each region.

Sources: Rosstat, *Regiony Rossii. 2005* (Moscow: Rosstat, 2005), 36–37, 402–3; Rosstat, *Regiony Rossii. 2007* (Moscow: Rosstat, 2007), 56–57, 401–2; Rosstat, *Regiony Rossii. 2008* (Moscow: Rosstat, 2008), 56–57, 406; author's calculations; private farm data from http://www.akkor.ru.

data are presented in the seventh data column in table 6.3. Instead of a net decline, the number of private farms increased nationwide and in three of the five European districts. Moreover, in the Southern district, where conditions are most favorable to agriculture, the net increase was over 29,000 new farms. In sum, since 2000, regional differences have become more pronounced, with one dominant regional winner—the Southern district—where land is fertile and geoclimatic factors are conducive to productive agriculture.

Landholdings

At the national level, a rapid growth in farmers' landholdings occurred during the 1990s, although not all registered land was used for food production, as noted in footnote 14. There are different categories of rural land. General land includes land that may not be suitable for agricultural uses, such as roads, land surrounding bodies of water, hills, marshes, and so on. A second category is agricultural land, defined as that which is suitable for agricultural production; within that category is arable land. Finally, there is cultivated land, which is a subcategory of arable land and indicates how much land was actually put into production.

More so than the number of private farms, trends in farmers' landholdings illustrate the unfolding success story, measurable in four ways, as shown in table 6.4. First, as the table shows, the total area registered to private farms continues to increase, from 14.3 million hectares in 1999 to almost 26 million hectares, according to the 2006 agricultural census. Second, nationwide, over 83 percent of farmers' land is classified as agricultural, and nearly 70 percent of agricultural land is actually in use. Farmers in the most fertile regions—the Southern and Volga districts—have 85 percent of their agricultural land in production. Third, almost 70 percent of agricultural land is considered arable, and in the Volga district, 79 percent of land is arable. Fourth, a high percentage of arable land is actually cultivated—88 percent for the nation, including 84 percent in the Southern district and 87 percent in the Volga district. This latter statistic is a dramatic improvement from 1999, when only 42 percent of farmers' land was cultivated, and shows that with government and regional assistance programs, farmers are doing an excellent job putting their land to use. Private farms have come far from their "Potemkin village" days of the early 1990s, as earlier described by Humphrey.

Furthermore, farmers account for a greater percentage of total cultivated land. Nationwide in 1999, they used only about 7 percent of all cultivated land; by 2006, it had increased to over 17 percent. Farmers' cultivated land area continued to increase even after the 2006 census and in 2009 reached 15.8 million hectares, accounting for 20.5 percent of all cultivated land and

TABLE 6.4

Characteristics of Land Use by Private Farms in July 2006, European Russia

	Total Area of Land Registered to Private Farms (thousands of hectares)	Of Total Area, Quantity That Is Classified as Agricultural Land (thousands of hectares)	Amount of Agricultural Land in Use (thousands of hectares)	Percentage of Agricultural Land in Use	Of Agricultural Land, Quantity That Is Arable (thousands of hectares)	Percentage of Agricultural Land That Is Arable	Farmers' Cultivated Land (thousands of hectares)	Percentage of Arable Land Cultivated
Russian Federation	25,972	21,588	17,903	69%	14,991	69%	13,200	88%
Central	2,518	2,425	1,856	74%	1,865	77%	1,548.2	83%
Northwestern	573	313	124	22%	85	27%	81.1	95%
Southern	7,350	7,215	6,277	85%	4,340	60%	3,624.3	84%
Volga	5,732	5,637	4,877	85%	4,461	79%	3,872.4	87%
Urals	1,498	1,197	903	60%	836	70%	724.1	87%

Note: Numbers and percentages have been rounded.

Sources: Rosstat, *Regiony Rossii. 2008* (Moscow: Rosstat, 2008), 30–33; author's calculations.

24 percent of cultivated land used for grain production.[49] In the most fertile areas of Russia, farmers use 24 percent of the cultivated land in the Southern district and 17 percent in the Volga district, impressive gains compared to 1999 (see table 6.2).

The Third Decade (2010–2019)

Private farmers are starting their third decade in much better condition than they started their second. As we saw above, by the end of their second decade, farmers played a key role in the production of certain plant commodities, especially grain, in some of the most fertile and productive agricultural areas in Russia.[50] Although farm popularity was low, as measured by the saturation rate, there was a net increase in the number of private farms in the fertile Southern district. Landholding trends were also positive, as increases occurred in total land, agricultural land, arable land, and cultivated land. Particularly important was the fact that the Southern and Volga districts ended the second decade with a high ratio of cultivated to arable land.

As the third decade begins, the Russian government recognizes farmers' economic significance to the nation's food security and is committed to the sector's continued economic growth. Vice Premier Viktor Zubkov confirmed the government's commitment to the private farm sector when he stated, "The government sees private farmers as the foundation of the middle class in the countryside, the representatives of small and middle-sized business, the guarantee of social stability in Russian villages. For this reason the government continues to adopt systematic measures for strengthening the private farming sector."[51] Prime Minister Putin stated that private farms "are a powerful segment of the domestic agroindustrial complex."[52] In February 2011, Minister of Agriculture Elena Skrynnik argued that "farmers play an important role not only in providing food security to the state, but also in maintaining and developing the socioeconomic potential and cultural-historical significance of rural areas."[53] Speaking at AKKOR's Twenty-Second Annual Congress in March 2011, Putin stated that "private farming in Russia is an economic and social force, and to a significant degree is a pillar of society, and is an important source for the development of Russian regions and revival of our countryside. Our task is to give rural entrepreneurs possibilities to conduct their business without barriers and obstacles, to remove baseless, onerous administrative, financial, and organizational costs." He then turned directly to the farmers in the audience and said , "The government . . . is doing everything it can to create conditions for your effective work, and in any case will show you assistance."[54]

The question is whether private farmers can build on the successful trends that emerged in the second decade. This section argues that they can do so on the basis of several policy levers that are likely to have a positive effect. One policy lever is the government's continued use of tariffs and import quotas to protect domestic agricultural producers, policies that benefit private farmers.[55] In October 2010, Prime Minister Putin announced that import quotas for poultry—Russia's largest meat import—would decrease during 2010–2012 so that in 2012 the volume would be only 58 percent of the 2009 level.[56] In December 2010, trade tariffs and import quotas for 2011 were established for beef, pork, and poultry—530,000 tons of beef, 472,000 tons of pork, and 350,000 tons of poultry.[57] Putin expressed hope that in the coming years, Russia could do without meat imports at all, and the general director of the Russian Poultry Union predicted that perhaps by 2012, Russia "would turn from an importer to an exporter of poultry meat."[58] Trade protection, particularly in animal husbandry, is important for private farmers because the branch is underdeveloped and the government has just started a concerted effort to strengthen it.[59] Private farmers will need protection from foreign competitors that are more mechanized and more efficient, and the government's intent to use trade policies to provide protection until Russian farmers are able to compete more effectively is an important step.

A second policy lever that portends continuing success is government support for small and medium-size businesses. Speaking in January 2009, Prime Minister Putin explained to the plenary session of the Davos forum that "we have passed a bill to entitle regions to the right to reduce taxes on small and medium businesses from 15% to 5%. We have established funds to support such businesses. They function either through banks as they receive federal funds or through regional agencies.[60] We will support small and medium businesses in every economic branch on our priority list, farming being no exception."[61] In early January 2011, Vice Premier Viktor Zubkov stated that "the leadership of the country considers support for small agrobusiness one of the most important priorities of the government." In early February 2011, Minister Skrynnik indicated in a video press conference that support for small forms of farming is a governmental priority, and toward this end the government subsidizes 95 percent of the Central Bank's interest rate for refinanced loans and regional budgets the remaining 5 percent.[62] She also promised that a "hotline" would be established that would provide consultative service to agricultural producers about the government's subsidization programs.

A third policy lever is the commitment to address problems that still confront private farmers. In December 2010, Putin argued that "undoubtedly, we should resolve the systemic problems that are holding back the development of entrepreneurship in the countryside. All the problems that are restraining the development of entrepreneurship in the countryside should be eliminated as quickly as possible. We need to build a functioning mechanism for consumer cooperatives, to give farmers the opportunity to sell their products. We need to make cheaper and faster the procedure for formulating boundaries of land shares so that the peasantry can become a full-fledged master who defends his land and is freely able to use this resource, including mortgaging the land to raise capital from financial institutions."[63] Toward this end, Putin indicated that instructions had been given to continue government subsidies for fuel, seed, and fertilizer during 2011.

A fourth policy lever is the revival of the "Russian Farmer" program. At the end of November 2010, the dominant party in Russia's political system, United Russia (which has had the Kremlin's backing for many years and is headed by Vladimir Putin), adopted the new program, which will run to 2020, "an important event not only for the leading political party in the country and for the Russian farmer, but also for the agrarian branch as a whole and all rural dwellers."[64] The significance of United Russia's support for private farming is that this party controls nearly every regional legislature and that almost every regional head (oblast or republic) is a member of the party, at least nominally. As Darrell Slider has argued, United Russia remains a Kremlin-controlled party, and there are few institutional mechanisms for the party to develop independence.[65] Therefore, United Russia represents the means for the Kremlin to pursue its goals, and tangible results in the Russian Farmer program are more likely since United Russia controls regional policy and budgets.

The Russian Farmer project will "assist the development and strengthening of the farmer sector and other small forms of farming in the agroindustrial complex, increase the effectiveness of measures for the development of agricultural production, and [assist] in the revival of the Russian countryside."[66] Specifically, the goals of the program are 1) to increase the number of private farms, 2) to create employment opportunities in the countryside and increase rural incomes, 3) to help retain rural youth in the countryside, 4) to improve the demographic situation in the country, and 5) to help to develop sustainable rural communities.[67] The two people responsible for the program are Minister of Agriculture Skrynnik and the president of AKKOR, Vladimir Plotnikov. Skrynnik emphasized that the adoption of the Russian Farmer program "is a guarantee for receiving state assistance. . . . The implementation of the program permits us to integrate all the directions of state support for small entrepreneurship in the countryside into a single program that will promote the development of farming."[68] In turn, Plotnikov argued that "a system of state support of small forms of farming in the countryside is one of the key tasks of agrarian policy in the country."[69] This new program fits within

Medvedev's modernization plan for Russia's economy as a whole, a theme that the president has touched on repeatedly in recent years and one that he made a central theme of his annual address at the end of November 2010.[70]

A fifth and final consideration is AKKOR's policy to strengthen corporatist relationships between AKKOR and major financial actors in the agribusiness complex. An original agreement of cooperation was signed in 2007 between AKKOR and the state-owned and -operated company Rosagrolizing, an organization that purchases foreign equipment and then leases or sells it at subsidized interest rates to large farms and private farms within Russia. The chairman of AKKOR, Vladimir Plotnikov, noted that this agreement was important for providing agricultural equipment and pedigree livestock to private farms, and in particular he drew attention to the advantageous terms that allowed private farmers to acquire machinery and that helped those who were affected by the 2010 drought. In mid-January 2011, the leadership of Rosagrolizing and AKKOR met to discuss the signing of a new agreement of cooperation. The new agreement allows Rosagrolizing to provide financing for rural housing for farmers and facilitates supplying agricultural machinery directly to farmers through regional branches of AKKOR.[71]

In addition, in February 2010, AKKOR signed an agreement of cooperation with Rossel'khozbank that is to run to the end of 2012.[72] The agreement directs subsidized credit through Rossel'khozbank to private farmers, operators of private plots, and small agricultural agribusinesses. In January 2011, the leadership of Rossel'khozbank and AKKOR met to discuss the signing of a new agreement of cooperation that would help to develop small forms of farming, including private farming, by channeling subsidized credit through rural credit cooperatives.[73] The new agreement was signed in February 2011 and will make is easier for farmers to obtain credit from Rossel'khozbank by reducing the number of required documents and creating AKKOR information-consulting centers in branch offices.[74]

Thus, at the national level, a number of policy levers and initiatives support the conclusion that private farming is poised for further growth. The government is willing to spend financial resources and intends to remain active in assisting the development of private farming. The government has shown a willingness to use policy levers to help the agricultural sector. The government has a commitment to develop small business and entrepreneurship in the countryside. A variety of government financial assistance programs exist and are funded. There is a deepening relationship between AKKOR and important financial actors that serves the interests of private farmers.

At the regional level, the importance of vanguard regions—such as the Volga and Southern federal district—may have wider beneficial effects. Farmers in regions where private farming is more developed have higher standards of living and greater productivity. In turn, the prosperity of farmers in advanced regions may provide incentives for farmers in other regions to introduce new technologies or methods of farming. Further, the successes of the vanguard regions may lead the central government to fund programs that apply the experiences of advanced regions elsewhere. In addition, a coalition of regional AKKOR leaders, successful private farmers, and other agricultural producers may push for policies in trade and domestic support that are favorable for all. In other words, vanguard regions may lead a movement that leads to more agrarian change and wider prosperity for all.

Of course, there is significant variation depending on the financial resources of a region and its leadership, but even in places where natural factors are not favorable to agriculture, attempts are being made to modernize and innovate. Hard data are difficult to come by that pertain specifically to private farmers, but one would expect that as risk takers and entrepreneurs, private farmers are active in introducing new methods and technologies. One example is in Tyumen oblast, where a special regional program to develop animal husbandry was introduced in 2002 and continues to the present. The purpose of the program is to introduce French and American breeds of cattle to Russian farms; these breeds produce more milk per cow and yield much more meat per head than Russian breeds.[75] Budget assistance from the regional government supports the creation of special farms where the new breeds are raised. In another example, a regional innovation center was created by the Siberian Regional Branch of the Russian Agricultural Academy (Rossel'khozakademii), the most prestigious educational and scientific organization devoted to agriculture in Russia. The center and its academics are working to introduce new technologies, methods, grain cultures, and animal breeds throughout farms located in Siberia.[76] These examples illustrate that policy initiatives are occurring at the regional level as well.

Conclusion

From the beginning of the first decade to the beginning of the third, continuities and significant change are evident in Russia's private farming sector. This chapter has analyzed four factors and their relevance to private farmers: government policy, food output, the popularity of private farming, and landholdings. The conclusion summarizes which factors experienced change and which show continuity.

Policy from the federal government has undergone significant change. Although the early post-Soviet government under Boris Yeltsin hoped to supplant collective farms with private farms, in real terms its support was short lived and not effective. A lot of financial assistance was wasted or stolen, the Russian Farmer program existed only two years, and the level of federal support decreased dramatically after 1994, coming to a complete end starting with the 1996 budget. The general consensus is that the government's actions did not match its rhetoric. In contrast, since the mid-2000s, private farmers have been eligible to participate in and benefit from government assistance programs that were introduced to help the agricultural sector. In addition, several programs that are specific to private farming have been adopted and are fully funded. Numerous high-level governmental leaders have gone on record that they consider private farming an integral part of Russia's strategy to become a global food supplier and to attain national food security.

Food output contains elements of continuity and change. In terms of change, private farmers today contribute more to the nation's food supply than ever in terms of physical volume, ruble value of their production, and percentage of total value of output. In particular, we saw that private farmers produce significant quantities of grain, sugar beet, and sunflower. Grain output is more than 20 million tons a year and has allowed Russia to become a major exporter, ranking third in the world in 2008 and 2009. Large farms produce enough grain to meet the domestic needs of the country, but it is the production of grain on private farms that constitutes the surpluses for export and brings in revenue. Thus, while former state and collective farms remain the backbone of the nation in terms of food production (measured in volume, not ruble value), private farming is an important supplement that is growing in significance. In terms of continuity, the product mix that private farmers produce best has not changed much from the 1990s, and this is mostly a result of government policy and the incentives that flow from those policies. Going forward, the government's stated intent is to develop the animal husbandry and poultry sectors. A further element of continuity is that the highest-producing regions in the 1990s remain the best-producing regions today.

The popularity of private farming shows mostly continuity. The saturation rate of private farms remains low, about 1.7 to 1.8 private farms per 1,000 persons nationwide, a number that has not changed much since 1993. The total number of private farms has fluctuated during the years but in the aggregate is not much different from the mid-1990s. The specific regions (oblasts and krays) that had most of the private farms in the 1990s continue to do so today. At the same time, distributional patterns have changed, with the emergence of one clear winner (the Southern federal district), whereas other districts in European Russia have experienced a net decline in the number of private farms.

Finally, farmers' landholdings show significant change in terms of total land area registered, the percentage of their total land that is considered agricultural, the amount of their agricultural land that is arable, and the amount of their arable land that is cultivated. On all these dimensions, the trends are clearly positive, especially because higher percentages of total land are arable and cultivated. In particular, each federal district shows a high percentage of arable land that is being cultivated, more than 80 percent, whereas in the 1990s only about 40 percent of arable land was cultivated. In short, private farmers not only have more land but also have better land and are making fuller use of that land, a fact that no doubt impacts the upward trajectories in food production.

Notes

1. The original RSFSR "Law on Peasant Farms" was adopted in November 1990 and then amended in December 1990. The 1990 law was replaced in 2003 by an updated law of the same name, and the 2003 law continued to be amended thereafter.

2. Stephen K. Wegren, "Russia's Food Policies and Foreign Policy," *Demokratizatsiya: The Journal of Post-Soviet Democratization* 18, no. 3 (2010): 189–207.

3. Formed in January 1990, AKKOR is the main organization that represents the interests of private farmers and private plot operators.

4. Stephen K. Wegren, "Private Farming in Russia: An Emerging Success?," *Post-Soviet Affairs* 27, no. 3 (2011): 211–14.

5. Stephen K. Wegren, *Agriculture and the State in Soviet and Post-Soviet Russia* (Pittsburgh, PA: Pittsburgh University Press, 1998), 77–107; Ziv Lerman, Csaba Csaki, and Gershon Feder, *Agriculture in Transition: Land Policies and Evolving Farm Structures in Post-Soviet Countries* (Lanham, MD: Lexington Books, 2004), 105–62.

6. *Rossiiskii fermer*, no. 40, 1993, 2.

7. *Krest'yanskie vedomosti*, no. 7, 1992, 4–5.

8. Don Van Atta, "The Return of Individual Farming in Russia," In *The "Farmer Threat": The Political Economy of Agrarian Reform in Post-Soviet Russia*, ed. Don Van Atta, 75–91 (Boulder, CO: Westview Press, 1993), 20–21.

9. Goskomstat, *Tseny v Rossiiskoi Federatsii* (Moscow: Goskomstat, 1995), 24.

10. Z. F. Belikova, "Razvitiyu fermerstva—Gosudarstvennii protektsionizm," in *Gosudarstvennoe regulirovanie deyatel'nosti agrarnikh i promyshlennikh predpriyatii*, ed. A. G. Zel'dner (Moscow: Institut ekonomiki, 1997), 64.

11. Van Atta, "The Return of Individual Farming in Russia," 83–89; Stefan Zhurek, "Transforming Russian Agriculture: Why Is Privatization so Difficult?," *The Soviet and Post-Soviet Review* 21, no. 2–3 (1994): 263–74. A governmental survey of more than 187,000 private farms in 1999 revealed that six of ten private farms were unprofitable. Only 55 percent of private farmers used all their arable land, and nearly a quarter used less than 50 percent. Most private farms were undercapitalized, and while significant difference existed between large and small private farms, on average the numbers were strikingly low. See A. P. Zinchenko, "Tendentsii i problemy ispol'zovaniya proizvodstvennogo potentsiala krest'yanskikh (fermerskikh) khozyaistv," *Ekonomika sel'skokhozyaistvennikh i pererabatyvayushchikh predpriyatii* 10

(2001): 17–18. For example, in 1999, the average for all private farms was one hired worker per farm, thirty-seven head of horned cattle per 100 farms, sixteen pigs per 100 farms, and seventy-six tractors and thirty-six trucks per 100 farms. On private farms that specialized in producing plant products, there was an average of twenty-eight combines, fifty-four plows, forty-nine seeding machines, and twenty harvesters per 100 farm. Goskomstat, *Sel'skokhozyaistvennaya deyatel'nost' krest'yanskikh (fermerskikh) khozyaistv v Rossii* (Moscow: Goskomstat, 2000), 36–37, 42.

12. "O deyatel'nost'i krest'yanskikh (fermerskikh) khozyaistv v Rossiiskoi Federatsii," *Statisticheskii Byulleten'* 10 (2000): 5–13.

13. Stephen Handelman, *Comrade Criminal: Russia's New Mafiya* (New Haven, CT: Yale University Press, 1995), 22.

14. *Krest'yanskie Rossiya*, no. 22, 1993, 2.

15. As the rate of farm creation stagnated, private farm bankruptcies increased dramatically: 5,000 in 1993, 14,000 in 1994, 26,000 in 1995, and more than 25,000 in 1996. During 1995, twenty-five regions of Russia experienced a net decline in the number of private farms; in 1996, that number rose to forty-nine regions. During 1996, for every 100 farms created, ninety-six went out of business; I. Terent'ev, "Agrarnaya reforma i krest'yanskie (fermerskie) khozyaistva," *Ekonomist* 7 (1996): 94.

16. *Finansovie izvestiya*, no. 15, 1994, 3.

17. Belikova, "Razvitiyu fermerstva—Gosudarstvennii protektsionizm," 64.

18. N. Popov, "Krest'yanskie (fermerskie) khozyaistva," *APK: Ekonomika, upravlenie* 5 (1996): 59.

19. Popov, "Krest'yanskie (fermerskie) khozyaistva."

20. From 1991 through 1995, prices for industrial goods used by food producers increased 2,230 percent, while purchase prices for agricultural products rose only 752 percent (*Zemlya i trud*, 1996, 3).

21. Sergei Sazonov, "Sotsial'no-ekonomicheskie aspekty razvitiya fermerskogo dvizheniya v Rossii," *APK: Ekonomika, upravlenie* 5 (1995): 57.

22. Goskomstat, *Rossiiskii statisticheskii ezhegodnik* (Moscow: Goskomstat, 2003), 201. In 1999, private farms accounted for 3.1 percent of the ruble value of the nation's plant production and 1.7 percent of the value of its animal husbandry production; Goskomstat, *Sel'skokhozyaistvennaya deyatel'nost' krest'yanskikh (fermerskikh) khozyaistv v Rossii*, 20.

23. According to the 2006 agricultural census, the bankruptcy rate increased in each successive time period: 1995–1997, 1998–2000, and 2001–2003; Rosstat, *Osnovnie itogi Vserossiiskoi sel'skokhozyaistvennoi perepisi 2006 goda*, vol. 1, bk. 2 (Moscow: Rosstat, 2008), 57.

24. Goskomstat, *Sel'skokhozyaistvennaya deyatel'nost' krest'yanskikh (fermerskikh) khozyaistv v Rossii*, 83–87.

25. Jessica Allina-Pisano, *The Post-Soviet Potemkin Village: Politics and Property Rights in the Black Earth* (New York: Cambridge University Press, 2008), 85–112.

26. Caroline Humphrey, *Marx Went Away but Karl Stayed Behind*, rev. ed. (Ann Arbor: University of Michigan Press, 2001), 449.

27. Timothy Heleniak, "Out-Migration and Depopulation of the Russian North during the 1990s," *Post-Soviet Geography and Economics* 40, no. 3 (1999): 155–205.

28. A. A. Lichman, "Regional'nie aspekty raspredeleniya nekotorikh pokazateley malogo sel'skokhozyaistvennogo biznesa Rossii," in *Krupnii i malyy biznes v sel'skom khozyaistve: tendentsii, razvitiya, problemy, perspektivy*, ed. I. N. Buzdalov (Moscow: Russian Academy of Agricultural Science, 2006),

29. During the 1990s and up to the adoption of the 2001 Land Code, a number of regions had legislation that did not permit private landownership or had legislation that was silent on the issue. The inability to use land as collateral was important because a survey of farmers found that the single most important factor that limited the expansion of production was insufficient monetary capital for investment, expressed by almost three-quarters of farmers who were surveyed, Goskomstat, *Sel'skokhozyaistvennaya deyatel'nost' krest'yanskikh (fermerskikh) khozyaistv v Rossii*, 41.

30. Goskomstat, *Sel'skokhozyaistvennaya deyatel'nost' krest'yanskikh (fermerskikh) khozyaistv v Rossii*, 15. The remaining 5 percent of agricultural land had other uses.

31. *Rossiiskaya zemlya*, no. 21, 2010, 2.

32. Stephen K. Wegren, "Russian Agrarian Policy under Putin," *Post-Soviet Geography and Economics* 43, no. 1 (2002): 26–40.

33. A. Semenov and D. Ageyev, "Sotsial'nie prioritety podderzhki malogo predprinimatel'stva," *Ekonomist* 10 (2000): 77.

34. V. I. Kudryashov and M. P. Kozlov, "Integratsiya krest'yanskikh (fermerskikh) khozyaistv v sistemu mnogoukladnoi ekonomiki APK," *Ekonomika sel'skokhozyaistvennikh i pererabatyvayushchikh predpriyatii* 9 (2003): 44.

35. Rosstat, *Rossiya v tsifrakh. 2006* (Moscow: Rosstat, 2006), 436–37.

36. The federal program (Development of the APK) was supplemented with regional programs of assistance. The size of the regional assistance programs varied by region and financial resources. Generally, in northern areas where agriculture was weak, regional financial assistance was considerably less.

37. "Gosudarstvennaya programma razvitiya sel'skogo khozyaistva i regulirovaniya rynkov sel'skokhozyaistvennoi produktsii, syr'ya i prodovol'stviya na 2008–2012 gody," 2007, http://www.mcx.ru (accessed June 15, 2010).

38. Some of those assistance measures in the program include: a price support system for grain crops and a degree of purchase guarantees; the subsidization of interest rates for investment loans; the extension of subsidized credit and loans to purchase agricultural machinery and farm equipment or pedigree livestock; subsidized credit for the construction of buildings to house livestock or for food storage; subsidized credit for obtaining fuel, spare parts, or mineral fertilizer; subsidized credit for obtaining materials to repair farm buildings; subsidized credit for the purchase of young livestock; direct production subsidies for meat and milk delivered to state-licensed purchasing agents; a leasing program that allows producers to lease farm machinery with the state subsidizing the cost; and subsidized credit in order to develop rural tourism.

39. "Razvitie krest'yanskikh (fermerskikh) khozyaistv i drugikh malykh form khozyaistvaniya v APK na 2009–2011," 2009, 10, http://www.mcx.ru, under link "malie formy khozyaistvovaniya" (accessed June 15, 2010).

40. "Razvitie krest'yanskikh (fermerskikh) khozyaistv i drugikh malykh form khozyaistvaniya v APK na 2009–2011," 11–12.

41. To fulfill the first task, the project would subsidize 500 infrastructural projects in eighty-one regions for a total cost of R3.7 billion. To stimulate innovation, the program allocated R1.2 billion. According to the program, innovation was defined as acquiring pedigree milk cows and increasing the genetic potential for productivity, acquiring high-yield seed, and acquiring high-value breeds of livestock. To achieve the third task, the program allocated R5 million, and for the fourth task up to R3.6 billion was assigned.

42. *Sel'skaya zhizn'*, October 29–November 4, 2009, 1; *Rossiiskaya zemlya*, no. 4, 2010, 4.

43. Elena B. Skrynnik, "Povyshenie proizvoditel'nosti i finansovoi ustoichivosti malykh form khozyaistvenniya na sele," *Ekonomika sel'skokhozyaistvennikh i pererabatyvayushchikh predpriyatii* 2 (2010): 4.

44. "Za dva goda otraslevoi programmy Ministerstva sel'skogo khozyaistva RF fermery postroili 311 zhivotnovodcheskikh ferm," 2011, http://goo.gl/nx9Np.

45. About 88 percent of farmers' cultivated land is devoted to crops that are processed, such as grain, sunflower, and sugar beet.

46. Reyting, "Reyting krupneyshikh fermerskikh khozyaistv Rossii-Klub 'Fermer-300,'" *Ekonomika sel'skokhozyaistvennikh i pererabatyvayushchikh predpriyatii* 2 (2010): 22.

47. I should note that the number of private farms is only a rough measure and not necessarily the best indicator of farmers' success because not all registered farms are actually engaged in agricultural production. For example, the current president of AKKOR, Vladimir Plotnikov, revealed that 49,000 private farms did not have any land according to the 2006 agricultural census, a fact that reflects "anarchy and corruption"; see Vladimir N. Plotnikov, "Doklad Prezidenta AKKOR Vladimiria Nikolaevicha Plotnikova na XIX s'ezde AKKOR," *Fermerskoe samoupravlenie* 3–5 (2008): 3–8. Further, the 2006 agricultural census revealed that only 50 percent of registered farms are engaged in agricultural production nationwide; regions varied from a low of 18 percent in the Northwestern federal district to a high of 64 percent in the Southern federal district; Rosstat, *Osnovnie itogi Vserossiiskoi sel'skokhozyaistvennoi perepisi 2006 goda*, vol. 1, bk. 2 (Moscow: Rosstat, 2008), 155, 229. For this reason arable landholdings, cultivated land, and agricultural production are better measures of farmers' success. Nonetheless, the number of private farms is important because those numbers document regional shifts and reflect a general popularity of private farming over time.

48. Rosstat, *Osnovnie itogi Vserossiiskoi sel'skokhozyaistvennoi perepisi 2006 goda*, vol. 1, bk. 1 (Moscow: Rosstat, 2008), 56–57.

49. Krest'yanskie (fermerskie) khozyaistva, "Krest'yanskie (fermerskie) khozyaistva Rossii v 2009 g. (ekonomicheskii obzor)," *APK: Ekonomika, upravlenie* 5 (2010): 72.

50. "22 Dekabrya V. A. Zubkov vstretilsya s predstavitelyami AKKOR i Tsentrosoyuza Rossii," 2010, http://www.akkor.ru/news/podrobnee/707.

51. *Sel'skaya zhizn'*, February 18–24, 2010, 5.

52. *Rossiiskaya zemlya*, no. 24, 2010, 1.

53. "Pod predsedatel'stvom Ministra sel'skogo khozyaistva RF Eleny Skrynnik sostoyalos' rasshirennoe zasedanie kollegii Ministerstva 'O gosudarstvennoi podderzhke malykh form khozyaistvovaniya v APK,'" 2011, http://www.mcx.ru/news/news/show_print/4454.78.htm.

54. *Rossiiskaya zemlya*, no. 5, 2011, 3, 5.

55. Wegren, "Russia's Food Policies and Foreign Policy," 198–99.

56. *Rossiiskaya zemlya*, no. 20, 2010, 2.

57. "Utverzhdeny tarifnie kvoty na 2011gg," 2010, http://www.akkor.ru/news/podrobnee/718.

58. *Rossiiskaya zemlya*, no. 20, 2010, 2.

59. In 2010, the federal government adopted a special program for its development that included steps to reduce meat imports and increase domestic production (Dmitri Medvedev, "Vystuplenie prezidenta Rossiyskoi Federatsii D. A. Medvedeva na zasendanii prezidiuma Gossoveta," *Ekonomika sel'skokhozyaistvennikh i pererabatyvayushchikh predpriyatiy* 8 [2010]: 6–7). The name of the program is "On Measures for Accelerating Development of Animal Husbandry" and was adopted in July 2010. In 2011, the federal government intends to spend R7.5 billion in support of this program, which also receives funding from regional governments (*Sel'skaya zhizn'*, November 2, 2010). In October 2010, the Ministry of Agriculture introduced a program to prevent the spread from one territory to another of a plague that affected pigs, with Minister Skrynnik stating that "this program not only permits us to minimize the risk to animal husbandry but also promotes the strengthening of food security in the country" (*Sel'kaya zhizn'*, October 21–27, 2010, 2).

60. In 2009, as part of its anticrisis program, about R30 billion of credit was extended to all small businesses from banks, and another R10 billion was extended from the federal budget. See Prezident AKKOR, "Prezident AKKOR V. Plotnikov prinyal uchastie vo vstreche V. Putina s pukovoditelyami obedinenii predprinimateley malogo i srednego biznesa," 2010, http://www.akkor.ru/news/podrobnee/712. For 2010, the federal government budgeted R5.6 billion to subsidize interest rates for loans taken out by small business. By December 2010, R5.2 billion had already been dispersed; the remainder was to be spent by the end of the year; Viktor Zubkov, "Viktor Zubkov vyravnivaet kooperatsiyu," 2011, http://www.agronews.ru.

61. "S tochki zreniya," 2009, http://premier.gov.ru.

62. "3 Fevralya sostoyalas' videopress-konferentsiya Ministra sel'skogo khozyaistva RF Eleny Skrynnik," 2011, http://www.mcx.ru.

63. Vladimir Putin, "Vystupitel'noe slovo Vladimira Putina," 2010, http://www.akkor.ru.

64. *Rossiiskaya zemlya*, no. 21, 2010, 1.

65. Darrell Slider, "How United Is United Russia? Regional Sources of Intra-Party Conflict," *Communist Studies and Transition Politics* 26, no. 2 (2010): 257–75.

66. "Edinaya Rossiya pristupaet k realizatsii partiinogo proekta 'Rossiiskii fermer,'" 2011, http://www.akkor.ru/news/podrobnee/656. The program is discussed in *Rossiiskaya zemlya*, no. 21, 2010, 1–2.

67. "Partiinii proekt 'Rossiiskii fermer,'" 2011, http://er.ru/print.shtml?17/1675.

68. "Edinaya Rossiya pristupaet k realizatsii partiinogo proekta 'Rossiiskii fermer.'"

69. "Gospodderzhka malykh form khozyaistvovaniya v APK dolzhna byt' effektivnoi," 2010, http://www.akkor.ru/news/podrobnee/697.

70. Hans-Henning Schroder, "In Search of Modernization without Irritation: Medvedev's Third Address to the Federal Assembly," *Russian Analytical Digest* 90 (2011): 2–5. Although most Western attention in the press has been given to

Medvedev and his expressed urgency for modernization, in reality, the real modernizer in agriculture has been Putin, who introduced assistance programs starting in 2005, long before Medvedev was on the political radar. President Medvedev has emphasized modernization of the food-processing industry in particular within the agricultural sector.

71. "18 Yanvarya sostoyalas' vstrecha rukovodstva AKKOR i Rosagrolizing," 2011, http://www.akkor.ru (under the link "novosti").

72. *Rossiiskaya zemlya*, no. 24, 2010, 6. Rossel'khozbank is a 100 percent state-owned agricultural bank that has seventy-eight regional branch offices and another 1,500 local offices, making it the second-largest banking network in Russia, with more than 2 million clients (see www.rshb.ru/en/about/profile.php).

73. "19 Yanvarya sostoyalas' vstrecha rukovodstva AKKOR i OAO Rossel'khozbank," 2011, http://www.akkor.ru (under the link "novosti").

74. "Podpisano soglashenie o sotrudnichestve AKKOR i Rossel'khozbanka," 2011, http://www.akkor.ru/news/podrobnee/842.

75. *Sel'skaya zhizn'*, October 28–November 3, 2010, 4.

76. *Sel'skaya zhizn'*, November 2, 2010, 1–2.

7

Russia's Potential Role in the World Oil System

Reciprocal Dependency, Global Integration, and Positive Unintended Consequences

Andrew Barnes

Russia is one of the two largest oil producers in the world, often besting Saudi Arabia for the top position. While there is more to the Russian economy than just oil, the petroleum sector supports the country's economic growth and fiscal balance, as many analysts have noted (see chapter 2). Less frequently discussed, however, is whether and how that oil wealth might give Russia the power to affect the global oil system.

Russia's endowments as an oil producer and transporter appear to give it potential influence in the international political economy of oil. After a slight dip in 2008, production increased in 2009, and the country provided almost 13 percent of the petroleum consumed in the world in 2010. Similarly, exports rebounded in 2010, and Russia sends more than 5 million barrels a day to customers around the world.[1] Most of those barrels go to Europe, as Russian oil has helped fill the void left by declining production in the North Sea—thus, even if European demand for oil never grew any further, the continued falloff from North Sea fields would provide a growing market for Russian oil. In the east, meanwhile, demand is most assuredly growing, and Russia is positioning itself to be a key supplier to China.

Russia's place in the regional pipeline system also gives it a potential role in the world oil economy despite the efforts of others to develop alternate routes. Most westward-flowing oil from Kazakhstan still runs through Russia, via either the Soviet-built pipeline to Samara or the foreign-built Caspian Pipeline Corporation (CPC) pipeline around the Caspian Sea. The recently opened pipeline from Russia to China could make Russia a significant player in that enormous economy. And while the Baku–Tbilisi–Ceyhan pipeline allows much oil from Azerbaijan to circumvent Russia, that pipeline still lies within Russia's sphere of influence. In the long run, more alternative pipelines will be built, but constructing them is no easy task, so Russia remains a hub in the regional transit system.

What can Russia do with these potential levers of power? Russian leaders have long desired to be significant players in the global oil system, and in the contemporary world, where petroleum is central to so many economies, the country would seem well positioned to wield considerable influence on the world stage. The oil economy, however, is a large and fluid system, and Russia is only one of many players in it. Furthermore, other oil powers have had mixed success, at best, translating their oil wealth into international power.

This chapter explores actions that Russia could take to influence its neighbors, reshape the world oil system to its advantage, or both. The possibilities are many, but few are easy, and none is without cost. The chapter therefore concludes by cautioning against seeing Russian actions only in terms of the damage they might do. Instead, Russia's dependence on oil revenues will make it harder to exploit other countries' dependence on its oil or transport networks, and the interconnected nature of the world oil system means that some of the strategies that would most benefit Russia would benefit the rest of the world as well.

Physical Levers

The size of the world's oil industry is remarkable, to say the least. Drilling equipment reaches miles into the earth, pipelines traverse entire countries, and ships carry hundreds of thousands of barrels of oil at a time, all of which makes the modern economy possible. This section examines how Russia could use its physical control over parts of the oil system in order to affect the world around it.

Context: The Size and Structure of the Russian Oil Sector

During the Soviet era, the Soviet Union used its oil wealth to subsidize industrial production, support allies, and bring in hard currency (through either exports or oil-collateralized international loans).[2] It developed a massive petroleum industry, but it also encouraged wasteful approaches to using that oil. After 1991, the command economy was gone, but the importance of oil remained. In the 1990s, domestic oil prices remained below world prices, thus continuing to subsidize industrial activity, although this was not enough to sustain the economy in the context of the myriad shocks it faced during the decade. As oil prices began to rise at the turn of century, the government began to tax oil exports heavily, and the system began to look more and more like a traditional rentier state.[3] In 2004, raw materials accounted for over 60 percent of exports, with oil at 40 percent and natural gas around 15 percent.[4] Furthermore, nearly 40 percent of revenues came from taxes on oil and gas in 2003, and that number had risen to about 48 percent by 2010.[5]

Further demonstrating the importance of oil for the Russian economy and budget was the country's performance during the recent global economic downturn. The drop in oil prices in the second half of 2008 hit Russia hard, as several years of economic growth and budget surpluses were radically reversed in 2009. While real growth had been positive in every year since the financial crisis of 1998, including a rate of 5.2 percent in 2008, real gross domestic product (GDP) fell by 7.8 percent in 2009. Expected oil and gas revenues to the budget dropped by more than half between November 2008 and April 2009, and the planned budget balance fell from more than 3.7 percent of GDP to less than 7.4 percent. While much of the rest of the world remained mired in recession, however, Russian GDP growth moved back into positive territory in 2010 (growing at a rate of 4 percent), as world oil prices rebounded from an average of about $60 per barrel in 2009 to almost $80 per barrel in 2010.[6]

The budget is still in deficit, but if oil prices remain in the neighborhood of $100 to $120 per barrel official forecasts see Russia returning to balanced budgets by 2015; if prices hover in the vicinity of $90 per barrel, the country would run a deficit of 1 or 2 percent of GDP.[7]

The participants in the Russian oil sector are numerous and varied. First is the state itself, which affects the system in at least three significant ways, two of them active and one passive. Perhaps most obviously, the Russian government affects the oil sector through regulation, including taxes, privatization plans, allocation of exploration and production licenses, and approval or disapproval of mergers. In addition, the state exerts direct control through its ownership of Rosneft and Gazprom Neft, two of the five largest producers in the country, as well as Transneft, the pipeline company. Finally, the state serves as an object to be lobbied by the major Russian companies as well as foreign suitors.

In addition to the state, the sector includes several major oil companies that vary in terms of ownership, production, and operation (see table 7.1). Rosneft is the largest (in terms of production), although it began its post-Soviet life as essentially an afterthought. When LUKoil, Surgutneftegaz, and Yukos were created as separate, state-owned companies in 1992, the rest of the oil sector was left in a holding company called Rosneft. Over the next several years, additional companies, including Sibneft and Sidanko, were broken out of Rosneft and

TABLE 7.1
Major Russian Oil Companies (2010)

Company	Million Tons per Year	Million Barrels per Day	Percent Russian Total	Ownership Type	Five-Year Production Trend
Rosneft	115.8	2.3	22.9	State	Increasing
LUKoil	89.8	1.8	17.8	Private	Increasing
TNK-BP	87.5	1.75	17.3	Private	Stagnant
Surgutneftegaz	59.5	1.2	11.8	Private	Declining
Gazprom Neft	50	1	9.8	State	Stagnant
Other (<6 percent each)	102.4	2.04	20.4		
Total	505	10.09	100		

Sources: Company annual reports; calculations from GKS data.

sold off. It was not until Vladimir Putin appointed Igor Sechin, his erstwhile KGB associate, as head of Rosneft that the company became a major player. Most important, Rosneft became the vehicle for the state's takeover of Yukos in 2003–2004, vaulting it overnight to the rank of the country's leading producer. Since then, however, it has also invested in new production (often with state assistance in procuring development licenses) and has continued to grow. The most important greenfield development to date has been the Vankor oil field in Eastern Siberia. It currently produces more than 250,000 barrels a day and is the main source of oil to fulfill a twenty-year contract with China that went into effect in January 2011.

The other large, state-owned oil company in Russia is Gazprom Neft, operated by the natural gas behemoth, Gazprom. Early in his first term, Putin replaced the Yeltsin-era management of Gazprom and strengthened the company's control over its subsidiaries (especially the trading company Itera, which had siphoned revenues from Gazprom in the 1990s). Originally expected to take over Yukos, Gazprom was outmaneuvered by Rosneft and Sechin as well as some of the legal tactics of Yukos. In the end, it had to be content with taking over Sibneft from oligarch Roman Abramovich. Since then, the company has not been especially dynamic economically or politically. It is the fifth-largest Russian oil producer, but its output has been essentially stagnant since 2006. And unlike its parent company, Gazprom, which is able to use the state to push competitors out of natural gas fields, Gazprom Neft has made no such moves.

Three other large firms—LUKoil, Surgutneftegaz, and TNK-BP—are majority privately owned, although they vary widely in how they operate economically and in how they approach politics. LUKoil was one of the first oil companies to be privatized, with company insiders acquiring a significant stake. Over the past decade, its expansion efforts have focused most heavily on international opportunities, and its political strategy has been to avoid antagonizing the government. (In the wake of the Yukos affair, for example, LUKoil began to advertise just how happy it was to contribute to the social development of the country, perhaps even overpaying its taxes.) It has not been a stagnant company, however. It was once 20 percent owned by Cono-coPhillips (although it recently completed a buyback of those shares), it acquired a 25 percent stake in new fields in the Timan-Pechora basin earlier this year, and its newest effort at partnership involves talk of a joint venture with Rosneft in the Black Sea.

Surgutneftegaz was also privatized to insiders initially, but it has been less dynamic than LUKoil, preferring a slow-and-steady approach. Its business plan has relied on drilling high numbers of exploratory wells in the fields it owns, and it has been very quiet politically. Its risk-averse strategy has not paid great dividends in production rates, but it is still the fourth-largest producer in the country, and it has holdings in East Siberia that show promise of increased output.

TNK-BP, Russia's third-largest producer, by contrast, has caused much greater stirs in the political realm. Formed in 2003 as a fifty-fifty joint venture between the Russian group Alfa-Access-Renova (AAR) and the international oil major BP, the company has conflict built into its ownership structure, and it has not disappointed. In 2008, AAR tried to drive BP out of the partnership and succeeded in pushing chief executive officer Robert Dudley out of the country temporarily. This past year, the group successfully scuttled a joint venture between BP and Rosneft, as will be discussed in more detail below. The company still produces a great deal of oil, but in some ways it seems like the least stable of the Russian majors.

Transneft, which ships 93 percent of Russia's domestically produced oil through its pipeline network, is another major player in the Russian oil system. Although some of its equity is in private hands, all its voting shares are still owned by the state, and it exhibits the lack of transparency often associated with such enterprises. (Minority shareholder, lawyer, and blogger Alexei Navalny has leveled sensational embezzlement charges against the company, which the government has so far unsuccessfully tried to sweep under the rug.) Its behavior, however, is driven not only by its state ownership but also by its position as a profit-seeking monopoly, demonstrated most clearly in its efforts to raise transportation tariffs.

Despite the enormous size of the Russian oil sector and its importance for the state and the economy, it is important to recognize that there are significant differences between Russia and an archetypal natural resource economy, such as Saudi Arabia or Kuwait. Significantly, the Russian economy is much more complex, containing opportunities for backward linkages that are not present in other settings. That is, when the Russian oil sector grows, it can (and does) buy inputs from domestic producers, and its employees can (and do) buy goods from domestic producers. In less developed economies, growth of the oil sector may simply generate more imports. In addition, many governments today have learned to deal more effectively with such challenges as exchange rate appreciation that can accompany large inflows of capital from natural resources exports. Most notably, they heavily tax the exports and invest those revenues internationally, using such vehicles as Eurobonds or U.S. Treasury bonds, and Russia has followed this approach for several years.[8]

Nevertheless, while there is more to the Russian economy than just oil, taxes on and revenues from the petroleum sector have been a central component of the country's fiscal and economic successes since the early 2000s. When oil prices have been high, Russia has grown its economy and balanced its budget; when they have been low, growth has reversed, and deficits have returned. Russia depends on oil revenues, so it cannot cavalierly shut off supplies to its neighbors, as will be discussed in more detail in the next section.

Exports

The most obvious source of leverage for an oil producer is the threat of supply cutoffs, and the West has feared such actions at least since the 1973 Arab oil embargo. Russian President Vladimir Putin explicitly argued that Russia should consider just such a strategy, writing in his (possibly partially plagiarized and likely ghostwritten) dissertation that the Russian government should use the oil and gas sectors to reassert Russian power in the world.[9] He also appointed energy minister Viktor Khristenko as his envoy to the Commonwealth of Independent States.[10] Furthermore, Russia has either cut off or threatened to cut off hydrocarbon supplies to its customers in the course of several disagreements, albeit more frequently and successfully with natural gas than with oil.[11]

As tempting a tool as the "oil weapon" might seem, however, and as disruptive as it would be for the target country, its effectiveness should not be overstated.[12] There are several reasons why using oil as a coercive tool might be less successful than a major oil exporter might hope. First, in the short run, the target country can survive by tightening its belt. In the meantime, the exporting country would lose revenues at it implemented the strategy. Second, in the medium and long run, the target country can purchase oil elsewhere. Prices would be higher, but embargoed supplies could be replaced. Third, in the long run, industries in the target country can shift to less oil-intensive practices. They might use less energy overall, or they might change to alternative fuels. Finally, target countries can prepare for such cutoffs by, for example, building up strategic reserves. In this way, they can mitigate even short-run problems and severely undermine the effectiveness of an embargo.

Russia is particularly vulnerable to these kinds of responses because of the role oil revenues play in its own economy. Thus, even though Europe depends on Russia for a great deal of its oil (approximately 5 million barrels a day), those shipments provide Russia with surprisingly little leverage over Europe. This is because the limitations of the cutoff threat are all clearly on display in the European context. Europe has several short- and medium-term supply alternatives. Major European states have well-established strategic reserve systems. And, perhaps ironically, the large size of European imports mean the revenues lost by cutting off those imports would be exceptionally damaging to Russia. Furthermore, the goals of an oil embargo against Europe would probably be nebulous and only indirectly related to oil.[13]

On all these dimensions, China is in a somewhat less advantageous position than Europe. Therefore, while China imports far less oil from Russia than Europe, Russia appears to have enjoyed some success in its oil-related negotiations with China. Almost a decade ago, Russia and China reached a tentative agreement on the construction of an eastbound pipeline running from Siberia to the Chinese terminal of Daqing. The Putin government, however, was unwilling to allow the private company Yukos to take the leading role in this arrangement and for a number of reasons effectively renationalized the company in 2003–2004. In the short run, another private company, LUKoil, was pressed into service to make up for the lost exports to China, and volume totaled 6 million tons in 2004.[14]

During the takeover of Yukos, the state-owned Rosneft was able to secure a $6 billion "advance payment" from the Chinese company CNPC, allowing Rosneft to purchase Yukos's main production asset in a convoluted auction in December 2004. The payment was to secure the shipment of approximately 50 million tons of oil to China through 2010. The purchase price for the oil would be $3 below the published price for Brent crude.[15]

Over the next several years, Russia eventually met the arrangement's overall target for oil exports to China, although it fell short of annual targets each year. More important, in 2007 and 2008 Russia sought to renegotiate the price China was paying for the oil. Deliveries dropped by about 10 percent in 2007, and China agreed to accept a discount from Brent of only $2.325 per barrel.[16]

In the second half of 2008, the context of negotiations changed as the collapse in world oil prices, and the financial crisis began to hit Russia. Russia, of course, could still use oil shipments—and the potential denial of such shipments—as leverage, but the Russian companies Rosneft and Transneft were in a much more difficult economic position. The Russians had long sought to limit Chinese investment in their oil sector and to maintain several export options. At the end of 2008, however, they agreed to accept a $25 billion loan from China ($15 billion to Rosneft and $10 billion to Transneft) and pledged to ship 15 million tons of crude oil a year to China.[17] Chinese companies were also able to take direct ownership positions in Russian oil companies, although they are minority positions.

China, then, is not helpless in this relationship despite Russia's ability to cut off oil flows. Even 15 million tons a year represent only a fraction of China's oil consumption, so its dependence on Russia is limited. China is also famously pursuing oil sources in many other areas of the world, from Central Asia to Africa and beyond.

Still, Russia was able to extract concessions of its own. First, while China hoped to peg the interest on the $25 billion loan to the LIBOR rate in Europe, Russia negotiated a lower rate.[18] Second, the Chinese agreed to buy the oil at the market price at Kozmino Bay in the Russian Far East. That price includes the cost of rail transit from Skovorodino to Kozmino, while the oil that China receives in Daqing travels through a pipeline, which one would expect to be cheaper. In fact, China has protested the high price of ESPO oil since the deal was signed, but so far Russia has been able to hold the Chinese side to the original agreement.[19] Thus, Russia currently appears to be on even footing with China on questions related to oil, although its leverage will probably continue to decline as China develops more supply options.

Transit

Interestingly, in some cases oil *exporters* in Russia's vicinity may be more vulnerable than are oil importers. That is, rather than threatening to cut off its own supplies to other countries, Russia could block the pipelines that carry *other* countries' oil across or near its territory.[20] The Western-financed CPC line runs from Kazakhstan around the northern edge of the Caspian Sea to the Russian port of Novorossiisk, and a Soviet-era pipeline carries oil from Turkmenistan and Kazakhstan to central Russia and the main export lines to Europe. Those exporting countries are therefore in a relatively weak position when negotiating transit tariffs or volume quotas. Kazakhstan, in particular, has been boxed in in this regard since most Kazakhstani oil is still exported through Russia despite the construction of a pipeline directly to China. Azerbaijan, by contrast, decided in the early 1990s to build the Baku-Tbilisi-Ceyhan pipeline that bypassed Russia, even though it was not the most cost-effective export route at the time.[21]

Russia itself has encountered trouble in exporting oil through Belarus. In response, Transneft, the Russian pipeline company, has proposed building a pipeline that would circumvent the country. It also built a pipeline around Chechnya in the 1990s. Pipeline control is an important source of potential power in the world of oil.

Even if transit routes do not cross Russian territory, they could still be affected by Russia. In certain strategic areas, most notably the Caucasus and Central Asia, Russia could cause uncertainty and instability at fairly low cost to itself. Gains, too, might not be large, but they would probably include a short-term jump in oil prices. Disrupting trade beyond its own neighborhood would also be possible in theory, but such options—blocking maritime trade in a particular region, for example—would be extremely risky, and they would produce uncertain gain.

Production

While we tend to think of oil power coming from the ability to cut off supplies, another source of influence lies in the capacity to *increase* supplies or refuse to do so. Swing producers (Saudi Arabia today but Kuwait, Iraq, and others in the past) are treated differently than other states. Being in a position to ease world oil shocks grants a state potential leverage in international affairs.

There are three paths by which spare production capacity could emerge in Russia. First, and most obviously, Russian oil companies could find and develop new fields faster than they exhaust old ones. Certainly, high world prices make this at least feasible if not likely. Russia's undeveloped oil regions are inhospitable and expensive to work, but if prices remain in the neighborhood of $100 per barrel, the necessary investment capital and economic incentive will drive companies in that direction. Indeed, significant eastern Siberian fields have come online since 2009, and overall Russian production increased slightly in 2009 and 2010 after declining in 2008.[22]

Still, it would take a near-miraculous find for Russia to grow its way into the role of swing producer. The other two paths, however, involve the reduction of consumption, which may be more feasible. As developed countries continue to struggle through their recessions and as economic and political pressure mounts for them to reduce their consumption of fossil fuels, Russian companies may be able to keep some of their production capacity in reserve. Similarly, Russia could increase its excess capacity by reducing its own consumption. Both the Russian government and some independent analysts, such as Renaissance Capital, believe that such a development is possible in the next few years. Generally, then, it seems feasible that Russia could enhance its role in the world oil system by developing excess production capacity, but doing so could be good for the rest of the world as well as for Russia.

Finally, it is worth noting that Russia could enhance its role in all three of these areas—production, export, and transit—by expanding its presence in oil sectors beyond its borders. The region in which it has done so most prominently is Central Asia. LUKoil, with the support of the Russian state, has ownership stakes in Kazakhstani oil deposits, the CPC pipeline, and the eastbound pipeline from central Kazakhstan to China.[23] In addition, much of the oil flowing through the Kazakhstan–China pipeline at this point is from Russia. Of course, these positions leave Russia more exposed to certain dangers: its deposits, pipelines, and transit oil are all at the mercy of the government of Kazakhstan. Nevertheless, they also give it a more direct say in Kazakhstani affairs and provide it with more oil and more connections to the rest of the world. The regional expansion of Russian oil holdings will bear monitoring in the coming decade.

Financial Levers: Manipulating or Reshaping Futures Markets

The world of oil includes more than the physical extraction and transportation of crude and products around the world. Enormous futures markets constitute another major component. Futures contracts—promises to buy or sell a certain amount of oil at a certain price on a certain date—are traded in volumes far greater than the total oil produced in the world each day. The prices that result from trading on the two biggest markets, the New York market for West Texas Intermediate (WTI) and the London market for Brent, play a central role in determining the prices companies pay for physical oil. At least two strategies for using the futures market to gain some advantages are available to Russia. One is short term, market disrupting, and difficult; the other is long term, potentially constructive, and also difficult.

Context: The Oil Futures Market and Its Role

Significant paper markets have developed around petroleum, just as they have for agricultural products, mineral ores, currencies, and many other commodities. Most readers are probably aware of trade in soybean or pork belly futures or in foreign exchange derivatives.[24] The paper markets eventually come to dwarf the physical market, and this has happened in oil as well, although there is still considerable room for growth.

The New York Mercantile Exchange introduced futures contracts for WTI crude oil, as well as some petroleum products, in the 1980s, and in the ensuing years options and other derivatives were developed. Such paper can provide attractive investments or hedges against inflation or a declining dollar, both of which have been important issues in the 2000s. In 2004, the paper oil market expanded further as institutional investors (especially pension funds) entered and began to take significant positions in WTI futures that they rolled over every month. Hedge funds, whose activities are harder to track because they are subject to fewer disclosure requirements, also appear to have established significant positions. Finally, a large but unmeasured over-the-counter market exists for oil futures and other derivatives.[25]

It is natural, therefore, to wonder whether and how paper markets affect physical ones. In the case of crude oil, the link can be quite direct: the one-month futures price for WTI forms the base price for most exchanges of physical oil in the Western Hemisphere. The link between the futures price and the contract price can vary over time and from deal to deal—unlike, say, mortgage rates that are pegged to the prime rate—but the prices paid generally track with the paper market.

Supply and demand are the usual suspects when it comes to finding a cause for the price of oil. Anyone who has taken introductory economics (and many who have not) expect rising demand or falling supply to drive up prices and falling demand or rising supply to drive them down. Furthermore, every time prices spike, Congress holds hearings and calls for investigations, but each time, they report back that the "fundamentals" of the market—the simple supply and demand for oil—are the main culprits.

Scholars and market analysts as well seek causes in relative supply and demand of physical oil.[26] The most familiar explanation for a price increase is a cutoff of supply, perhaps because of a natural disaster or a political event. More recently, the alleged culprit is growing demand in the face of stagnant supply. In either case, it is the supply/demand imbalance that is suspected of causing the change in price.

Much of the evidence for this position, however, is too unsystematic and/or unfocused to be convincing. One can always find a "supply shock" to explain a price hike after the fact, but one can also find examples of disruptions that did *not* seem to affect price. In 2008, for example, both the Russian invasion of Georgia and the Kurdish sabotage of the Baku–Tbilisi–Ceyhan pipeline in Turkey occurred in August, but world oil prices continued to slide. Had they been rising, these events would no doubt have been used to explain the increase. Longer-term explanations are similarly suspect. Increasing demand (especially from China) is often blamed for rising oil prices, but those demand increases have been visible during periods of price increases *and* of price decreases. An unchanged trend, of course, should not be used to explain contradicting outcomes.

Interestingly, while the supply and demand argument is widely popular among those who conceive of the oil market as a physical one, analysts of *financial* markets often look elsewhere. Scholars and practitioners are not satisfied with the explanatory power of supply and demand trends. They analyze short-term perturbations of long-term trends in search of greater information about future prices. They follow trading strategies that they believe will allow them to win more than they lose.[27]

One approach is "fundamental analysis." Fundamental analysts believe that there exists a "correct" price for an asset (including an oil future), and their job is to determine that price. If the asset is trading above its correct value, they should sell it; if it is trading below its correct value, they should buy it. Fundamental analysis usually includes tracking supply and demand for the asset in question, but it can also include methods that do not rely on such information. In particular, analysts may have mathematical formulas for determining the correct value of an asset at any given time. The most famous of these is the Black–Scholes model for derivatives pricing, but there are many others.[28] The beauty of such models is that they can be solved quickly (with a computer) and do not rely on more time-consuming analysis of fundamental data.[29]

Fundamental analysts also try to ascertain how fast a price is likely to return to its appropriate level (whether that level is stable or drifts at a predictable rate). They seek to know whether the market's response to a shock is "appropriate" or whether the market has somehow overdone it. Likewise, they want to know whether the return to the mean is of a normal speed or is faster or slower than it should be. The focus, again, is on determining when a future is a bargain and when it is not.[30]

"Technical analysis," by contrast, does not worry about what the "right" price is. Rather, it tries to predict future trends in an asset's price based on past trends. The most familiar technical approach reads charts of trading results from the preceding days, weeks, months, or years in an effort to spot rallies or declines as they are getting started.[31] Technical analysts are not looking for the causes of the trends; they are simply trying to ride them. Interestingly, this approach means *buying as prices start to rise* and *selling as prices start to fall*.

Another approach (not mutually exclusive of the others) might be called "social network trading." Traders following such a strategy (or their assistants) patrol the halls or the trading pits to learn what others are thinking. This is intended to help them see trends coming and hop on them early.

Note that all three types of traders just discussed believe that there is more to prices than simple supply and demand for the physical product. People who play in the market think that there is room for other forces, including the force of the market itself.

A final group of traders are the "index traders." These are investment houses that have decided to offer their customers a return tied to the performance of commodities markets. Just as a broker might offer an investment that mimics the performance of the Standard & Poor's 500 or some other stock index, he or she might offer one that mimics the performance of a commodities index.[32] This type of investor is *not* an active one. He or she is not trying to catch trends or to adjust trading strategies based on whether an asset is selling for the "right" price or not. Instead, index traders simply buy and sell enough commodities futures to balance their portfolios in accordance with the proportions laid out in the index.[33] Furthermore, since futures expire each month, index traders must sell those expiring futures and buy new ones that expire further down the road—that is, they must "roll over" part of their portfolio each month.

Strategy 1: Manipulation

Overall, then, while futures markets are promoted as mechanisms allowing buyers and sellers of commodities to hedge prices, they also provide financial investors opportunities to profit on changes in price, just as they do in other securities markets. There is nothing nefarious about this arrangement, but it means that the price of futures may respond to more than the simple supply and demand of the physical product. Investors may buy oil futures in order to hedge against inflation or a declining dollar, to diversify their investment portfolios, to reap the rewards of riding a trend, or for other reasons. In that context, buying can beget more buying, which benefits oil producers. (Of course, selling can beget more selling, which harms them.)

One strategy available to Russia, therefore, is to try to foment another sustained rally in the futures markets. Any of the negative tactics discussed earlier—cutting exports, blocking pipelines, causing instability, and so on—might create an environment in which speculators return to oil as an attractive asset. Conceivably, Russia could funnel assets into the futures markets directly, again hoping to prompt an upward trend in prices. Such activities, however, are illegal, and today's constrained financial environment would make it very hard to attract a large enough wave of investment into the market to make the strategy work.

Strategy 2: Reshaping

A second approach to oil futures markets involves reshaping them in a way that could benefit Russia. As noted earlier, futures contracts allow both buyers and sellers of physical oil to hedge prices. Most blends of crude oil, however, do not have futures contracts that are traded widely; instead, buyers and sellers have to hedge their trades of, say, Bonny Light oil (Nigeria) with futures deals in WTI (United States) or Brent blend (Europe).

From the perspective of both the buyers and the sellers, this is an imperfect arrangement since the futures contracts actually lock in not the price of the oil being sold (Bonny Light in this example) but instead the price of an oil that is usually of similar worth. At least the three types of oil just mentioned, however, are relatively "light" and "sweet."[34] For crude oils that are relatively "heavy" and "sour," deciding how many futures contracts of WTI or Brent to buy or sell in order to hedge the physical deal becomes even more complicated. In practice, the world's supply of light, sweet oil is declining in comparison with heavy, sour crude, so this problem may become more significant over time.

The current system is imperfect from the perspective of the Russian government as well since it creates something of an artificial demand for WTI and Brent futures. Buyers and sellers of many different types of oil have to hedge with WTI and Brent, potentially driving up those prices more than the price for Russian oil. Russian leaders consistently express their frustration with what they believe to be an unjustifiably high spread between the price for the world's two "marker crudes" (especially Brent) on the one hand and Russian exports on the other.

There is therefore reason to believe that the world could use another widely traded futures contract, this one for heavier and more sour crude than WTI or Brent. Unfortunately for Russia, establishing a widely traded futures contract does not happen overnight. It requires a transparent, well-regulated market, perhaps denominating the contract in dollars or euros, and quite a bit of luck (just like trying to become the standard in anything else would). Furthermore, Russia is not the only country that wants to create such a contract, and, in fact, Dubai's is the most established in the region right now. In addition, the New York Mercantile Exchange, the Intercontinental Exchange, and Russia itself have all tried to launch a futures contract for Russian Urals blend oil, but their efforts have failed to date. Informal forward deals are conducted, but the formal futures market is moribund.

Nevertheless, many observers believe that the need for a heavy, sour futures contract will only grow over time, and Russia may be in position to provide it. It is a difficult task but perhaps not an impossible one. Importantly, it is also a strategy that would benefit not only Russia but much of the rest of the world as well. The development of a new futures contract would not only enhance Russia's position in the world political economy but also make global oil transactions easier.

Conclusion

Russia has the natural endowment to be a significant oil power, and this chapter has highlighted a number of ways in which it could capitalize on that endowment. Presented this way, the list can seem long and worrisome. This is especially true when we realize that some of the strategies discussed could be more successful if Russia collaborated with other countries. It might be difficult, for example, for Russia to affect world oil supplies significantly by itself or to shape futures markets on its own, but it might be able to do so by cooperating with other producers, including OPEC. Russian firms resisted such cooperation in the early 2000s, but conditions are different today, especially within Russia, where the oil sector is far less fractious than it once was, as the state is more firmly in control. If the Russian government decided to work with OPEC, either formally or informally, the sector could be expected to move in that direction in lockstep. Cooperation could fail, of course, given what we know about the troubles cartels often face, but it represents one more tool Russia has at its disposal for making political and economic use of its oil.

Still, it is important to recognize that not everything that benefits Russia hurts others. Furthermore, not every move Russia makes is aimed at coercing another state. Successful development of its oil resources is not pursued just because it will entrap the West or force China to do something. It also brings direct benefits to Russia and in some cases can be good for the rest of the world as well. Having an additional swing producer in the system, for instance, or a widely traded futures contract for heavy and sour oil would have positive implications well beyond Russia. The reciprocal dependency between Russia and its customers, along with the highly integrated nature of the world oil system, makes many positive unintended consequences possible.

More broadly, it is important to recognize that the world oil system is evolving in myriad ways. Some of the impending changes will result from Russian efforts, some will come from the work of other international actors, and some will be entirely unplanned. This chapter can thus be read as a frightening list of aggressive policies that Russia might pursue, but it can also be read as a discussion of some of the parts of the system that are most likely to change: new consumers are on the rise; major producers are growing less and less beholden to their historical patrons, but major consumers also have more and more options; transit routes will link countries that were in separate camps during the Cold War; and new marker crudes may eventually take the place of WTI or Brent. For Russia, the West, and the rest of the world, being alert to those possibilities will be key to adapting successfully.

Notes

Earlier versions of parts of this chapter appeared as a conference paper at the annual meeting of the American Association for the Advancement of Slavic Studies or as policy memos at conferences under the auspices of PONARS Eurasia. I am grateful to participants for their critiques and suggestions.

1. British Petroleum, *BP Statistical Review of World Energy* (London: British Petroleum, 2010).
2. Leslie Dienes, *The Soviet Energy System: Resource Use and Policies* (Washington, DC: V. H. Winston, 1979); Thane Gustafson, *Crisis amid Plenty: The Politics of Soviet Energy under Brezhnev and Gorbachev* (Princeton, NJ: Princeton University Press, 1989).
3. On rentier states, see, for example, Hussein Mahdavy, "The Patterns and Problems of Economic Development in Rentier States: The Case of Iran," in *Studies in Economic History of the Middle East*, ed. M. A. Cook, 37–61 (London: Oxford University Press, 2970); Hazem Beblawi, "The Rentier State in the Arab World," in *The Rentier State*, ed. Hazem Beblawi and Giacomo Luciani, 49–62 (London: Croom Helm, 1987); Michael L. Ross, "The Political Economy of the Resource Curse," *World Politics* 51, no. 2 (1999): 297–322; and Pauline Jones Luong and Erika Weinthal, *Oil Is Not a Curse: Ownership Structure and Institutions in Soviet Successor States* (Cambridge: Cambridge University Press, 2010).
4. Fiona Hill, *Energy Empire: Oil, Gas, and Russia's Revival* (London: Foreign Policy Centre, 2004), 13; Rudiger Ahrend, "Can Russia Break the 'Resource Curse'?," *Eurasian Geography and Economics* 46, no. 8 (2005): 595, fig. 6.
5. Hill, *Energy Empire*, 13; Carolyn Cohn, "Buy Russia, Sell Turkey as Oil Price Climbs," *National Post's Financial Post* (Canada), March 9, 2011; Interfax, "Russian Budget Parameters to Regain Pre-Crisis Levels in 2015: Kudrin," July 7, 2011.
6. Rosstat, "Valovoi vnutrennii produkt," http://goo.gl/j3vlB; British Petroleum. *BP Statistical Review of World Energy* (2010); British Petroleum, *BP Statistical Review of World Energy* (London: British Petroleum, 2011).
7. Interfax, "Russian Budget Parameters to Regain Pre-Crisis Levels in 2015."
8. Andrew Barnes, *Owning Russia: The Struggle over Factories, Farms, and Power* (Itathca, NY: Cornell University Press, 2006); Organization for Economic Cooperation and Development, *Russian Federation* (Paris: Organization for Economic Cooperation and Development, 2004).
9. Harvey Balzer, "The Putin Thesis and Russian Energy Policy," *Post-Soviet Affairs* 21, no. 3 (2005): 210–25.
10. Hill, *Energy Empire*, 20.
11. Adam N. Stulberg, *Well-Oiled Diplomacy: Strategic Manipulation and Russia's Energy Statecraft in Eurasia* (Albany: State University of New York Press, 2007).
12. Indeed, even the 1973 embargo did not force the United States to change its policy toward Israel, as was its intent.
13. For a discussion of why this would undermine the effectiveness of an embargo, see Stulberg, *Well-Oiled Diplomacy*. Note that these conditions do not hold nearly as

strongly in the case of European (and, especially, Ukrainian) imports of Russian natural gas, which probably makes Europe more vulnerable on that front.

14. Vladilen Kashchavtsev, "Great Oil Route to China," *Oil of Russia* 1, http://goo.gl/dAR9y.

15. Sergei Blagov, "Rosneft Seeks Stronger Chinese Connection," *Eurasia Daily Monitor* 5, no. 133 (2008).

16. Sergei Blagov, "Russia Faces Delays in Far Eastern Pipeline," *Eurasia Daily Monitor* 5, no. 75 (2008). Even the $3 discount seems like a good deal for Russia. The Russian crude blend that is exported to Europe ("Urals blend") typically traded at more than $3 below Brent in 2007 and 2008. The blend exported to China may have been of slightly higher quality, but it is not at all clear that it would have fetched such a high price on an open market.

17. Sergei Blagov, "Moscow Strengthens Its Energy Ties with China," *Eurasia Daily Monitor* 6, no. 89 (2009); Vladimir Socor, "Oil-for-Loans Deal Will Increase Russian Oil Deliveries to China," *Eurasia Daily Monitor* 6, no. 34 (2009).

18. Stephen Blank, "The Russo-Chinese Energy Follies," *China Brief* 8, no. 23 (2008).

19. Jake Rudnitsky, "China Pays Off Debt for Russia Crude Supply," *Platts Oilgram News*, June 1, 2010.

20. Russian control over pipelines is even more important in the natural gas sector than in the petroleum sector for several reasons: natural gas is controlled by one state-owned company in Russia; customers have little choice but to receive their gas through pipelines, while they could receive oil via tankers; and Russia has shown a greater inclination to use its gas pipeline dominance to try to influence neighbors, especially Turkmenistan and Ukraine. For more on this sector, see Jonathan P. Stern, *The Future of Russian Gas and Gazprom* (Oxford: Oxford University Press, 2005), and Stulberg, *Well-Oiled Diplomacy*. Similar issues surround oil pipelines, although the existence of other options for both exporters and importers weakens Russia's position.

21. Stulberg, *Well-Oiled Diplomacy*.

22. Andrew Barnes, "Russian-Chinese Oil Relations: Dominance or Negotiation?," policy memo for *Program on New Approaches to Research and Security in Eurasia (PONARS Eurasia)*, 124; British Petroleum, *BP Statistical Review of World Energy* (2011).

23. Kimberly Marten, "Russian Efforts to Control Kazakhstan's Oil: The Kumkol Case," *Post-Soviet Affairs* 23, no. 1 (2007): 18–37; Sergei Blagov, "Russia's Long-Term Export Strategy for Asia Remains China-Oriented," *Eurasia Daily Monitor* 3, no. 210 (2006).

24. Of course, any trade in foreign exchange, whether for derivatives or for currencies themselves, is part of a "paper market," but one can still make an analytical distinction between FOREX trading for the purposes of making a physical purchase across state borders and trading that is not directly linked to a physical exchange.

25. The over-the-counter market makes it possible for some players in the market to get around position limits. Those players approach an investment bank wanting returns that mirror those from an investment in oil (or other commodity) futures. The bank provides those returns and is allowed to hedge its commitment by buying

and selling futures. The Commodity Futures Trading Commission, which is charged with regulating the market, limits the positions that financial investors can hold in the market but *not* those that physical traders can hold in order to hedge themselves. The arrangements just described would appear to circumvent that restriction on financial investors. The Commodity Futures Trading Commission does not believe that this is a significant loophole, but it has begun collecting data in the past two years. It has also created a category in its reporting system for institutional financial investors.

26. See James D. Hamilton, *Causes and Consequences of the Oil Shock of 2007–08*, NBER Working Paper Series 15002 (Cambridge, MA: National Bureau of Economic Research, 2009) and Jan-Hein Jesse and Coby van der Linde, *Oil Turbulence in the Next Decade* (Clingendael: Netherlands Institute of International Relations, 2008).

27. Note that they do not have to be right more often than they are wrong. They just have to let their correct guesses play out longer than their incorrect ones.

28. See, for example, Dragana Pilipovic, *Energy Risk: Valuing and Managing Energy Derivatives* (New York: McGraw-Hill, 1998).

29. This approach might be considered "technical analysis" by some (see below) since it relies on math and on data about asset prices rather than supply and demand. I am treating it as a type of fundamental analysis, however, since it rests on the assumption that assets have "correct" prices and tries to see if they are trading above or below those levels.

30. Many scholars have written on mean reversion, drift, and shocks. For two textbooks that include such subjects, see Terence C. Mills and Raphael N. Markellos, *The Econometric Modelling of Financial Time Series*, 3rd ed. (Cambridge: Cambridge University Press, 2008), and Pilipovic, *Energy Risk*.

31. Frank Cholly and Jeffrey Friedman, "Beginner's Guide to Grain Trading," *Futures*, 2004, http://goo.gl/IiCAa offer a primer.

32. By far the most popular of these is the Goldman Sachs index, although there are others available.

33. In the case of the Goldman Sachs index, this means that a large percentage of the investment needs to be in WTI futures.

34. "Light"/"heavy" and "sweet"/"sour" are industry descriptors. Relatively dense crude oils are called heavy, and they produce less of the most desirable petroleum products, such as gasoline or diesel fuel, than light streams do. Sour crudes contain more sulfur than sweet ones and so are more expensive to process, all else being equal. Russia's Urals blend (sometimes called Russian Export Blend) is relatively heavy and sour, while its Siberian blend is light and sweet.

8

Russia as Semiperiphery

Political Economy, the State, and Society in the Contemporary World System

Paul T. Christensen

THE DEBATE ABOUT WHAT Russia is now—the nature of its economy, its state and politics, its society, and where it fits into the international system—remains robust and at times heated; a few examples from recent works will suffice as illustration. Daniel Treisman argues that Russia today is neither "the 'petro-fascist' state depicted in much recent writing" nor the "old Soviet Union in disguise, a Marxist bureaucratic meat grinder of a state" bent on undermining the West.[1] As he puts it, Russia is "something more prosaic"—a country "with problems that are painful but not unusual for middle income states, and with medium-run prospects that remain relatively promising." For Treisman, Russia politically occupies "the foggy zone" between democracy and authoritarianism; for Steven Levitsky and Lucan Way, Vladimir Putin had by 2008 "succeeded in consolidating authoritarian rule mainly by eliminating key organizational sources of vulnerability. In a context of very low leverage and a weak opposition, he met virtually no resistance as he eliminated the last vestiges of democracy."[2] In terms of the state, there are those like Levitsky and Way who see state capacity increasing and those who focus more on personal power networks, inside the state and out, while recognizing that the state still plays a major role. In Michael Urban's words, "Despite this relative weakness, however, the Russian state remains a presence: arbitrary, lawless, corrupt, extortionist, unpredictable—but a presence all the same."[3] Similarly, Brian Taylor argues that under Putin, "the achievements of the state-building project were modest and partial, with the greatest gains in capacity taking place in rebuilding a regime of repression to implement extraordinary decisions of the Kremlin."[4] Ivan Krastev goes further, arguing that "the current regime in Moscow" is a "weak state weakly connected to a weak society."[5]

In economic terms, while everyone agrees that the oil and gas sectors are central to the story, there is much less agreement on what impact Russia's energy economy has had and will continue to have internally and externally and economically and politically, particularly when viewed in the context of Russia's overall economic situation.[6] In most accounts of Russia's present and future, Russian society plays a relatively minor role, except for those parts of society that make up political and economic elites. Most accounts that do address society focus mainly—and not without reason—on the problems associated with civil society development or on the causes of social "passivity."[7] Finally, there is the question of Russia's "status" in the international system: is it a great power, a regional power, an existential threat to the West, or a victim of Western and particularly U.S. policy aimed at isolating Russia?[8]

As much as they differ interpretively, all the above analyses implicitly or explicitly examine Russia in comparative terms, highlighting the fact that Russia has become increasingly integrated into the existing global system. Looking back historically, Fernand Braudel referred to Russia as a "world apart," writing that "the world economy centered on Europe did not extend to the whole of the old continent. Beyond Poland, there was always the remote and marginal world of Muscovy."[9] While this is clearly no longer true, something of that sense of Russia as "remote" or at least fundamentally different long remained part of perceptions in the West in spite of Russia's now three-centuries-old process of integration into the capitalist world economy—a process that was temporarily and only partially interrupted by the Soviet interlude. That this process has been uneven and contradictory is perhaps an understatement, but the underlying argument of this chapter is that the processes often referred to as "globalization"[10] have a long history and that any assessment of Russia's position and prospects now is best made by examining Russia's relationship to the modern world system in the long historical term even while taking due consideration of the particularities of Russia's past and the legacies of the Soviet period.

An examination of this relationship leads me to three central arguments. First, since "connecting" to the world capitalist economy in the eighteenth century, Russia has been and remains a semiperipheral state. While the policies of the Russian/Soviet/Russian state were designed to move Russia from the semiperiphery to the core of the international system, these policies ultimately failed. Second, in the postcommunist period, the policies of the Russian state and those of the core countries of the system (including the international institutions representing the interests of the core states such as the International Monetary Fund [IMF] and the World Bank), in combina-

tion with some structural legacies of the Soviet political economy, have solidi-
fied Russia's semiperipheral status. These policies have also weakened Russia
among the semiperipheral states, and the real issue may well be whether
Russia moves not to the core but farther down the ladder of countries within
the semiperiphery. And third, the combination of structural legacies and
conscious policies that have shaped Russia's reintegration into the capitalist
world system has had a deleterious effect on most social groups within the
country (although I will limit my discussion on this point primarily to workers) while at the same time creating some (at this point mostly potential)
avenues for social organization and resistance.

Central to these arguments is the point that in assessing the daily, monthly,
or yearly fluctuations in Russia's economy, positive and negative indicators
in various sectors, or changes in Russia's "assertiveness" in international politics, one cannot lose sight of the longer-term structural realities of the global
system in which Russia is embedded. We have witnessed the very rapid (in
historical terms) economic collapse of Russia in the 1990s, followed by an
equally rapid recovery in the 2000s, punctuated by severe crises at the end of
each decade. As noted above, arguments continue over the extent of political
consolidation and its direction in more authoritarian or democratic directions, with Putin and Medvedev now at the center of that debate. Questions
also persist about whether we are likely to see increased social unrest or continued social passivity, as polling data track Russians' levels of life satisfaction,
trust in government, and willingness to participate in protests.[11] It is not that
these things do not matter; rather, they make sense only in terms of broader
trends—political, economic, and social—that are consolidating Russia's position as a second-tier state despite its putative equality as a permanent member
of the Security Council, its membership in the G-20, and its residual geopo-
litical power based on its nuclear arsenal and its expansive territory.

Russia as Semiperiphery, from Peter the Great to Gorbachev

It is common in the academic literature and certainly among many in Russia
to refer to Russia for most of its history as a great power or even as a superpower for a short period of Soviet history. Given this, it may seem counter-
intuitive to refer to Russia/Soviet Union as a semiperipheral state; however,
when viewed against the backdrop of the global political economy taken as a
whole, the designation is more accurate than "great power" in describing Russia's position. Russia's claim to great-power status, whether before, during,
or after the Soviet period, was based primarily on its military might and geo-
political centrality in Eurasia rather than on its overall level of development

in economic, technological, or social terms.[12] This became immediately clear with the winding down of the Cold War and with the greater openness that began under Gorbachev well before the collapse of communism.

The exact nature and definition of a "semiperipheral state" has always been a subject of some dispute within the world systems literature and among its critics,[13] but the general parameters become clear when described in the context of the other states in the capitalist world economy, the core, and the periphery:

> The core-periphery distinction . . . differentiates those zones in which are concentrated high-profit, high-technology, high-wage diversified production (the core countries) from those in which are concentrated low-profit, low-technology, low-wage, less diversified production (the peripheral countries). But there has always been a series of countries which fall in between in a very concrete way, and play a different role. The productive activities of these semiperipheral countries are more evenly divided. In part they act as a peripheral zone for core countries, and in part they act as a core country for some peripheral areas.[14]

These countries, therefore, have relatively diversified economies, generally second- or third-generation technologies, and overall higher levels of "development," particularly in relation to the peripheral states in the region of the semiperipheral country in question. The description is more analytically helpful than the term "developing country" because that includes states in both the periphery and the semiperiphery and also because—and this is one of the central claims of world systems theory—there is no a priori claim being made that these states are actually developing. Some may develop or not, and in this theoretical model, certainly not all of them will. Countries can rise and fall, like individuals between classes, but the structure is long enduring.[15] It is also more descriptive of the nature of the economy than the term "middle-income country" given its definitional focus on the nature of productive processes.

Braudel makes the case that Russia has occupied this position historically, in the prerevolutionary period, convincingly in the work cited above. The more controversial claim is that Russia, during the Soviet period (and along with the rest of the socialist bloc), in fact remained a semiperipheral state that was never entirely separated from the world capitalist system. The original impulse of revolutionaries in Russia may well have been to create a new and superior social system, but the Soviet Union's reintegration into the world capitalist system arguably began in earnest soon after the limits of forced industrialization—that is, "extensive" versus "intensive" growth in Soviet parlance (see chapter 2)—started to be felt. Indeed, even in the NEP and Stalinist periods, the Soviet Union retained contacts and traded with the major capitalist powers, as the involvement of Ford and many other companies in the

1930s illustrates. The major forces of reintegration began to accelerate under Brezhnev, not only in the Soviet Union and Eastern Europe but in China as well. As Simon Clarke argues in the Soviet case, "By the Brezhnev period the Soviet Union had become dependent on its exports of oil and gas to finance its imports of machinery and even of food, and the reproduction of the Soviet system depended increasingly on transactions on the world market."[16] As one world systems scholar puts it, "The big transformations that occurred in the Soviet Union and China after 1989 were part of a process that had long been underway since the 1970s. The big sociopolitical changes were a matter of the superstructure catching up with the economic base."[17] The vulnerability of the Soviet economy to fluctuations in the international economic system became obvious during the oil shocks, and the technological lag increasingly made Soviet products uncompetitive on international markets.

If the Soviet Union was semiperipheral in relation to the core states of the international system, it was also the supplier of many industrial midrange goods for many peripheral states and smaller semiperipheral states. These would include not only the other "republics" of the Soviet Union but also much of Eastern Europe and the series of client states that made up the "Second World." There was also significant trade between the Soviet Union and other nonsocialist states in the periphery and semiperiphery, once again illustrating the linkages and the vulnerabilities (as when COMECON goods began to lose markets to the newly industrialized countries and other semiperipheral states) of the Soviet Union to the global system.

While the arguments surrounding the issue of why the Soviet Union ultimately fell apart remain heated and divisive, there is widespread agreement that the inability of the Soviet economy to deliver the goods to the Soviet population and to provide adequate support to the Soviet state was a major factor. In the terms of this argument, it became clear by the late 1980s that the state-led and -controlled model of economic development had been unsuccessful in moving the Soviet Union from the semiperiphery to the core of the world economic system, and indeed the country was in danger of slipping farther down the semiperiphery, particularly due to the rise of China and the newly industrialized countries. The dynamic of how this played out is well described by Simon Clarke, who argues that as "repression was increasingly tempered by negotiation" from the 1950s on,

> attempts to overcome the deficiencies of the system by providing material incentives to workers and managers necessarily implied the expansion of market relations and the further weakening of centralised control. This was the stumbling block of reform throughout the Brezhnev period. As export growth slowed and the terms of trade turned against the Soviet Union in the 1980s, the new wave of reform was unleashed. The course of reform, from ending the state monopoly of

foreign trade to abandoning state control of prices and wages, was not simply the transition from an administrative-command system to a market economy in Russia, but was more specifically a process of integration of the soviet economy into the global capitalist economy through its subordination to the world market.[18]

The same dynamic played out across the former communist world but with very different political-economic outcomes, depending on how the countries of the former communist world and the West responded to that dynamic.

Semiperipheral Globalization in the Post-Soviet Period

If the entire Soviet experience was at base an ultimately failed attempt on Russia's part to break out of its semiperipheral position through a massive state-led program of modernization couched in socialist rhetoric, the post-Soviet Russian experience has been an attempt on the part of successive Russian leaders to at least retain if not improve Russia's position through a combination of sectorally segmented economic policies controlled by and benefiting a small elite and increasingly hollow "democratic" rhetoric, designed mainly with foreign audiences in mind. This attempt has so far failed for Russia as a whole; what has emerged is a highly polarized society in which the elite and a small section of the population are deeply integrated into the global system while the rest of the country stagnates or even slips farther behind. In another time and context, one might have referred to system in Russia as a "comprador regime."[19]

The policies adopted in the wake of the abolition of the Soviet Union were ostensibly designed to transform Russia into a "normal, civilized" country, that is, a democratic capitalist state. The centerpiece of the economic policy that emerged in 1991 was of course shock therapy and privatization, the primary effect of which was to transfer the bulk of the wealth and property in Russia into the hands of the old party and industrial nomenklatura while undercutting the social foundations for either widespread societal development or serious opposition to the new ruling, capitalist elite.[20] There is substantial argument over how great a negative effect shock therapy and privatization had on the Russian economy and society and whether the problems derived from the policies being too radical or not radical enough,[21] but the key issue is what kind of political economy these policies created in Russia.

First, there is the relatively small but extremely powerful sector of the elite that is centered on the extractive industries, particularly oil and natural gas but also metals. These sectors of the Russian economy account for approximately 80 percent of Russia's exports. Not only does this make the Russian economy highly vulnerable to fluctuations in the price of these commodities on global markets, but it also makes the state highly dependent on revenues from this sector and accounts for the extensive influence of the "oligarchs" in Russia in the 1990s as well as for Putin's drive over the past decade to reconsolidate state control over these sectors under the leadership of his *siloviki* allies.[22]

Second, there is the sector of the "new Russians," people who became wealthy either through involvement in organized crime or, for an even more significant group, because they tapped into the burgeoning import/export and service sectors centered on the big cities and closely linked to outside actors in the global economy. Closely linked to this group are the members of the ever-larger Russian state bureaucracy who have done well through a combination of corruption and creativity in managing Russia's real and virtual economies.

Third, and finally, there is everyone else, including the bulk of industrial workers, workers in the agricultural economy, pensioners, people living in smaller cities or towns, that is, approximately two-thirds of the population. In the 1990s, their standard of living fell, the social infrastructure and state services on which they depended either collapsed or shrunk markedly, and their livelihoods became more and more precarious. In the words of Stefan Hedlund, these people, along with the enterprises and towns in which they live, made up the middle of the "Soviet Sandwich." As he explains the situation,

> The logic is that we have two pieces of fresh and appetizing bread. The top one is the energy complex, and the bottom one is the equally vibrant private sector or small start-ups, which has attracted a good deal of justifiable attention. Wedged in between, however, we may find a decaying filling of Soviet-era manufacturing industries that nobody want to touch.[23]

Hedlund goes on to cite Peter Lavelle, commenting on the sandwich theory, on what is perhaps its most important implication, namely, that the filling is the state and most of the politically homeless electorate from the Soviet period. As the wealthiest stratum of society derives its vast income from the natural resources sector, it does not have much of a need for the rest of society.[24]

The situation that existed in Russia when Putin took over was due to the way in which Yeltsin and his radical reformers pushed Russia into the global economy while at the same time—by design or default—dismantling the state. The raw materials sector had been important before 1991 and was destined to be so after 1991, but the difference was that the state lost control over the property and revenues. In addition, it was clear to almost everyone prior to shock therapy and privatization that most Russian industries could not compete in an open market economy since their plant and equipment were outdated, their structures of production were not geared toward profit and loss considerations, and their ability to invest or to attract investment was virtually nonexistent. As a result, entire sectors of Russian industry virtually collapsed, there was a massive outflow of capital from industry as large-scale asset stripping occurred, and the production of domestic goods plummeted to be replaced by "cheaper" imports that further undercut Russia's productive base.[25] An examination of production indicators for nineteen sectors of Russia's industrial economy indicates that by 2010, only five of those sectors were producing at levels that were equal to or greater than the level of production in those same sectors in 1990.[26]

The entire reform process that led to these outcomes was not only encouraged by but also insisted on by the core states of the world system and the international institutions that represent their interests, in this case the IMF in particular. As Reddaway and Glinski, among others, have demonstrated, from undercutting of the Shatalin-Yavlinsky Plan in 1990 to pushing shock therapy in its most radical form in 1991 to effectively encouraging Yeltsin to violate the Russian constitution and "remove" parliament during the confrontation in 1993, the IMF (and the United States directly) used the market and political structures that evolved in this most recent period of "globalization" to construct—along with their elite allies in Russia at the time—the Russia they thought they wanted.[27]

The internal Russian forces and the external core forces seemingly achieved their aim, as certain sectors of the old Soviet elite secured their power while the core states gained much greater access to and control over Russia's political economy. Viewed again from the perspective of the world system, Russia looked more like a typical semiperipheral state in 1999 than it did ten years before. It retained a relatively diversified though highly vulnerable economic structure based largely on second-tier technologies, wealth and power were concentrated in a small and geographically concentrated sector of the population, and most of society struggled to get by and found it difficult to effectively organize and challenge existing arrangements. One might point to countries like Mexico, South Africa, Brazil, India, and Indonesia, among others, as structurally similar examples of semiperipheral states in this regard.

The years 2000–2011, under the presidencies of Putin and Medvedev, have been in many ways transformative for Russia, but they have not changed the underlying factors that keep Russia in a semiperipheral position. At best, the combination of policy initiatives and luck—the latter consisting in the vastly improved terms of trade in the energy sector over the past decade—has strengthened, at least temporarily, Russia's position within the semiperipheral. Russia in 2011 in many ways appears stronger than it did in 2000: the economy has enjoyed relatively high growth; the state and political system have, from a certain vantage point, increased in capacity even while becoming less democratic; and social stability and cohesion—again, based on certain indicators—have increased. There remain serious questions, however, as to how robust and enduring these changes will be and even more how real and significant they are when viewed from the broader perspective of Russian and global political economy.

Russia's economic recovery after the crisis of 1998 was rapid and sustained if viewed from the perspective of growth in gross domestic product, which averaged over 6 percent from 1999 to 2008 before contracting in 2009 and rebounding again in 2010.[28] The Russian state also reduced its foreign debt from $133 billion in 1999 to $38.83 billion as of May 1, 2011.[29] Gross national income per capita (PPP International dollars) rose from $7,260 in 2000 to $19,750 in 2008, falling back to $18,300 in 2009. As noted by Treisman, the Russian Central Bank built up the third-largest reserves in the world by 2008, and the country underwent a "consumer boom," with retail trade, wages levels, and the stock market all rising considerably.[30] In addition, poverty rates fell, life expectancy climbed marginally upward, and official unemployment fell from its peak of 13.2 percent in 1998 to a low of 6.1 percent in 2007 before edging upward to 8.2 percent in 2009. Net inflows of foreign direct investment increased from $2.7 billion in 2000 to $75 billion in 2008, dropping to $36.7 billion in 2009.[31] So, given where Russia was economically in 1998, the turnaround has been substantial.

Politically, the 2000s were dominated by the attempts, in many ways successful from one perspective, of Vladimir Putin to recentralize state power in his own hands and that of his mainly *siloviki* allies. Analyses of this process and its implications are numerous, and the broad contours of the story are relatively clear.[32] As Rick Simon put it, "Putin's overarching aim has been to re-establish the 'power vertical' with the Kremlin at its apex."[33] This has been accomplished through a series of policies and political maneuvers, including the elimination of the election of governors, the appointment of presidential overseers in seven superregions, the effective renationalization of important sectors of the economy, and the appointment of members of his administration and other allies to posts on the boards of directors of major Russian companies. Another important aspect of this process has been the construction of United Russia and the constriction of the influence and operation of other political parties, which has served Putin's interests as he moved from the presidency to the post of prime minister; it has also brought a greater measure of control to regional politics as United Russia expands its national infrastructure.

The increasing level of central state control extended to the social sphere as well, although this was not as much of a departure from the Yeltsin years as were the policies in the economic and political spheres. As noted above, the period from 1991 to 2000 saw the collapse of the admittedly limited Soviet welfare state, increasing polarization of society, rising unemployment and underemployment, demographic decline, increasing incidence of disease, and increasing levels of crime. The period also witnessed an explosion of social organization in the form of "associationalism" in a number of quarters, if not the rise of what Western literature refers to as "civil society." In large measure, the semiperipheral reintegration of Russia deconstructed and disempowered much of Russia society by 2000, and the years under Putin have done little to change that. The one thing that the decline in Russian state capacity under Yeltsin did was to provide an opening for Russian society to assert itself in limited ways; the Putin administration has largely reversed that and offered in exchange a measure of greater economic and general security. As this aspect of Russia's experience over the past two decades is often overlooked, the following section explores some of the major issues of semiperipherality in Russia from a social perspective.

Semiperipherality and Russian Society

As far as associational life and the material bases necessary to support it are concerned, post-Soviet Russia provides evidence for some very cautious optimism and rather less cautious pessimism. Russia has seen the emergence of tens of thousands of associations concerned with the most varied of interests and issues and not only in the major cities of Moscow and St. Petersburg but across the country as well. The issue, however, is not merely what globalization theorists would call the extensity of associational life but also its intensity and the internal qualities of the associations themselves. There is also the issue of resource mobilization and the question of Russian society's relationship to global civil society actors and the process of globalization more generally.

The rebuilding of Russia's associational life in the 1990s was in many ways remarkable. While a complete catalog of these associations is impossible here, it is also not necessary to make the point. We have seen the rise (and fall) of a plethora of political parties from the serious to the absurd, the (partial) restructuring of trade unions, and the proliferation of business-related associations in response to economic change. The emergence of these latter groups, particularly those concerned with small business and professional interests, is certainly of great interest given the importance to the development of capitalism (and civil society) of similar groups in other historical contexts. In the Russian case, the difficulties encountered by such groups in dealing with both organized crime and state corruption are important indicators of how far Russia has come and how far it has yet to go.

A significant amount was written in Russia and the West about the emergence of independent women's organizations from the Gorbachev period to the early 2000s.[34] The hundreds of women's groups in Russia reflected a wide range of attitudes and political/ideological positions as well as of interests and issues. Some were extremely conservative and traditional, wishing to return women to the home and family. Others were concerned with the problem of domestic violence, still others with women's economic empowerment, and some with providing educational opportunities to women and men, specifically in terms of women's studies programs.

The picture in terms of environmental groups looked similar. According to Mirovitskaya, by 1992 there were "more than 840 non-governmental environmental organizations in the Russian Federation alone—operating at the local, inter-regional and international levels.[35] Many organizations dealing with the urban environment and the preservation of cultural and historical heritage were not included in this total." The focus of these groups' activities varied from expanding protected areas in Russia to preserving Lake Baikal to cleaning up rivers to the inventorying and recycling of industrial waste. The 1990s also saw the publication of numerous environment-oriented newspapers in diverse regions of Russia.

These examples could be multiplied to include associations concerned with virtually every type of social issue or group. There were organizations made up of activists from and people interested in the welfare of the indigenous peoples of Siberia, as described by Marjorie Mandelstam Balzer.[36] Numerous associations attempted to work on behalf of the gay, lesbian, and transsexual community in Russia, as noted in Laurie Essig's *Queer in Russia*.[37] One could mention groups like "Mothers of Soldiers" and others concerned with things military, neofascist organizations, religious associations—and the list goes on. And these are just the groups that might be considered directly or indirectly political.

Perhaps the most interesting feature of these social movement organizations apart from their rapid expansion after 1989 is their virtual disappearance since the late 1990s as central figures in discussions and activities pertaining to the issues with which they were or are concerned. There are a number of explanations for this, but chief among them is the increasing control exercised by the state over nongovernmental organizations and other "unsanctioned" societal groups—along with the establishment of the Public Chamber, which "was inaugurated to bring together favored representatives of civil society organizations"—and increasing control over the activities of foreign nongovernmental organizations and aid organizations.[38] It is perhaps also indicative of the current relationship between state and society in Russia that Russians now lead all other Europeans in applications to the European

Court of Human Rights for redress of rights violations on a whole host of issues.[39] This is not particularly surprising if Michael Urban is correct in his assessment that Russian elites evince a widespread contempt for society. He writes that since the 1990s,

> references to "the people" in the language of Russia's political class have become both infrequent and not uncommonly execrative. Above all, "the people" are assigned no agency. In the best light, they appear as supplicants: either immediately and with their conscious participation; or from a distance, as receivers of supposed benefactions of which they are themselves unaware or toward which they may even be negatively disposed. The narratives of respondents who did direct remarks to "the people" can be subdivided into four general orientations: the people as inert; as in need; as degraded; as manipulable.[40]

To the extent that this is true, it does not bode well for any turn away from an authoritarian politics that relies primarily on a form of instrumental legitimacy that continues to be based on global gas and oil prices; thus, one has to question the durability of the social foundations on which Russia's semiperipheral regime rests.

The situation for workers in Russia is extremely complicated at the level of the firm and with regard to the trade unions. Labor activism was the first and most powerful sign of the reemergence of social movements in the late Soviet period, and the founding of independent unions and admittedly limited attempts to reform the "official" trade unions provided some grounds for optimism. The period since 1991, however, has seen whatever gains were made largely erased. Shock therapy and privatization undercut workers' wages, job security, and the ability to organize. One of the main effects of opening up Russia to the forces of global capitalism has been to reinforce workers' dependence on the enterprise—already a central fact in workers' lives during the Soviet period. During the 1990s, workers and managers clearly had a mutual interest in keeping enterprises in operation, particularly in a context in which unemployment was increasing and when workers had few opportunities for upward job mobility. Since managers of many large enterprises knew that they could not compete on the global market even if they wanted to, they adopted other methods of keeping factories in operation, including nonpayment of wages and administrative leave. Workers were loath to quit jobs even under such conditions since leaving would remove them from pension rolls and insurance programs and since it was difficult to find commensurate employment because of the vagaries of the Russian labor market.[41] Across the entire transition period, unemployment in Russia has not been as high as might have been expected given the severity of the economic shocks, but Russian workers are faced with high levels of wage variation and changes in working hours that breed insecurity. As noted by Gimpelson and Kapeliushnikov,

> If workers are afraid of unemployment, they are more likely to accept flexible wages. . . . In Russia, such fear has always been very strong against the background of low UBs [unemployment benefits] and the impotent PES [Public Employment Service]. Using household survey data for 1994–2008, we documented that Russian workers express very strong fear of losing their job and, if this happens, of not finding a new one of similar quality. . . . Fear indexes for Russian workers are much higher than those in the OECD [Organization for Economic Cooperation and Development] countries, but are close to those observed in Latin America.[42]

The nature of the Russian labor market has far-reaching structural implications not only for workers and the social relations of production but for the nature of Russia's political economy as a whole. The fact that in relation to workers' responses to the labor market Russia resembles not the Organization for Economic Cooperation and Development but rather Latin America is instructive.

The role of trade unions and strikes has been problematic for Russia's workers as well. The traditional trade unions that were part of the Soviet state apparatus were viewed with a great deal of skepticism by Russian workers, and their behavior in the post-Soviet period has done little to improve their image. Rather than serving as a genuine resource for labor organization and mobilization, the trade union umbrella organization the Federation of Independent Trade Unions has remained what it essentially was in the Soviet period, that is, an adjunct of the ruling elite, only now the state and large business interests as opposed to the Communist Party. The new, "independent" trade unions were always very small and professionally specific, and most of those ended up discrediting themselves for many workers by siding with the neoliberal reformers in the early years of the postcommunist period. The most common form of worker protests from the mid-1990s to the mid-2000s consisted of either "wildcat" strikes by individual groups of workers or strikes organized jointly by enterprises and local union or worker groups in an effort to gain resources from the state in an effort, enterprise managers say, to avoid social unrest.

The past five years or so have witnessed some interesting developments on the Russian labor front in terms of levels of labor unrest and organization as well as regarding the state's continued attempts to control Russia's workers. While the unions of the Federation of Independent Trade Unions generally remain comfortable adjuncts of the state, workers employed either by foreign firms or in sectors that have extensive dealings with the global economy show greater signs of being willing and able to organize and strike than those in other sectors. The best known of these strikes and union organizing drives took place at the Ford motor plant outside St. Petersburg in 2007 and subsequent similar drives in other auto plants connected to Western multinationals. While these new forms of organizing and resistance remain relatively small in comparison to the overall labor force, they may suggest, as Clarke argues, that "capitalism in Russia is not in the end so different from capitalism everywhere else and that Russian workers are ready to take their place in the global struggle of workers to resist the tyranny of capital."[43]

These developments are particularly interesting in light of the fact that official statistics show that strike activity in Russia dropped to virtually zero by 2010. This reflects not the absence of labor unrest in Russia as much as the fact that the Russian labor code makes it virtually impossible to carry out a strike legally, and any industrial action that is taken without legal sanction is simply not recorded. So the impression one gets from the Russian state varies widely from that one derives from examining the materials collected by the All-Russian Confederation of Labor and other labor-monitoring groups in Russia.[44] Recent moves on the part of the Russian state to change the labor code so as to even further disempower workers raises further questions about how successful the state views its current mechanisms to control the labor process, which remains a vital component in its attempts to bolster the state and capital internally and externally.[45] Whether viewed from the perspective of economic recovery, the reconsolidation of state power, or control over society, the position of Russia's ruling elites (or at least some sectors of them)— if not Russia more generally—in 2011 is certainly stronger than it was in 2000, but that has to be viewed against the position from which it began at the end of the Yeltsin era and in comparison to other semiperipheral states. Economically, Russia remains overwhelmingly dependent on its extractive industries in terms of export income and inward-directed foreign direct investment as well as in terms of subsidizing other economic sectors and its social services. As Ted Hopf points out, Russia's outward investment also "underscores its semi-peripheral status.[46] Russian foreign investment, totaling $257 billion in 2007, began in the 1990s and is concentrated mostly in the Commonwealth of Independent States (CIS)," mainly in Armenia, Georgia, and Uzbekistan. As another indication of the concentration of Russia's economic relationships with regional peripheral states (a common feature of semiperipheral states), 76 percent of all officially recognized foreign workers in Russia in 2010 were from countries of the Commonwealth of Independent States, predominantly from Central Asia—a figure that is increasing over time.[47]

The persistence and consistency of the patterns of Russia's economic activity—sectorally, geographically, and in terms of trade and investment—and continued existence of the constituent elements of the "Soviet Sandwich," or what in more technical terms Simon Clarke refers to as "the uneven subsumption of labour under capital," means that Russia remains vulnerable to fluctuations in limited commodity markets for its continued economic health. The use of resource rents to continue social subsidies works in tandem with the dynamic of the Russian labor market to undercut large-scale structural change.[48] Gimpelson and Kapeliushnikov argue that the Russian labor market system "does not facilitate enterprise restructuring. On the contrary, it helps to save old jobs at the cost of creating new ones. Supporting . . . inefficient firms it keeps them afloat, preserves large segments of low productive and technologically obsolete jobs." I would agree with Gimpelson and Kapeliushnikov that the prospects for breaking this cycle "in the medium term are slim." In the context of this analysis, the Russian labor market system at once reflects and reinforces semiperipheral social relations of production. The fact that the political popularity of the regime and its ability to control social mobilization has also been linked to the economic performance of the country also urges caution when considering the long-term prospects for the stability of Russia's position in the semiperiphery.

Conclusion

The reintegration of Russia into the world system as a semiperipheral state—at least for the time being—is relatively complete. It is the character and durability of the political economy and regime that have emerged out of this reintegration that remain open to serious question. Thus, two recent discussions of Russia's semiperipheral status come to rather different conclusions, although they agree (as I do) about the underlying structural determinants. Rick Simon, writing in 2009 in reference to the 2008 financial crisis, argues that the crisis "will thus enhance many aspects of Russia's semi-peripherality," adding that

> the conflict between different "clans" will be exacerbated as the frailty of many of Russia's oligarchs and entrepreneurs will be revealed. This will serve to strengthen the autonomy of the state even further as the latter decides which to bail out and which to let sink. Nevertheless, if the crisis is prolonged and energy revenue is substantially diminished, the capacity of the state to broker deals will be eroded, enhancing the political struggle around the succession to Medvedev.

This view of political and economic conflict among elites and the overall fragility of the system as currently constituted contrasts with the view of Ted Hopf. He maintains that since 2003,

> a new Russian identity has emerged, one that has broad and deep social support. This is a Russia that no longer defines itself in terms of Western or Eurasian "Others," but sees itself instead as restoring Russia's "natural" identity. Its components include a strong and centralized authoritative state in Moscow, social protections for the population, secure sovereign borders, and, consequently, engagement with Western hegemony on a strictly selective basis.

He goes on to argue that Russia remains "existentially secure behind its nuclear arsenal, and a possessor of enormous natural resources desired by the core members of the Western hegemonic system" and as a result that "Russia has become a deliberately self-limiting participant in the perpetuation of that system."[49]

On my reading of the evidence overall, not only emanating from Russia but derived from analyses of semiperipheral states in general, I would argue that Russia's future is much less secure and rather more conflictual than Hopf's analysis suggests. There is little evidence to support the assertion that semiperipheral states can successfully "self-limit" their positions in relation to core powers over long historical periods. Second, analyses from many sources seem to underscore Simon's arguments that "clan" conflicts (or, in some accounts, individually based power networks) dominate Russia's politics as opposed to the unified "elite national identity project" suggested by Hopf.[50] Finally, I would take issue with Hopf's suggestion that Russian society has bought into a sort of "organic corporatist" project to restore Russia's "natural identity." The dynamics of labor politics in past years, at the very least, seems to suggest otherwise or at least that the issue is much more complex than that.

The focus of this chapter has been primarily on making the case for Russia's semiperipherality and therefore has concentrated on Russia's relational vulnerabilities in relation to the core states of the world system. Two other points bear mentioning at this juncture.

First, since the position of any state in the world system is relational, it is important to take into consideration the position of Russia in comparison to other semiperipheral states. From a different perspective, this is what the designation of the "BRIC" countries is designed to convey. Hopf makes an important point in this regard when he notes that "according to the Boston Consulting Group, only seven Russian companies are 'global challengers,' compared to 21 from India and 44 from China."[51] It is on the basis of broader comparisons such as this that the question of whether we should remove the "R" from that "BRIC" wall will be determined.

Second, to argue that Russia is a semiperipheral state—and a vulnerable one at that in many ways—is not to argue that Russia is powerless. It wields significant geostrategic and economic power in the "near abroad," as events in Georgia in 2008 and the disputes over gas supplies and prices with Ukraine (among others) attest. Its control over gas resources also gives Russia substantial leverage on energy issues (at least for the time being, as noted earlier) in the core area of the European Union, which is rather atypical for a semiperipheral state. The role of Russia's nuclear arsenal in all of this is less clear. Russia may be "existentially secure" behind its nuclear weapons if that means that no other country is likely to attack it, but that does not seem to be a particularly immanent threat. Nor does it seem likely that Russia would threaten nuclear war if and when the global terms of trade turn against it—though anything is possible. At the very least, the relevance of Russia's military capabilities to its semiperipheral status in the existing global system requires further consideration.

To turn the tables a bit in this discussion of Russia's semiperipheral status, it is important to recognize that Russia, like all other countries in the world system, is operating in a context in which the hegemonic domination of the core powers in the system is also in question. Whether one views the current global situation as "the terminal crisis of US hegemony"[52] or merely as evidence that "an increasingly centrifugal world is going to become progressively harder for Washington to manage,"[53] the underlying argument is that power and control in the world system is in serious flux. The argument advanced here is that among the semiperipheral states, Russia is not particularly well placed in the long term to take advantage of the opportunities that such a breakdown of the "global vertical of power" might provide, even if Russia's position in the short to medium term looks rather more positive, as both Hopf and Treisman contend.

On a final socially oriented point, in light of the current crisis of the world system, it is worth noting that some world systems theorists view the semiperiphery as the most likely place from which systemic challenges to the capitalist world system will occur. In the words of Chase-Dunn, "Core workers may have the experience and opportunity, but a sizable segment of the core working classes lack motivation because they have benefited from a non-confrontational relationship with core capital."[54] Peripheral workers may have the motivation, but they lack the opportunity. Semiperipheral workers (and we might say semiperipheral societies more generally) in this analysis have both. They are large enough and diversified enough to mount a challenge to the core should conditions arise, and conditions are more likely to arise because of the level of social and economic development typical of the semiperiphery. The current situation in Russia is an interesting test of and, in my view, a challenge to this view, and much will depend on the way Russian society ultimately responds to the current economic and political situation in which the country currently finds itself.

Notes

1. Daniel Treisman, *The Return: Russia's Journey from Gorbachev to Medvedev* (New York: Free Press, 2011), 388.

2. Steven Levitsky and Lucan Way, *Competitive Authoritarianism: Hybrid Regimes after the Cold War* (New York: Cambridge University Press, 2010), 200.

3. Michael Urban, *Cultures of Power in Post-Communist Russia* (Cambridge: Cambridge University Press, 2010), 71.

4. Brian D. Taylor, *State Building in Putin's Russia: Policing and Coercion after Communism* (Cambridge: Cambridge University Press, 2011), 111.

5. Ivan Krastev, "Paradoxes of the New Authoritarianism," *Journal of Democracy* 22, no. 2 (2011): 7.

6. See, for example, Simon Clarke, "Globalisation and the Uneven Subsumption of Labour under Capital in Russia," in *Global Economy Contested*, ed. Marcus Taylor, 32–50 (New York: Routledge, 2008); M. Steven Fish, *Democracy Derailed in Russia: The Failure of Open Politics* (Cambridge: Cambridge University Press, 2005), esp. chap. 5; Marshall Goldman, *Petrostate: Putin, Power, and the New Russia* (Oxford: Oxford University Press, 2008); Edward Lucas, *The New Cold War* (New York: Palgrave, 2008); and Treisman, *The Return*, 362–67.

7. Simon Clarke and Sarah Ashwin, *Russian Trade Unions and Industrial Relations in Transition* (New York: Palgrave, 2003); Sarah Henderson, *Democracy in Contemporary Russia: Western Support for Grassroots Organizations* (Ithaca, NY: Cornell University Press, 2003); James Richter, "Integration from Below? The Disappointing Effort to Promote Civil Society in Russia," in *Russia and Globalization*, ed. Douglas W. Blum, 181–203 (Washington, DC: Woodrow Wilson Center Press, 2008); Urban, *Cultures of Power in Post-Communist Russia*, 34–90.

8. Alex Callinicos, *Imperialism and Global Political Economy* (Cambridge: Polity, 2008), 213–17; Levitsky and Way, *Competitive Authoritarianism*, 185; Lucas, *The New Cold War*; Stephen F. Cohen, *Soviet Fates and Lost Alternatives* (New York: Columbia University Press, 2009), chap. 7.

9. Fernand Braudel, *The Perspective of the World: Capitalism and Civilization, 15th–18th Century, Volume 3* (New York: Harper and Row, 1986), 441.

10. The term "globalization," in my view, is a misnomer; the processes now taking place are better described by John Darwin: "What we call globalization today might be candidly seen as flowing from a set of recent agreements, some tacit, some formal, between the four great economic 'empires' of the contemporary world: America, Europe, Japan, and China"; cited in Callinicos, *Imperialism and Global Political Economy*, 7. Note that Russia is not included among them.

11. Analiticheskii Tsentr Iuriia Levadyi, *Obshchestvennoe Mnenie-2009* (Moscow: Levada-Tsentr, 2009).

12. This is not to say that Russia, particularly during the Soviet period, did not have sectors of its overall system that challenged those of core states. The Soviet scientific establishment is one case in point. One might point out, however, that to achieve the advanced level that Soviet science did entailed massive state investment of available capital, which in turn led to the systematic underdevelopment of other sectors of the Soviet economy and society.

13. Anthony Brewer, *Marxist Theories of Imperialism: A Critical Survey* (London: Routledge and Kegan Paul, 1980), 166.

14. Immanuel Wallerstein, *The Capitalist World-Economy* (Cambridge: Cambridge University Press, 1979), 97.

15. From a different theoretical perspective but making a similar point, see John Passe-Smith, "The Persistence of the Gap between Rich and Poor Countries, 1960–1998," in *Development and Underdevelopment: The Political Economy of Global Inequality*, ed. Mitchell A. Seligson and John Passe-Smith, 17–31 (Boulder, CO: Lynne Rienner, 2003).

16. Simon Clarke, "Globalisation and the Subsumption of the Soviet Mode of Production under Capital," in *Anti-Capitalism: A Marxist Introduction*, ed. Alfredo Saad-Filho (London: Pluto Press, 2003), 191–92.

17. Christopher Chase-Dunn, "Globalization: A World-Systems Perspective," *Journal of World-Systems Research* 5, no. 2 (1999): 205. See also Boris Kagarlitsky, *Russia under Yeltsin and Putin: Neo-Liberal Autocracy* (London: Pluto Press, 2002), 60. For Eastern Europe, see Stephen Kotkin and Jan T. Gross, *Uncivil Society* (New York: Modern Library, 2010), 25–30.

18. Clarke, "Globalisation and the Uneven Subsumption of Labour under Capital in Russia," 42.

19. Colin Leys, *Underdevelopment in Kenya: The Political Economy of Neo-Colonialism* (Berkeley: University of California Press, 1975); Kagarlitsky, *Russia under Yeltsin and Putin*, 99–101; Clarke, "Globalisation and the Subsumption of the Soviet Mode of Production under Capital," 196.

20. The strongest case made for this position is Peter Reddaway and Dmitri Glinski, *The Tragedy of Russia's Reforms: Market Bolshevism against Democracy* (Washington, DC: United States Institute of Peace Press, 2001), esp. chaps. 5 and 9, epilogue. See also Kagarlitsky, *Russia under Yeltsin and Putin*, and Steven Rosefielde and Stefan Hedlund, *Russia since 1980* (New York: Cambridge University Press, 2009), chaps. 6 and 7.

21. The literature here is large and diverse. For a pessimistic view, see Reddaway and Glinski, *The Tragedy of Russia's Reforms*; for others, see Anders Åslund, "Ten Myths about the Russian Economy," in *Russia after the Fall*, ed. Andrew Kuchins, 110–24 (Washington, DC: Carnegie Endowment for International Peace, 2002), and Treisman, *The Return*.

22. See, in particular, Karen Dawisha, "Is Russia's Foreign Policy That of a Corporatist-Kleptocratic Regime?," *Post-Soviet Affairs* 27, no. 4 (2011): 331–65.

23. Stefan Hedlund, "A 'Soviet Sandwich' for Mr. Putin?," *Russia and Eurasia Review* 2, no. 11 (2003), http://goo.gl/pxOxW.

24. Hedlund, "A 'Soviet Sandwich' for Mr. Putin?"; see also Urban, *Cultures of Power in Post-Communist Russia,* 69–90.

25. These trends began to reverse themselves after the financial shock of 1998. This is not surprising given the collapse of the ruble, which made imports more expensive and also scared off foreign capital investment, combined with the continued strength of particularly oil prices. But this is rather the point: semiperipheral states, particularly ones in which real economic diversity is limited, are dependent on external economic actors and conditions in ways that core states are not, and the growth that Russia has seen over the past decade could still very quickly change on the basis of external factors and the continued weakness of its internal economic base. Putin recognized this early on. See Vladimir Putin, "Transcript of Putin's State of the Nation Address," BBC Monitoring, May 16, 2003, reprinted in *Johnson's Russia List,* no. 7186, May 19, 2003.

26. Rosstat, "Dinamika osnovnyikh sotsial'no-ekonomicheskikh pokazatelei," 2011, http://goo.gl/s5Lqf.

27. Reddaway and Glinski, *The Tragedy of Russia's Reforms,* 175–82, 292–98, 414–17.

28. Rosstat, "Dinamika osnovnikh sotsial'no-ekonomicheskikh pokazatelei."

29. Export.BY, "Russian Finance Ministry: Russia's External Debt Totals $38.8 bln as of May 1," 2011, http://goo.gl/QeW4p.

30. Treisman, *The Return,* 233.

31. All data from World Bank, "Indicators: Russian Federation," 2011, http://goo.gl/H2qAc.

32. See, for example, the April 2009 special issue of *Journal of Democracy* 20, no. 2; Anna Politkovskaya, *Putin's Russia: Life in a Failing Democracy* (New York: Holt Paperbacks, 2007); and Treisman, *The Return,* 80–122.

33. Rick Simon, "Upper Volta with Gas? Russia as a Semi-Peripheral State," in *Globalization and the "New" Semi-Peripheries,* ed. Owen Worth and Phoebe Moore (Basingstoke: Palgrave Macmillan, 2009), 133.

34. Mary Buckley, *Post-Soviet Women: From the Baltic to Central Asia* (Cambridge: Cambridge University Press, 1997); Nanette Funk and Magda Mueller, *Gender Politics and Post-Communism* (New York: Routledge, 1993); Lisa McIntosh Sundstrom, "Women's NGOs in Russia: Struggling from the Margins," *Demokratizatsiya* 10, no. 2 (2002): 7–24; Anastasia Posadskaya, *Women in Russia* (London: Verso, 1995); Valerie Sperling, *Organizing Women in Contemporary Russia: Engendering Transition* (Cambridge: Cambridge University Press, 1999).

35. Natalia Mirovitskaya, "The Environmental Movement in the Former Soviet Union," in *Environment and Society in Eastern Europe,* ed. Andrew Tickle and Ian Welsh (New York: Longman, 1998), 30.

36. Marjorie Mandelstam Balzer, *The Tenacity of Ethnicity: A Siberian Saga in Global Perspective* (Princeton, NJ: Princeton University Press, 1999).

37. Laurie Essig, *Queer in Russia: A Story of Sex, Self, and the Other* (Durham, NC: Duke University Press, 1999).

38. Simon, "Upper Volta with Gas?," 132; Richard Sakwa, *Russian Politics and Society* (London: Routledge, 2008), 330–44.

39. Valerie Sperling, *Altered States: The Globalization of Accountability* (Cambridge: Cambridge University Press, 2009), 22–176.

40. Urban, *Cultures of Power in Post-Communist Russia*, 79.

41. Simon Clarke, *The Formation of a Labour Market in Russia* (Cheltenham: Edward Elgar, 1999), 35–46. While Gimpelson and Kapeliushnikov point to persistently high labor turnover throughout the 1990s and 2000s, it is unclear the extent to which this was the result of the same workers moving a number of times versus the high turnover of a large percentage of workers; that is, the evidence of Clarke and Morrison points to the maintenance of the "core" of labor collectives, particularly in the 1990s. See V. Gimpelson and R. Kapeliushnikov, *Labor Market Adjustment: Is Russia Different?*, Working Paper WP3/2011/04 g45 (Moscow: Publishing House of the Higher School of Economics, 2011), 5–6.

42. Gimpelson and Kapeliushnikov, *Labor Market Adjustment*, 24–25.

43. Clarke, "Globalisation and the Subsumption of the Soviet Mode of Production under Capital," 48. This statement to a certain degree conflicts with some of Clarke's other analyses that capitalism in Russia has in fact been rather different. See Clarke, *The Formation of a Labour Market in Russia*; see also Claudio Morrison, *A Russian Factory Enters the Market Economy* (London: Routledge, 2008).

44. For the former, see Rosstat, "Zabastovki," 2011, http://goo.gl/3ESAe; for the latter, see the VKT website at http://goo.gl/5qvjW and Petr Biziukov, "Monitoring TsSTP: Trudovie protesti v Rossii za 2008–2010 gg" and "Monitoring TsSTP: Trudovie protesti v Rossii za aprel' 2011g," 2011, http://goo.gl/oOhYm.

45. See, for example, Profsoiuzyi segodnya, "Liudoedii i Trudovoi kodeks," 2011, http://goo.gl/8tkrc. For a rather different perspective, see Beiten Burkhardt, *Labor Law in Russia, Edition 2006–2007*, 2007, http://goo.gl/iGG2P.

46. Ted Hopf, "Russia's Place in the World: An Exit Option?," *PONARs Eurasia Policy Memo* 79 (2009): 2.

47. Rosstat, "Chislennost' inostrannikh rabotnikov," 2011, http://goo.gl/5ynVv; see also chapter 5 in this volume.

48. Clarke, "Globalisation and the Uneven Subsumption of Labour under Capital in Russia."

49. Hopf, "Russia's Place in the World," 4–5.

50. Hopf, "Russia's Place in the World," 5.

51. Hopf, "Russia's Place in the World," 2.

52. Giovanni Arrighi, *The Long Twentieth Century: Money, Power, and the Origins of Our Time* (London: Verso, 2010), 384.

53. Callinicos, *Imperialism and Global Political Economy*, 225.

54. Chase-Dunn, "Globalization," 207–8.

9

Conclusion

The Political Dysfunctions of Russian Capitalism

Neil Robinson

THE ESSAYS IN THIS BOOK HAVE presented a broad picture of Russia's developing political economy and its history, evolution, dysfunctions, and place
in the world. Two issues stand out: the nature of Russian capitalism and its
political problems of Russian capitalism. As we argued in chapter 1, Russia's capitalism is political, and there is a tension within it between "good"
(developmental) and "bad" (parasitic) political capitalism. Efforts to create a
"good" state capitalism in which the state plays the major role in promoting
economic development in Russia run up against (and thus far have foun-
dered) the political system's inability to lead reform in the economy or even
begin to reform itself so that it can promote economic change and growth.

Figure 9.1 illustrates the depth of the program and its longevity and puts
Russia's problems into context. Figure 9.1a and figure 9.1b are based on the
World Bank's Governance Indicators. The World Bank measures six governance issues. In figure 9.1a, all six (for voice and accountability, political
stability, government effectiveness, regulatory quality, rule of law, and control
of corruption) are aggregated into a single score for Russia, for the states of
the Organization for Economic Cooperation and Development[1] (essentially
the advanced liberal capitalist world), for the former Soviet Union (excluding Russia and the Baltic states), and for Brazil, India, and China, the other
large developing economies put together in the BRIC category (Brazil, Russia,
India, and China). Figure 9.1b does the same but just for those indicators that
deal with economic governance (government effectiveness, regulatory quality,
rule of law, and control of corruption). Aggregated figures like these are not
the hardest of hard data, but they do provide some indication of countries'

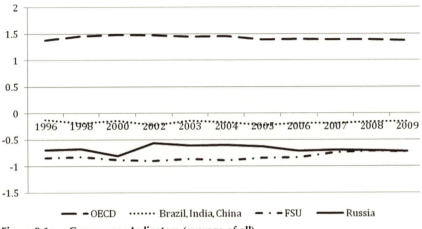

Figure 9.1a.   Governance Indicators (average of all)

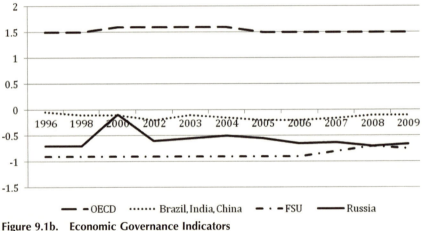

Figure 9.1b.   Economic Governance Indicators

FIGURE 9.1
Governance in Russia, the Organization for Economic Cooperation and Development, the former Soviet Union, Brazil, India, and China. *Source:* **Calculated from data in World Bank, "Governance Indicators," 2011, http://goo.gl/sU5wU.**

Note: Scores runs from 2.5 to –2.5, with higher scores signaling better governance.

general patterns of governance. Russia is far from the standard of governance either generally or specifically in its economy that is common to the Organization for Economic Cooperation and Development.

There is also considerable lag between its standards of governance and the standards in the other BRIC nations of China, India, and Brazil: this is one of the reasons why they have attracted greater inward investment than Russia has and why improving the quality of governance around investment has been such a theme in Medvedev's speeches in the last years of his presidency.[2] Russia, as Christensen notes in chapter 8, may not always be the "R" in BRIC. Overall, Russia's governance is not that much better than in the rest of the former Soviet Union. Moreover, improvements in its governance have been temporary. There was an upward spike in governance generally and in economic governance particularly after the 1998 crisis and as Putin replaced Yeltsin. This did not last, however. Gradually and after 2002, the upward estimation of the quality of Russia's governance declined; there had been some improvement because Yeltsin's retirement and the actions taken against oligarchs looked to have cleaned up Russian politics at the apex, but overall there was not that much of an improvement, and other events, such as the instances of raiding discussed in chapter 4, brought its governance score down again. This makes it hard to believe that the Russian state, even if political control over the economy has been tightened, has developed institutions that are effective and capable of being the core of a developmental state. Broadly, and even if its economic situation has improved, Russian governance generally and specifically in the economy is not much better after a decade of Putinism–Medvedevism than it was in 1996, the date when the first World Bank Governance Indicators were published.

The failure to improve the quality of rule at the same time that political control over the economy was being expanded would seem to indicate that the view of political capitalism that paints it as parasitic is the more accurate where Russian political capitalism is at currently. This view, as was argued in chapter 1, emphasizes that the state is an economic resource to be consumed as well as a vehicle through which rapacious elite groups commandeer the resources and property of others. Office holding in such a political capitalist system is proprietorial and associated with high levels of corruption; public trust in political institutions is low, and government efficacy is weakened. All these things are true for Russia, as figure 9.1 shows. Ganev associates this form of political capitalism with the collapse of the old bureaucratic order at the end of communism and the absence of social alternatives to regulate the behavior of public officials in the new order.[3] As we saw in chapter 2, Russia fits this path of development. The seeds of a political capitalism that feeds off the state lay in the Soviet system, in the relationships that economic actors had to escape from the vagaries of the command-administrative system. Once these began to privatize and protect themselves as the Soviet system collapsed at the end of the 1980s and start of the 1990s, they formed a powerful layer of resistance to the post-Soviet Russian state. The state was able, albeit with difficulty, to formally reconstitute itself as a legal structure in the 1990s but was never able to develop public administration that was effective and legally based. The result was Sakwa's "dual state," a constitutional state married to a corrupted and corrosive informal polity based on factionalism and loyalty. The rot started at the top with the relations developed in the Yeltsin era between regional leaders and oligarchs. Putin changed the terms of those relationships and did so to the fiscal advantage of the state, but the relationships themselves remained. So too did the factionalism and the corruption and the importance of political logics over market rationalities. Putin's intentions may have been good, and he may have wanted some version of political capitalism that prioritized development, but he did not get it. Putin himself admitted as much on the eve of handing over the presidency to Medvedev: "Although we have had some successes over these last years we have still not yet succeeded in breaking away from the inertia of development based on energy resources and commodities . . . even with the economic situation in our favour at the moment, we are still only making fragmentary attempts to modernise our economy."[4] The reason for this was that Putin prioritized stability, as Sakwa notes in chapter 4.

How likely is Russia to escape from the political problems of its economy? Comparison with other cases of venal political capitalism suggests that escape is hard. Russia's problems are far from unique; they are very common problems faced by states that want to pursue developmental agendas but that are also afraid of political instability and weak. The state is necessary for development—as Robert H. Bates has put it, "no state, no development"[5]—but putting in place institutions that can overcome obstacles to change and manage a market is politically very costly. Developing a state that can lead reform and spur growth is a matter of political calculation. Economic development is a public good: the basic aims of development (greater availability of goods and services, higher per capita gross domestic product) are, if achieved, enjoyed by society as a whole, even if they are accessed unequally. Consequently, there are collective action problems in achieving economic reform. A majority may have what Geddes calls a "latent interest" in development in that they might gain from it, but they have low incentives to organize and agitate for reforms that will lead to development; they will incur costs if they do organize and agitate for reform but will gain from the public goods economic reform might create if they free-ride.[6] The uncertainty of reforms needed to produce developmental success reinforces free-rider problems. The immediate benefits of free riding are clear (the avoidance of the personal costs of political or market activity and the continued derivation of benefit from traditional economic activity and relationships), but the benefits of reform and hence development are deferred. On the other hand, losers from change—those who enjoyed consumption before policies to create development were put in place—have incentives to oppose reform. Their losses (privileged access to goods and resources and undisturbed consumption) are borne directly by them and outweigh the gains that they would derive from the public good of reform. Consequently, not all states take action, and some that do back down. The reason for this is that popular demand rarely transforms itself simply and directly into pressure for politicians to provide a public good so that the delivery of reforms to secure such goods is not routinized.[7] Information asymmetries (it is difficult for voters to determine whether a politician is responsible for providing the benefits of a public good) and influence asymmetries (politicians may service small constituencies to accrue resources necessary to fight political campaigns rather than the larger constituency of voters with a latent interest in reform) mean that the delivery of public goods will be inconsistent. This means that politicians have a degree of choice about providing public goods and building the political structures that can help to deliver them. They must choose whether to reform, to build up state institutions so as to facilitate the provision of public goods or to accumulate resources that they can use for their own ends, or to consolidate the state or compromise it in the interest of servicing some important group or groups for their own advantage. As a result, politicians' calculations about state building and development turn on what Geddes calls the "politician's dilemma": "politicians who might otherwise consider offering reforms as a strategy for attracting support will not be able to afford the cost in lost political resources as long as they compete with others able to use such resources in the struggle for votes."[8]

The depth of the politician's dilemma can be influenced by contestation over the question of development itself and the ability and willingness of politicians to adapt development over time. In the first instance the extent to which politicians build states depends on the degree to which there are divisions within political society first, over development, and then over other issues that may politicize development policy by creating divisions over it to back up policy preferences in other areas. If development has occurred ability and willingness to adapt development complicates reform decisions because politicians need to restructure political and social formations that have generated earlier development. In particular they might need to change the terms on which investment is made through the state in order to force higher productivity or incentivize investment in higher value products in order, for example, to move from import substitution to export led growth.

Where divisions over development (or other issues that politicize development) are great, there is little chance of developing a developmental state that can sustain development over the long term by *both* forcing a transfer of resources from "old wealth" and consumption in to investment *and* ensuring that this investment is targeted and concerned to move from basic industrialization to economic diversity and competitiveness, which includes enhanced economic productivity, cost control, production of high-value goods, and so on. As Waldner has argued, where there is a high degree of conflict and elites are divided, they will seek to co-opt actors from wider society to stabilize their hold on or access to power.[9] Some economic development will occur in such a situation since the state will have some residual power to alter the overall balance between investment and consumption to generate some industrial growth. But the broad base of power will also encourage investment in inefficient sectors and equalize the claims of consumption and investment. The result at best is that a low level of development is secured or politicians do not adapt development over time so that development lags behind advanced states or more adaptive states.

In short, obstacles to launching development are great, and the incentives to backtrack from development by, for example, skewing the market to favor a particular group (domestic or international) or subverting the market when it proves too hard to manage are numerous for the late developer.[10] Russia suffers from all these problems. Economic reform was and is contentious and overlaps with other major and dangerous political issues. In the 1990s, the onset of reform was contentious, the source of reform in a small team of radical economists was divisive, the backing of the reformers by the West was disliked, and the whole reform issue was overlapped by struggles over the balance of power within central political institutions and between central and regional governments. Coalition therefore became the order of the day to save Yeltsin but at the cost of reform and development prospects. The market was too hard to manage for the Russian state, and political relationships were used instead of the institutions needed to regulate some variety of capitalism.[11] The situation remained the same under Putin. Although there was much discussion of reform and of the "dictatorship of law," political relations continued to supplant other means of regulation. Coalitions also endured, although their membership changed, and they were somewhat cowed by Putin's avenging displays of disloyalty, and they continued to obstruct development.[12]

What then of the future? Two points need to be made. The first is that there is no easy escape from this situation. The reason for stressing that the problems that Russia confronts are not unique to it is to illustrate this: there are many more cases of economic stasis—of slow growth or stagnation—than there are of success in breaking out of these conditions. Statistically, the odds are probably against Russia. "Systemic stalemate," as chapter 4 is called, is the norm rather than the exception. The lock on development that the political capitalist system creates is too great to overcome, and, as chapter 8 makes clear, there is little historically or socially to make us think that Russia can break out of its position in the global economy. Protest and dissatisfaction might lead Russian politicians to think more seriously about reform. There is currently, however, a problem with reform being generated from below. Protest in a hybrid system like Russia's shows up the weaknesses of the regime. Dealing with this weakness through pleasing protesters by launching reform is a possibility, but the very weakness that protest reveals might make achieving reform more difficult. The problem is the same as in the 1990s and 2000s: one or more of weakness in leadership, lack of credible commitment to change, or desire for political stability among competing elite groups can lead to compromise, to the promotion of consensus, and to the broadening of access to power rather than the construction of a tight reformist administration.

The second point is, unfortunately, that exogenous forces or shocks cannot shift this systemic stalemate at the moment either. Oil and gas wealth simply create too large a cushion for Russia to divert it from a developmental path decided by domestic forces. This means that change toward a nonpolitical form of capitalism, perhaps with political change or at least with the triumph of the constitutional order over the patrimonial administrative system, will not come on us rapidly. Change will in all likelihood need to build up over time. Smaller adjustments, such as the changes discussed in the agricultural sector by Wegren in chapter 6, will mount up to create some pressure for modernization from below. The oil cushion will shrink (if prices fall) or be spent (on arms probably given budget increases of recent years) and/or wasted. Political stability will be strained by some elite squabble over office or prerogatives, and some external economic stress will impact on Russia. On their own, one of these developments will probably not be enough to shift Russia from its systemic torpor. But at some point, these factors, like ill-favored stars, will align to create a moment when change is possible. How many of them combine and to what extent will determine the scope of possible change. Unfortunately, there will, as there is every day in the speeches and pronouncements of the Russian leadership, be more talk of change than there is successful reform.

Notes

1. Austria, Australia, Belgium, Canada, Chile, Czech Republic, Estonia, Finland, France, Germany, Greece, Hungary, Iceland, Ireland, Israel, Italy, Luxembourg,

Mexico, the Netherlands, New Zealand, Norway, Poland, Portugal, Republic of Korea, Slovakia, Slovenia, Spain, Sweden, Switzerland, Turkey, the United Kingdom, and the United States.

2. See, for example, Dmitri Medvedev, "Zasedanie Komissii po modernizatsii i tekhnologicheskomu razvitiyu ekonomiki Rossii. 30 marta 2011 goda," 2011, http://kremlin.ru/transcripts/10777.

3. Venelin I. Ganev, "Postcommunist Political Capitalism: A Weberian Interpretation," *Comparative Studies in Society and History* 51, no. 3 (2009): 648–74.

4. Valdimir Putin, "Speech at Expanded Meeting of the State Council on Russia's Development Strategy through to 2020," *Johnson's Russia List* 29 (February 11, 2008).

5. Robert H. Bates, "The Role of the State in Development," in *The Oxford Handbook of Political Economy*, ed. Barry R. Weingast and Donald A. Wittman (Oxford: Oxford University Press, 2006), 708.

6. Barbara Geddes, *Politician's Dilemma: Building State Capacity in Latin America* (Berkeley: University of California Press, 1994), 24.

7. Geddes, *Politician's Dilemma*, 38–41.

8. Geddes, *Politician's Dilemma*, 42.

9. David Waldner, *State Building and Late Development* (Ithaca, NY: Cornell University Press, 1999), 2.

10. Karin Aziz Chaudry, "The Common History of Late Developers," *Politics and Society* 21, no. 3 (1993): 245–74.

11. Neil Robinson, "The Presidency: the Politics of Institutional Chaos," in *Institutions and Political Change in Russia*, ed. Neil Robinson, 11–40 (Basingstoke: Macmillan, 2000).

12. See Neil Robinson, "Political Barriers to Economic Development in Russia: Obstacles to Modernization under Yeltsin and Putin," *International Journal of Development Issues* 10, no. 1 (2011): 5–19, and Neil Robinson, "Russian Patrimonial Capitalism and the International Financial Crisis," *Journal of Communist Studies and Transitional Politics* 27, no. 3–4 (2011): 434–55.

References

Abdullah, Nabi. "Boosting Population a Vague Science." *Moscow Times*, July 11, 2008.

Adachi, Yuko. "Subsoil Law Reform in Russia under the Putin Administration." *Europe-Asia Studies* 61, no. 8 (2009): 1393–414.

Ahrend, Rudiger. "Can Russia Break the 'Resource Curse'?" *Eurasian Geography and Economics* 46, no. 8 (2005): 584–609.

———. "Russia's Post-Crisis Growth: Its Sources and Prospects for Continuation." *Europe–Asia Studies* 58, no. 1 (2006): 1–24.

Aitken, Brian. "Falling Tax Compliance and the Rise of the Virtual Budget." *IMF Staff Papers* 48, Special Issue (2001): 180–208.

Akindova, N. K., S. V. Alekashenko, and E. G. Yasin. *Scenarios and Challenges of Macroeconomic Policy. Report at XII International conference on economic and social development, Moscow, April 5–7 2011.* Moscow: Higher School of Economics Publishing House, 2011.

Alexseev, Mikhail A. "Migration and Ethno-Religious Hate Crimes in Russia: Risk Profiles 2000–2010." Paper presented at the annual meeting of the American Political Science Association, 2006.

Allina-Pisano, Jessica. *The Post-Soviet Potemkin Village: Politics and Property Rights in the Black Earth.* New York: Cambridge University Press, 2008.

Analiticheskii Tsentr Iuriia Levady. *Obshchestvennoe Mnenie-2009.* Moscow: Levada-Tsentr, 2009.

Arrighi, Giovanni. *The Long Twentieth Century. Money, Power, and the Origins of Our Time.* London: Verso, 2010.

Åslund, Anders. *Gorbachev's Struggle for Economic Reform.* 2nd ed. London: Pinter, 1989.

————. "Ten Myths about the Russian Economy." In *Russia after the Fall*, edited by Andrew Kuchins, 110–24. Washington, DC: Carnegie Endowment for International Peace, 2002.

————. "Russia's Energy Policy: A Framing Comment." *Eurasian Geography and Economics* 47, no. 3 (2006): 321–28.

Avdeyeva, Olga. "Population Decline, Welfare State Restructuring, and Pro-Natalist Policies in Russia: Evaluation of Policy Response." Paper presnted at the annual meeting of the American Association for the Advancement of Slavic Studies, 2008.

Balzer, Harvey. "The Putin Thesis and Russian Energy Policy." *Post-Soviet Affairs* 21, no. 3 (2005): 210–25.

Balzer, Marjorie Mandelstam. *The Tenacity of Ethnicity: A Siberian Saga in Global Perspective*. Princeton, NJ: Princeton University Press, 1999.

Bank of Finland Institute for Economies in Transition. *Russian Economy—The Month in Review* 6 (2000).

Barnes, Andrew. 2006. *Owning Russia. The Struggle over Factories, Farms, and Power*. Ithaca, NY: Cornell University Press, 2006.

————. "Putin as Gerschenkron + Hamilton + Baldwin? Understanding the Russian Approach to Global Integration." In *Post-Cold War Challenges to International Relations*, edited by Yuri Akimov and Dmitri Katsy, 24–50. St. Petersburg: St. Petersburg University Press, 2006.

————. "Russian-Chinese Oil Relations: Dominance or Negotiation?" Policy memo for *Program on New Approaches to Research and Security in Eurasia (PONARS Eurasia)* 124 (2010).

Basmannoe pravosudie. *Basmannoe pravosudie: Uroki samooborony: Posobie dlya advokatov*. Moscow: Publichnaya reputatsiya, 2003.

Bates, Robert H. "The Role of the State in Development." In *The Oxford Handbook of Political Economy*, edited by Barry R. Weingast and Donald A. Wittman, 708–23. Oxford: Oxford University Press, 2006.

Beblawi, Hazem. "The Rentier State in the Arab World." In *The Rentier State*, edited by Hazem Beblawi and Giacomo Luciani, 49–62. London: Croom Helm, 1987.

Belikova, Z. F. "Razvitiyu fermerstva—Gosudarstvennii protektsionizm." In *Gosudarstvennoe regulirovanie deyatel'nosti agrarnikh i promyshlennikh predpriyatii*, edited by A. G. Zel'dner. Moscow: Institut ekonomiki, 1997.

Belkovsky, Stanislav. *Imperiya Vladimira Putina*. Moscow: Algoritm, 2008.

Bernstein, Jonas. "Experts Doubt That Russia's Population Decline Can Be Halted." *Eurasia Daily Monitor* 5, no. 8 (2008).

Biziukov, Petr. "Monitoring TsSTP: Trudovie protesti v Rossii za 2008-2010 gg." 2011. http://goo.gl/oOhYm.

————. "Monitoring TsSTP: Trudovie protesti v Rossii za aprel' 2011 g." 2011. http://goo.gl/oOhYm.

Blagov, Sergei. "Russia's Long-Term Export Strategy for Asia Remains China-Oriented." *Eurasia Daily Monitor* 3, no. 210 (2006).

————. "Russia Faces Delays in Far Eastern Pipeline." *Eurasia Daily Monitor* 5, no. 75 (2008).

———. "Rosneft Seeks Stronger Chinese Connection." *Eurasia Daily Monitor* 5, no. 133 (2008).

———. "Moscow Strengthens Its Energy Ties with China." *Eurasia Daily Monitor* 6, no. 89 (2009).

Blank, Stephen. "The Russo-Chinese Energy Follies." *China Brief* 8, no. 23 (2008).

Blyth, Mark, ed. *Routledge Handbook of International Political Economy (IPE): IPE as a Global Conversation.* London: Routledge, 2010.

Bradshaw, Michael J., and Nicholas J. Lynn. "After the Soviet Union: The Post-Soviet States in the World System." *Professional Geographer* 46, no. 4 (1994): 439–49.

Bradshaw, Michael, and J. Prendergast. "The Russian Heartland Revisited: An Assessment of Russia's Transformation." *Eurasian Geography and Economics* 46, no. 2 (2005): 83–122.

Braudel, Fernand. *The Perspective of the World. Capitalism and Civilization, 15th–18th Century, Volume 3.* New York: Harper and Row, 1986.

Bremmer, Ian. "The Return of State Capitalism." *Survival* 50, no. 3 (2008): 55–63.

———. "State Capitalism Comes of Age." *Foreign Affairs* 88, no. 3 (2009): 40–55.

Brewer, Anthony. *Marxist Theories of Imperialism: A Critical Survey.* London: Routledge and Kegan Paul, 1980.

British Petroleum. *BP Statistical Review of World Energy.* London: British Petroleum, 2010.

———. *BP Statistical Review of World Energy.* London: British Petroleum, 2011.

Buckley, Cynthia J. "Introduction: New Approaches to Migration and Belonging in Eurasia." In *Migration, Homeland, and Belonging in Eurasia*, edited by Cynthia J. Buckley, Blair A. Ruble, and Erin Trouth Hofmann. Baltimore: Johns Hopkins University Press and Woodrow Wilson Center, 2008.

Buckley, Cynthia J., Erin Trouth Hofmann, and Yuka Minagawa. "Does Nativity Matter? Correlates of Immigrant Health by Generation in the Russian Federation." *Demographic Research* 24, no. 32 (2011): 801–24.

Buckley, Mary. *Post-Soviet Women: from the Baltic to Central Asia.* Cambridge: Cambridge University Press, 1997.

Burkhardt, Beiten. *Labor Law in Russia, Edition 2006–2007.* http://goo.gl/iGG2P.

Callinicos, Alex. *Imperialism and Global Political Economy.* Cambridge: Polity Press, 2008.

Castles, Francis. "The World Turned Upside Down: Below Replacement Fertility, Changing Preferences, and Family-Friendly Public Policy in 21 OECD Countries." *Journal of European Social Policy* 13, no. 3 (2003): 209–27.

Chandler, Andrea. "The Truant Society: Gender, Nationalism and Social Welfare in Russia." Unpublished manuscript, 2008.

Chase-Dunn, Christopher. "Globalization: A World-Systems Perspective." *Journal of World-Systems Research* 5, no. 2 (1999): 186–215.

Chaudry, Karin Aziz. "The Common History of Late Developers." *Politics and Society* 21, no. 3 (1993): 245–74.

Chernik, D. G., ed. *Nalogi.* Moscow: Finansy i statistiki, 1998.

Chernomyrdin, Viktor. *Так govoril Chernomyrdin: O sebe, o zhizni, o Rossii.* Moscow: Eksmo, 2011.

Chilcote, Ronald H. *Theories of Comparative Political Economy.* Boulder, CO: Westview Press, 2000.

Cholly, Frank, and Jeffrey Friedman. "Beginner's Guide to Grain Trading." *Futures.* 2004. http://goo.gl/IiCAa.

Clarke, Simon. *The Formation of a Labour Market in Russia.* Cheltenham: Edward Elgar, 1999.

———. "Globalisation and the Subsumption of the Soviet Mode of Production under Capital." In *Anti-Capitalism: A Marxist Introduction,* edited by Alfredo Saad-Filho, 187–98. London: Pluto Press, 2003.

———. "Globalisation and the Uneven Subsumption of Labour under Capital in Russia." In *Global Economy Contested,* edited by Marcus Taylor, 32–50. New York: Routledge, 2008.

Clarke, Simon, and Sarah Ashwin. *Russian Trade Unions and Industrial Relations in Transition.* New York: Palgrave, 2003.

Cohen, Stephen F. *Soviet Fates and Lost Alternatives.* New York: Columbia University Press, 2009.

Cohn, Carolyn. "Buy Russia, Sell Turkey as Oil Price Climbs." *National Post's Financial Post* (Canada), March 9, 2011.

Collins, Susan, and Dani Rodrik. *Eastern Europe and the Soviet Union in the World Economy.* Washington, DC: Institute for International Economics, 1992.

Colton, Timothy J. *Yeltsin: A Life.* New York: Basic Books, 2008.

Connolly, Richard. "Financial Vulnerabilities in Russia." *Russian Analytical Digest* 65 (2009): 2–6.

Cook, Linda J. *Postcommunist Welfare States: Reform Politics in Russia and Eastern Europe.* Ithaca, NY: Cornell University Press, 2007.

———. "Eastern Europe and Russia." In *Oxford Handbook of the Welfare State,* edited by Francis G. Castles, Stephan Leibfried, Jane Lewis, Herbert Obinger, and Christopher Pierson, 671–88. Oxford: Oxford University Press, 2010.

———. "Re-Building Russia's Population: States and Markets, Mothers and Migrants." Paper presented at the Association for the Study of Nationalities 2011 World Convention, New York, 2011.

———. *The Soviet Social Contract and Why It Failed: Welfare Policy and Workers' Politics from Brezhnev to Gorbachev.* Cambridge, MA: Harvard University Press, 1994.

Cooper, Julian. "Of BRICS and Brains: Comparing Russia, China, India and Other Populous Emerging Economies." *Eurasian Geography and Economics* 47, no. 3 (2006): 255–84.

———. "Can Russia Compete in the Global Economy?" *Eurasian Geography and Economics* 47, no. 4 (2006): 407–26.

Cox, Robert W. "Civil Society at the Turn of the Millennium: Prospects for an Alternative World Order." *Review of International Studies* 25, no. 1 (1999): 3–28.

CPT. *Reiderstvo kak sotsial'no-ekonomicheskii i politicheskii fenomenon sovremennoi Rossii: Otchet o kachestvennom sotsiologicheskom issledovanii.* Moscow: Tsentr politicheskikh tekhnologii, 2008.

D'Arcais, Paolo Flores. "Anatomy of Berlusconismo." *New Left Review* 68 (2011): 121–40.

Dawisha, Karen. "Is Russia's Foreign Policy That of a Corporatist-Kleptocratic Regime?" *Post-Soviet Affairs* 27, no. 4 (2011): 331–65.

Deacon, Bob, Michelle Hulse, and Paul Stubbs. *Global Social Policy: International Organizations and the Future of Welfare.* London: Sage, 1997.

Desai, Raj M., and Itzhak Goldberg, eds. *Can Russia Compete?* Washington, DC: Brookings Institution, 2008.

Dienes, Leslie. *The Soviet Energy System: Resource Use and Policies.* Washington, DC: V. H. Winston, 1979.

Domcheva, Elena. "Kurs na demografiu." *Rossiiskaya gazeta*, September 21, 2006.

Dzarasov, S. "The Russian Crisis. Sources and Lessons." *Problems of Economic Transition* 52, no. 5 (2009): 52–73.

Easterly, William, and Stanley Fischer. "The Soviet Economic Decline." *The World Bank Economic Review* 9, no. 3 (1995): 341–71.

Eberstadt, Nicholas. "Russia's Demographic Straightjacket." *SAIS Review* 26, no. 2 (2004): 9–25.

Ellman, Michael. *Socialist Planning.* 2nd ed. Cambridge: Cambridge University Press, 1989.

Ericson, Richard. *The Post-Soviet Russian Economic System: An Industrial Feudalism?* Institute for Economies in Transition Working Paper 8. Helsinki: Bank of Finland, 2000.

Essig, Laurie. *Queer in Russia: A Story of Sex, Self, and the Other.* Durham, NC: Duke University Press, 1999.

European Bank for Reconstruction and Development. *Transition Report 1995. Investment and Enterprise Development.* London: European Bank for Reconstruction and Development, 1995.

———. *Transition Report 1997: Enterprise Performance and Growth.* London: European Bank for Reconstruction and Development, 1997.

———. *Transition Report 1999: Ten Years of Transition.* London: European Bank for Reconstruction and Development, 1999.

———. *Transition Report 2001: Energy in Transition.* London: European Bank for Reconstruction and Development, 2001.

———. *Transition Report 2003: Integration and Regional Cooperation.* London: European Bank for Reconstruction and Development, 2003.

———. *Doklad o perekhodnom protesse za 2009 goda.* London: European Bank for Reconstruction and Development, 2009.

———. "Data Base: Macro Economic Indicators." 2011. http://goo.gl/Nv5HB.

———. "Data Base: Structural Indicators." 2011. http://goo.gl/erjwX.

Evangelista, Matthew. "Stalin's Revenge: Institutional Barriers to Internationalization in the Soviet Union." In *Internationalization and Domestic Politics*, edited by R. O. Keohane and H. V. Milner, 159–85. Cambridge: Cambridge University Press, 1996.

Export.BY. "Russian Finance Ministry: Russia's External Debt Totals $38.8 bln as of May 1." 2011. http://goo.gl/QeW4p.

Fic, Tatiana, and Omar F. Saqib. "Political Instability and the August 1998 Ruble Crisis." *German Institute for Economic Research Discussion Papers* 626 (2006).

Filototchev, Igor, Mike Wright, and Michael Bleaney. "Privatization, Insider Control and Managerial Entrenchment in Russia." *Economics of Transition* 7, no. 2 (1999): 481–504.

Fish, M. Steven. *Democracy Derailed in Russia: The Failure of Open Politics.* Cambridge: Cambridge University Press, 2005.

Flynn, Moya. "Reconstructing 'Home/lands' in the Russian Federation: Migrant-Centered Perspectives of Displacement and Resettlement." *Journal of Ethnic and Migration Studies* 33, no. 3 (2007): 461–81.

Fortescue, Stephen. "The Russian Law on Subsurface Resources: A Policy Marathon." *Post-Soviet Affairs* 25, no. 2 (2009): 160–84.

Frye, Timothy. "Capture or Exchange? Business Lobbying in Russia." *Europe-Asia Studies* 54, no. 7 (2002): 1017–36.

Funk, Nanette, and Magda Mueller. *Gender Politics and Post-Communism.* New York: Routledge, 1993.

Gaddy, Clifford. "Statement of Clifford G. Gaddy, Senior Fellow The Brookings Institution, Committee on House Financial Services Subcommittee on Domestic and International Monetary Policy, Trade and Technology, 17 October 2007." *Johnson's Russia List* 219 (2007).

Gaddy, Clifford, and Barry Ickes. "Russia's Virtual Economy". *Foreign Affairs* 77, no. 5 (1998): 53–67.

———. *Russia's Virtual Economy.* Washington, DC: Brookings Institution, 2002.

Gaidar, Yegor. *Dni porazhenii i pobed.* Moscow: Znanie, 1996.

Ganev, Venelin I. "Postcommunist Political Capitalism: A Weberian Interpretation." *Comparative Studies in Society and History* 51, no. 3 (2009): 648–74.

Garrett, Geoffrey, and Peter Lange. "Internationalization, Institutions and Political Change." In *Internationalization and Domestic Politics*, edited by Robert O. Keohane and Helen V. Milner, 48–75. Cambridge: Cambridge University Press, 1996.

Geddes, Barbara. *Politician's Dilemma: Building State Capacity in Latin America.* Berkeley: University of California Press, 1994.

Gehlbach, Scott. *Representation through Taxation: Revenue, Politics, and Development in Postcommunist States.* New York Cambridge University Press, 2008.

Gel'man, Vladimir. "Introduction: Resource Curse and Post-Soviet Eurasia." In *Resource Curse and Post-Soviet Eurasia*, edited by Vladimir Gel'man and Otar Marganiya, 1–22. Lanham, MD: Lexington Books, 2010.

Gerschenkron, Alexander. *Economic Backwardness in Historical Perspective: A Book of Essays.* Cambridge, MA: The Belknap Press of Harvard University Press, 1962.

Gilman, Martin. *No Precedent, No Plan: Inside Russia's 1998 Default.* Cambridge, MA: MIT Press, 2010.

Gimpelson, V., and R. Kapeliushnikov. *Labor Market Adjustment: Is Russia Different?* Working Paper WP3/2011/04 g45. Moscow: Publishing House of the Higher School of Economics, 2011.

Goldman, Marshall. *Petrostate: Putin, Power, and the New Russia.* Oxford: Oxford University Press, 2008.

Goldstein, Joshua R., Tomas Sobotka, and Aiva Jasilioniene. "The End of Lowest-Low Fertility?" *Population and Development Review* 35, no. 4 (2009): 663–99.

Gontmakher, Yevgeny. "Goryachie tochki 2007 goda." *Rossiiskaya Gazeta*, January 2, 2007.

Goskomstat. *Tseny v Rossiiskoi Federatsii*. Moscow: Goskomstat, 2005.

——. *Finansy v Rossii: Statisticheskii sbornik*. Moscow: Goskomstat, 2000.

——. *Rossiiskii statisticheskii ezhegodnik*. Moscow: Goskomstat, 2000.

——. *Sel'skokhozyaistvennaya deyatel'nost' krest'yanskikh (fermerskikh) khozyaistv v Rossii*. Moscow: Goskomstat, 2000.

——. *Rossiiskii statisticheskii ezhegodnik*. Moscow: Goskomstat, 2003.

Goskomstat SSSR. *SSSR v tsifrakh v 1987 godu*. Moscow: Goskomstat, 1987.

Gosudarstvenii universitet—Vysshaya shkola ekonomiki (GU–VSE), Mezhvedomstvenii analiticheskii tsentr. "Otsenka antikrizisnikh mer po podderzhke real'nogo sektora rossiiskoi ekonomiki." *Voprosy ekonomiki* 5 (2009): 21–46.

Government of Russia. "Programma Pravitelstva Rossii: Osnovnii napravleniia sotsial'no-ekonomicheskoi politiki Pravitel'stva Rossiiskoi Federatsii na dolgosrochnuiu perspectivy." 2000. http://goo.gl/1Wi20.

Gramsci, Antonio. "Notes on Italian History." In *Selections from the Prison Notebooks of Antonio Gramsci*, edited and translated by Quintin Hoare and Geoffrey Nowell Smith, 104–20. London: Lawrence and Wishart, 1971.

Gregory, Paul. R. *The Political Economy of Stalinism: Evidence from the Soviet Secret Archives*. Cambridge: Cambridge University Press, 2004.

Guriev, Sergei, and Andrei Rachinsky. "The Role of Oligarchs in Russian Capitalism." *Journal of Economic Perspectives* 19, no. 1 (2005): 131–50.

Gustafson, Thane. *Crisis amid Plenty. The Politics of Soviet Energy Under Brezhnev and Gorbachev*. Princeton, NJ: Princeton University Press, 1989.

Hall, Peter A., and David Soskice. "An Introduction to the Varieties of Capitalism." In *Varieties of Capitalism: The Institutional Foundations of Comparative Advantage*, edited by Peter A. Hall and David Soskice, 1–70. Oxford: Oxford University Press, 2001.

Hamilton, James D. "On Testing for Self-Fulfilling Speculative Price Bubbles." *International Economic Review* 27, no. 3 (1986): 545–52.

——. "Understanding Crude Oil Prices." Unpublished manuscript, 2008.

——. *Causes and Consequences of the Oil Shock of 2007–08*. NBER Working Paper Series 15002. Cambridge, MA: National Bureau of Economic Research, 2009.

Handelman, Stephen. *Comrade Criminal: Russia's New Mafiya*. New Haven, CT: Yale University Press, 1995.

Hanson, Philip. *The Rise and Fall of the Soviet Economy: An Economic History of the USSR 1945–1991*. London: Longman, 2003.

——. "The Russian Economic Puzzle: Going Forwards, Backwards or Sideways?" *International Affairs* 83, no. 5 (2007): 869–89.

——. "The Turn to Statism in Russian Economic Policy." *The International Spectator* 42, no. 1 (2007): 29–42.

Hanson, Philip, and Elizabeth Teague. "Russian Political Capitalism and Its Environment." In *Varieties of Capitalism in Post-Communist Countries*, edited by David Lane and Martin Myant, 149–64. Basingstoke: Palgrave, 2007.

Hedlund, Stefan. "A 'Soviet Sandwich' for Mr. Putin?" *Russia and Eurasia Review* 2, no. 11 (2003). http://goo.gl/pxOxW.

———. *Russian Path Dependence: A People with a Troubled History.* New York: Routledge, 2005.

Heleniak, Timothy. "Out-Migration and Depopulation of the Russian North during the 1990s." *Post-Soviet Geography and Economics* 40, no. 3 (1999): 155–205.

———. "An Overview of Migration in the Post-Soviet Space." In *Migration, Homeland, and Belonging in Eurasia*, edited by Cynthia J. Buckley, Blair A. Ruble, and Erin Trouth Hofmann, 29–68. Baltimore: Johns Hopkins University Press and Woodrow Wilson Center, 2008.

———. "Russia's Population Perils." In *After Putin's Russia: Past Imperfect, Future Uncertain*, edited by Stephen Wegren and Dale Herspring, 133–58. New York: Rowman & Littlefield, 2010.

Hellman, Joel S. "Winners Take All: The Politics of Partial Reform in Postcommunist Transitions." *World Politics* 50, no. 2 (1998): 203–34.

Henderson, Sarah. *Democracy in Contemporary Russia: Western Support for Grassroots Organizations.* Ithaca, NY: Cornell University Press, 2003.

Herzer, Lauren, Sarah Dixon Klump, and Mary Elizabeth Malinkin, eds. *Transnational Migration to New Regional Centers: Policy Challenges, Practice, and Migrant Experience.* Conference Proceedings, Eurasia Migration Papers (2). Washington, DC: Woodrow Wilson Center International Center for Scholars, 2009.

Hewitt, Ed. *Reforming the Soviet Economy: Equality versus Efficiency.* Washington, DC: Brookings Institution, 1988.

Hill, Fiona. *Energy Empire: Oil, Gas, and Russia's Revival.* London: Foreign Policy Centre, 2004.

Hoffman, Erik, and Roy Laird. *The Politics of Economic Modernization in the Soviet Union.* Ithaca, NY: Cornell University Press, 1982.

Hopf, Ted. "Russia's Place in the World: An Exit Option?" *PONARs Eurasia Policy Memo* 79.

Humphrey, Caroline. *Marx Went Away but Karl Stayed Behind.* Rev. ed. Ann Arbor: University of Michigan Press, 2001.

Institut ekonomiki perekhodnogo perioda. *Krizisnaya ekonomika sovremennoi Rossii.* Moscow: Institut ekonomiki perekhodnogo perioda, 2010.

Illarionov, Andrei. "Mify i uroki Avgustskogo krizisa." *Voprosy ekonomiki* 10 and 11 (1999):4–19, 24–48.

Index Mundi. "Crude Oil (Petroleum) Monthly Price." 2011. http://goo.gl/XzSTu.

Inozemtsev, V. L., ed. *Demokratiya i modernizatsiya: K diskusii o vyzovakh XXI veka.* Moscow: Evropa, 2010.

Institute for Contemporary Development. *Rossiya XXI veka: Obraz zhelaemogo zavtra.* Moscow: Ekon-Inform, 2010.

Interfax. "Russian Budget Parameters to Regain Pre-Crisis Levels in 2015: Kudrin." July 7, 2011.

International Monetary Fund. "Russian Federation: Recent Economic Developments." *IMF Staff Country Report* 99/100. Washington, DC: International Monetary Fund, 1999.

————. *Russian Federation: 2007 Article IV Consultation—Staff Report: Staff Statement and Public Information Notice on the Executive Board Discussion.* Washington, DC: International Monetary Fund, 2007.

Ioffe, Grigory, and Zhanna Zayonchkovskaya. *Immigration to Russia: Why It Is Inevitable, and How Large It May Have to Be to Provide the Workforce Russia Needs.* NCEEER Working Paper. Seattle: University of Washington, 2010.

Jesse, Jan-Hein, and Coby van der Linde. *Oil Turbulence in the Next Decade.* Clingendael: Netherlands Institute of International Relations, 2008.

Johnson, Juliet. "Russia's Emerging Financial Groups." *Post-Soviet Affairs* 13, no. 4 (1998): 333–65.

Jones Luong, Pauline, and Erika Weinthal. *Oil Is Not a Curse: Ownership Structure and Institutions in Soviet Successor States.* Cambridge: Cambridge University Press, 2010.

Kagarlitsky, Boris. *Russia under Yeltsin and Putin: Neo-Liberal Autocracy.* London: Pluto Press, 2002.

————. *Periferiinaya imperiya: Tsikly russkoi istorii.* Moscow: Agoritm, 2009.

Karmalskaia, Elena. "'I Am Concerned about the Quality of Reproduction . . .': Russian State Demographic Policy in the Eyes of Youth Movement Activists in Tver." *Anthropology of East Europe Review* 26, no. 2 (2010): 56–67.

Kashchavtsev, Vladilen. "Great Oil Route to China." *Oil of Russia* 1 (2005). http://goo.gl/dAR9y.

Kim, T. "Bringing the State Back In? Rise of State Capitalism in Russia." Paper presented to the PSA annual conference, April 2009, Manchester, United Kingdom.

Kitashov, E. "Byt' li russkomu Bkhopalu?" In *Chelovek i zakon*, edited by Anton Samoilenkov, 42–53. Moscow: Chelovek i zakon, 2007.

Kitschelt, Herbert, Peter Lange, Gary Marks, and John D. Stephens. "Convergence and Divergence in Advanced Capitalist Democracies." In *Continuity and Change in Contemporary Capitalism*, edited by Herbert Kitschelt, Peter Lange, Gary Marks, and John D. Stephens, 427–60. Cambridge: Cambridge University Press, 1999.

Kornai, János. "The Soft Budget Constraint.'" *Kyklos* 39, no. 1 (1986): 3–30.

————. *The Socialist System: The Political Economy of Socialism.* Oxford: Clarendon Press, 192.

Koshkin, V. N. "O dopolnitel'nikh nalogakh i sborakh, vvodimykh organami vlasti sub'ektov RF." *Nalogovyi vestnik* 28 (1997): 33–35.

Kotkin, Stephen. *Armageddon Averted: The Soviet Collapse 1970–2000.* Oxford: Oxford University Press, 2001.

Kotkin, Stephen, and Jan T. Gross. *Uncivil Society.* New York: Modern Library, 2010.

Kozyrin, A. N., ed. *O federal'nikh organakh nalogovoi politsii: S postateynymi materialami.* Moscow: Statut, 2000.

Krastev, Ivan. "Paradoxes of the New Authoritarianism." *Journal of Democracy* 22, no. 2 (2011): 5–16.

Krest'yanskie (fermerskie) khozyaistva. "Krest'yanskie (fermerskie) khozyaistva Rossii v 2009 g. (ekonomicheskii obzor)." *APK: ekonomika, upravlenie* 5 (2010): 71–74.

Kroschenko, Mikhail, and Denis Zibarev. *Review of Current Approaches in Monitoring and Assessing Labour Shortages in the Russian Federation and Methods/Procedures in Migration Planning.* Moscow: International Labour Organization, 2009.

Kudryashov, V. I., and M. P. Kozlov. "Integratsiya krest'yanskikh (fermerskikh) khozyaistv v sistemu mnogoukladnoi ekonomiki APK." *Ekonomika sel'skokhozyaistvennikh i pererabatyvayushchikh predpriyatii* 9 (2003): 43–45.

Kulikov, Sergei, and Skliarov, Sergei. "Vyplaty materiam otlozhili na tri goda." *Nezavisimaia gazeta,* August 22, 2006.

Kumo, Kazuhiro. *Demographic Situations and Development Programs in the Russia Far East and Zabaikalye.* Working Paper Series 24. Tokyo: Hitotsubashi University Russian Research Center, Institute of Economic Research, 2010.

Kuzin, D. "Rossiiskaya ekonomika na mirovoi rynke: Problema konkurentosobnosti." *Obshchestvo I Ekonomika* 3 (1993): 32–44.

Kuznetsov, Andrei. *Foreign Investment in Contemporary Russia: Managing Capital Entry.* Basingstoke: Macmillan, 1994.

Kvintradze, Eteri. "Russia's Output Collapse and Recovery: Evidence from the Post-Soviet Transition." *IMF Working Paper* 10/89 (2010).

Lane, David. "What Kind of Capitalism for Russia? A Comparative Analysis." *Communist and Post-Communist Studies* 33, no. 4 (2000): 485–504.

———. "Emerging Varieties of Capitalism in Former State Socialist Societies." *Competition and Change* 9, no. 3 (2005): 221–41.

———. "From Chaotic to State-led Capitalism." *New Political Economy* 13, no. 2 (2008): 177–84.

Lane, David, and Martin Myant, eds. *Varieties of Capitalism in Post-Communist Countries.* Basingstoke: Palgrave, 2007.

Ledeneva, Alena. "Telephone Justice in Russia." *Post-Soviet Affairs* 24, no. 4 (2008): 324–50.

Legge, Jerome S., and John R. Alford. "Can Government Regulate Fertility? An Assessment of Pro-Natalist Policy." *Western Political Quarterly* 39, no. 4 (1986): 709–28.

Lerman, Ziv, Csaba Csaki, and Gershon Feder. *Agriculture in Transition: Land Policies and Evolving Farm Structures in Post-Soviet Countries.* Lanham, MD: Lexington Books, 2004.

Levina, Maria. "National Projects Under Crisis Watch." *Moscow Times,* November 14, 2008. http://goo.gl/Httb4.

Levitsky, Steven, and Lucan Way. *Competitive Authoritarianism: Hybrid Regimes after the Cold War.* New York: Cambridge University Press, 2010.

Lewis, Jane. "Work/Family Reconciliation, Equal Opportunities and Social Policies: The Interpretation of Policy Trajectories at the EU Level and the Meaning of Gender Equality." *Journal of European Public Policy* 13, no. 3 (2006): 420–37.

Leys, Colin. *Underdevelopment in Kenya: The Political Economy of Neo-Colonialism.* Berkeley: University of California Press, 1975.

Lichman, A. A. "Regional'nie aspekty raspredeleniya nekotorykh pokazateley malogo sel'skokhozyaistvennogo biznesa Rossii." In *Krupnii i malii biznes v sel'skom khozyaistve: Tendentsii, razvitiya, problemi, perspektivi,* edited by I. N. Buzdalov. Moscow: Russian Academy of Agricultural Science, 2006.

Lucas, Edward. *The New Cold War.* New York: Palgrave, 2008.

Mahdavy, Hussein. "The Patterns and Problems of Economic Development in Rentier States: The Case of Iran." In *Studies in Economic History of the Middle East*, edited by M. A. Cook, 37–61. London: Oxford University Press, 1970.

Makarenko, Boris. "Vozmozhna li v Rossii modenizatsiya?" *Pro et Contra* 12, no. 5–6 (2008): 33–47.

Malleret, Thierry, Natalia Orlova, and Vladimir Romanov. "What Loaded and Triggered the Russian Crisis?" *Post-Soviet Affairs* 15, no. 2 (1999): 107–29.

Mama i Malysh. "Maternskii kapital." 2011. http://www.2mm.ru/vote/9/result.

Mansfield, Edward D., and Jack Snyder. "Democratization and the Danger of War." *International Security* 20, no. 1 (1995): 5–38.

Marten, Kimberly. "Russian Efforts to Control Kazakhstan's Oil: The Kumkol Case." *Post-Soviet Affairs* 23, no. 1 (2007): 18–37.

Massey, Douglas S. "International Migration at the Dawn of the Twenty-First Century: The Role of the State." *Population and Development Review* 25, no. 2 (1999): 303–22.

Masters, Michael W. "Testimony before the Committee on Homeland Security and Governmental Affairs," United States Senate, May 20, 2008.

McAuley, Alastair. *Women's Work and Wages in the Soviet Union.* London: Allen and Unwin, 1981.

McKinnon, Roland. *The Order of Economic Liberalization.* 2nd ed. Baltimore: Johns Hopkins University Press, 1993.

McKinsey Global Institute. "Effektivnaya Rossiya: proizvoditel'nost' kak fundament rosta." 2009. http://goo.gl/9qgIq.

Medvedev, Dmitri. "Opening Address at a Meeting to Discuss Improving the Judicial System." 2008. http://goo.gl/39UYt.

———."Vystuplenie na V Krasnoyarskom ekonomicheskom forume 'Rossiya 2008–2020: Upravlenie rostom.'" 2008. http://goo.gl/1VmIz.

———. "Vystuplenie prezidenta Rossiyskoi Federatsii D. A. Medvedeva na zasendanii prezidiuma Gossoveta." *Ekonomika sel'skokhozyaistvennikh i pererabatyvayushchikh predpriyatiy* 8 (2010): 6–7.

———. "Zasedanie Komissii po modernizatsii i tekhnologicheskomu razvitiyu ekonomiki Rossii. 30 marta 2011 goda." 2011. http://kremlin.ru/transcripts/10777.

Mills, Terence C., and Raphael N. Markellos. *The Econometric Modelling of Financial Time Series.* 3rd ed. Cambridge: Cambridge University Press, 2008.

Ministry of Agriculture. *Agropromyshlennii kompleks Rossii.* Moscow: Ministry of Agriculture, 2000.

Ministry of Economic Development and Trade, Russian Federation. "Blueprint for Long-Term Socioeconomic Development of Russian Federation," Ministry of Economic Development and Trade, Russian Federation, June 22, 2008.

Mirovitskaya, Natalia. "The Environmental Movement in the Former Soviet Union." In *Environment and Society in Eastern Europe*, edited by Andrew Tickle and Ian Welsh, 30–66. New York: Longman, 1998.

Misikhina, Svetlana. "Could New Measures to Support Maternity, Increase Fertility, and Encourage Women with Children to Work Be Effective in Russia?" Paper presented at the conference "Challenges, Dynamics and Implications of Welfare Reforms: A Dialogue between Post-Soviet and East-Asian Scholars," University of Toronto, 2009.

Morrison, Claudio. *A Russian Factory Enters the Market Economy.* London: Routledge, 2008.

Mukomel, Vladimir. "Immigration and Russian Migration Policy: Debating the Future." *Russian Analytical Digest* 7 (2006): 2–6.

Myant, Martin, and Jan Drahokoupil. *Transition Economies: Political Economy in Russia, Eastern Europe, and Central Asia.* London: Wiley, 2011.

Nakachi, Mie. "N.S. Khrushchev and the 1944 Soviet Family Law: Politics, Reproduction, and Language." *East European Politics and Societies* 20, no. 1 (2006): 40–68.

National Intelligence Council. *Global Trends 2025: A Transformed World.* Washington, DC: U.S. Government Printing Office, 2008.

North, Douglass. *Institutions, Institutional Change and Economic Performance.* Cambridge: Cambridge University Press, 1990.

Nove, Alec. *An Economic History of the USSR.* Rev. ed. London: Penguin, 1993.

Organization for Economic Cooperation and Development. *Russian Federation.* Paris: Organization for Economic Cooperation and Development, 1995.

———. *Russian Federation.* Paris: Organization for Economic Cooperation and Development, 1997.

———. *Russian Federation.* Paris: Organization for Economic Cooperation and Development, 2004.

———. *Russian Federation.* Paris: Organization for Economic Cooperation and Development, 2009.

Ovcharova, L. N., ed. *Dokhody i Sotsial'nie Uslugi: neravenstvo, uiazvimost' i bednost': Kollektivnaia monographiia.* Moscow: GU-VShE, 2005.

Pappe, Ya.Sh. and Ya.S. Galukhina. *Rossiiskii krupnii biznes: Pervie 15 let. Ekonomicheskie khroniki 1993–2008.* Moscow: Izdatelskii dom GU VShE, 2009.

Pascall, Gillian, and Jane Lewis. "Emerging Gender Regimes and Policies for Gender Equality in a Wider Europe." *Journal of Social Policy* 33, no. 3 (2004): 373–94.

Passe-Smith, John. "The Persistence of the Gap between Rich and Poor Countries, 1960–1998." In *Development and Underdevelopment: The Political Economy of Global Inequality,* edited by Mitchell A. Seligson and John Passe-Smith, 17–31. Boulder, CO: Lynne Rienner, 2003.

Pavlovsky, Gleb. "Brat—3." *Ekspert: Luchshie materialy* 2 (2007): 63–67 (originally published in *Ekspert* 32 [September 1, 2003]).

Perov, A. V. *Nalogi i mezhdurodnie soglasheniia Rossii.* Moscow: Iurist, 2000.

Pilipovic, Dragana. *Energy Risk: Valuing and Managing Energy Derivatives.* New York: McGraw-Hill, 1998.

Plotnikov, Vladimir N. "Doklad Prezidenta AKKOR Vladimiria Nikolaevicha Plotnikova na XIX s'ezde AKKOR." *Fermerskoe samoupravlenie* 3–5 (2008): 3–8.

Politkovskaya, Anna. *Putin's Russia: Life in a Failing Democracy.* New York: Holt Paperbacks, 2007.

Popov, N. "Krest'yanskie (fermerskie) khozyaistva." *APK: Ekonomika, upravlenie* 5 (1996): 56–62.

Popov, Vladimir. "Life Cycle of the Centrally Planned Economy: Why Soviet Growth Rates Peaked in the 1950s." In *Transition and Beyond*, edited by Saul Estrin, Grzegorz W. Kolodko, and Milicia Uvalic, 35–57. Basingstoke: Palgrave, 2007.

———. "After 10 Years of Growth, the Russian Economy May Be Losing Steam." *Russian Analytical Digest* 48 (2008): 15–18.

Posadskaya, Anastasia. *Women in Russia*. London: Verso, 1995.

Prezident AKKOR. "Prezident AKKOR V. Plotnikov prinyal uchastie vo vstreche V. Putina s rukovoditelyami ob'edineniy predprinimateley malogo i srednego biznesa." 2010.

Profsoiuzyi segodnya. "Liudoedyi i Trudovoi kodeks." 2011. http://goo.gl/8tkrc.

Putin, Vladimir. "Rossiya na rubezhe tysyachiletii." In *Plan Prezidenta Putina. Rukovodstvo dlya budushchikh prezidentov Rossii*, 311–31. Moscow: Evropa, 1999.

——— "Transcript of Putin's State of the Nation Address." BBC Monitoring, May 16, 2003, reprinted in *Johnson's Russia List* 7186 (May 19, 2003).

———. "Politika: Poslanie Federal'nomu Sobraniiu Rossiiskoi Federatsii." *Rossiiskaya Gazeta*, April 26, 2005.

———. "Annual Address to the Federal Assembly, 10 May 2006." 2006. http://goo.gl/xVpR8.

———. "Beginning of the Session of the Presidential Council for the Implementation of Priority National Projects and Demographic Policy." 2008. http://goo.gl/ffS2p.

———. "Speech at Expanded Meeting of the State Council on Russia's Development Strategy through to 2020." *Johnson's Russia List* 29 (February 11, 2008).

———. "Vystupitel'noe slovo Vladimira Putina." 2010. http://www.akkor.ru, under the link "novosti."

Radygin, A. "Rossiya v 2000–2004 godakh na puti k gosudarstvenomy kapitalizmu?" *Voprosy ekonomiki* 4 (2004): 42–65.

Reddaway, Peter, and Dmitri Glinski. *The Tragedy of Russia's Reforms. Market Bolshevism against Democracy*. Washington, DC: United States Institute of Peace Press, 2001.

Renaissance Capital. *Oil and Gas Yearbook*. Moscow: Renaissance Capital, 2009.

Renz, Bettina. "Putin's Militocracy? An Alternative Interpretation of *Siloviki* in Contemporary Russian Politics." *Europe-Asia Studies* 58, no. 6 (2006): 903–24.

Reyting. "Reyting krupneyshikh fermerskikh khozyaistv Rossii-Klub 'Fermer-300,'" *Ekonomika sel'skokhozyaistvennikh i pererabatyvayushchikh predpriyatiy* 2 (2010): 22–27.

Richter, James. "Integration from Below? The Disappointing Effort to Promote Civil Society in Russia." In *Russia and Globalization*, edited by Douglas W. Blum, 181–203. Washington, DC: Woodrow Wilson Center Press, 2008.

Robinson, Neil. "The Global Economy, Reform and Crisis in Russia." *Review of International Political Economy* 6, no. 4 (1999): 531–64.

———. "The Economy and the Prospects for Anti-Democratic Development in Russia." *Europe-Asia Studies* 52, no. 8 (2000): 1391–415.

———. "The Presidency: The Politics of Institutional Chaos." In *Institutions and Political Change in Russia*, edited by Neil Robinson, 11–40. Basingstoke: Macmillan, 2000.

———. "The Myth of Equilibrium: Winner Power, Fiscal Crisis and Russian Economic Reform." *Communist and Post-Communist Studies* 34, no. 4 (2001): 423–46.

———. *Russia: A State of Uncertainty*. London: Routledge, 2002.

———. "Path Dependency, Global Economy and Post-Communist Change." In *Reforging the Weakest Link: Global Political Economy and Post-Soviet Change in Russia, Ukraine and Belarus*, edited by Neil Robinson, 106–26. Aldershot: Ashgate, 2004.

———. "So What Changed? The 1998 Economic Crisis in Russia and Russia's Economic and Political Development." *Demokratizatsiya: A Journal of Post-Soviet Democratization* 15, no. 2 (2007): 245–59.

———. "August 1998 and the Development of Russia's Post-Communist Political Economy." *Review of International Political Economy* 16, no. 3 (2009): 433–55.

———. "Political Barriers to Economic Development in Russia: Obstacles to Modernization under Yeltsin and Putin." *International Journal of Development Issues* 10, no. 1 (2011): 5–19.

———. "Russian Patrimonial Capitalism and the International Financial Crisis." *Journal of Communist Studies and Transitional Politics* 27, no. 3–4 (2011): 434–55.

Roland, Gérard. *Transition and Economics: Politics, Markets, and Firms*. Cambridge, MA: MIT Press, 2000.

Rosefielde, Steven, and Stefan Hedlund. *Russia since 1980*. New York: Cambridge University Press, 2009.

Ross, Cameron. *Local Politics and Democratization in Russia*. London: Routledge, 2008.

Ross, Michael L. "The Political Economy of the Resource Curse." *World Politics* 51, no. 2 (1999): 297–322.

Rosstat. *Rossiya v tsifrakh: 2004*. Moscow: Rosstat, 2004.

———. *Regiony Rossii: 2005*. Moscow: Rosstat, 2005.

———. *Rossiya v tsifrakh: 2006*. Moscow: Rosstat, 2006.

———. *Regiony Rossii: 2007*. Moscow: Rosstat, 2007.

———. *Rossiya v tsifrakh: 2007*. Moscow: Rosstat, 2007.

———. *Itogi Vserossiyskoi sel'skokhozyaistvennoi perepisi 2006 goda: Zemel'nie resursy*. Moscow: Rosstat, 2008.

———. *Osnovnie itogi Vserossiyskoi sel'skokhozyaistvennoi perepisi 2006 goda*. Vol. 1, bk. 1. Moscow: Rosstat, 2008.

———. *Osnovnie itogi Vserossiyskoi sel'skokhozyaistvennoi perepisi 2006 goda*. Vol. 1, bk. 2. Moscow: Rosstat, 2008.

———. *Regiony Rossii: 2008*. Moscow: Rosstat, 2008.

———. *Rossiya v tsifrakh: 2010*. Moscow: Rosstat, 2010.

———. "Chislennost' inostranniikh rabotnikov." 2011. http://goo.gl/5ynVv.

———. "Dinamika osnovniikh sotsial'no-ekonomicheskikh pokazatelei." 2011. http://goo.gl/s5Lqf.

———. "Valovoi vnutrennii produkt." 2011. http://goo.gl/j3vlB.

———. "Zabastovki." 2011. http://goo.gl/3ESAe.

Rudnitsky, Jake. "China Pays Off Debt for Russia Crude Supply." *Platts Oilgram News*, June (2011).

Russian Government. "Medium-Term Programme of the Economic Reforms of the Russian Government." *Russian Economic Trends* 1, no. 3 (1992): 43–69.

Rutland, Peter. *The Myth of the Plan: Lessons of Soviet Planning Experience*. London: Hutchinson, 1985.

———. "Oil, Politics and Foreign Policy. In *The Political Economy of Russian Oil*, edited by David Lane, 163–88. Lanham, MD: Rowman & Littlefield, 1999.

———. "The August 1998 Crash: Causes and Consequences." In *Business and the State in Contemporary Russia*, edited by P. Rutland, 173–86. Boulder, CO: Westview Press, 2001.

———. "The Impact of the Global Financial Crisis in Russia." *Russian Analytical Digest* 48 (2008): 2–5.

———. "Russia as an Energy Superpower." *New Political Economy* 13, no. 2 (2008): 203–10.

———. "The Oligarchs and Economic Development." In *After Putin's Russia: Past Imperfect, Future Uncertain*, edited by Stephen K. Wegren and Dale R. Herspring, 159–82. Lanham, MD: Rowman & Littlefield, 2010.

Sakwa, Richard. *Russian Politics and Society*. London: Routledge, 2008.

———. *The Quality of Freedom. Khodorkovsky, Putin, and the Yukos Affair*. Oxford: Oxford University Press, 2009.

———. *The Crisis of Russian Democracy: The Dual State, Factionalism and the Medvedev Succession*. Cambridge: Cambridge University Press, 2011.

Sazonov, Sergei. "Sotsial'no-ekonomicheskie aspekty razvitiya fermerskogo dvizheniya v Rossii." *APK: Ekonomika, upravlenie* 5 (1995): 55–61.

Schenk, Caress. "Open Borders, Closed Minds: Russia's Changing Migration Policies: Liberalization or Xenophobia?" *Demokratizatsiya: The Journal of Post-Soviet Democratization* 18, no. 1 (2010): 101–21.

Schröder, Hans-Hennig. "El'tsin and the Oligarchs: The Role of Financial Growth in Russian Politics between 1993 and 1998." *Europe-Asia Studies* 51, no. 6 (1999): 957–88.

Schroder, Hans-Henning. "In Search of Modernization without Irritation: Medvedev's Third Address to the Federal Assembly." *Russian Analytical Digest* 90 (2011): 2–5.

Schwager, Jack D. *Schwager on Futures: Fundamental Analysis*. New York: Wiley, 1995.

———. *Schwager on Futures: Technical Analysis*. New York: Wiley, 1996.

Semenov, A., and D. Ageyev. "Sotsial'nie prioritety podderzhki malogo predprinimatel'stva." *Ekonomist* 10 (2000): 75–81.

Sergeev, Mikhail. "Natsproekty v ozhidanii urezaniia." *Nezavisimaya Gazeta*, May 15, 2007.

Shakkum, M. L. *Ekonomika Rossii ot krizisa k stabil'nosti k ustoichivomu rostu*. Moscow: Globus, 1999.

Shevel, Oxana. "Identity, Citizenship, and Tolerance." In *Transnational Migration to New Regional Centers: Policy Challenges, Practice, and Migrant Experience*, edited by Lauren Herzer, Sarah Dixon Klump, and Mary Elizabeth Malinkin, 52–82. Conference Proceedings, Eurasia Migration Papers 2. Washington, DC: Woodrow Wilson Center International Center for Scholars, 2009.

Shkaratan, Ovsey. "The Russian Transformation: A New Form of Etacratism?" In *The Transformation of State Socialism. System Change, Capitalism or Something Else?*, edited by David Lane, 143–58. Basingstoke: Palgrave Macmillan, 2007.

Shlapentokh, Vladimir. "Wealth versus Political Power: The Russian Case." *Communist and Post-Communist Studies* 37, no. 2 (2004): 135–60.

Shleifer, Andrei, and Daniel Treisman. *Without a Map: Political Tactics and Economic Reform in Russia*. Cambridge, MA: MIT Press, 2000.

Sim, Li-Chen. *The Rise and Fall of Privatization in the Russian Oil Industry*. Basingstoke: Palgrave Macmillan, 2008.

Simon, Rick. "Upper Volta with Gas? Russia as a Semi-Peripheral State." In *Globalization and the "New" Semi-Peripheries*, edited by Owen Worth and Phoebe Moore, 120–37. Basingstoke: Palgrave Macmillan, 2009.

Sinitsina, I. *Experience in Implementing Social Benefits Monetization Reform in Russia: Literature Review*. Warsaw: Case Network Studies and Analyses, 2009.

Skolkovo. "The Official Website of the Skolkovo Foundation." 2011. http://goo.gl/GRuOj.

Skrynnik, Elena B. "Povyshenie proizvoditel'nosti i finansovoi ustoychivosti malykh form khozyaistvenniya na sele." *Ekonomika sel'skokhozyaistvennikh i pererabatyvayushchikh predpriyatii* 2 (2010): 1–6.

Slider, Darrell. "How United is United Russia? Regional Sources of Intra-Party Conflict." *Communist Studies and Transition Politics* 26, no. 2 (2010): 257–75.

Smolyakova, Tatyana. "140 Million and Not a Soul Less." *Current Digest of the Post-Soviet Press* 58, no. 21 (2006):4–5.

Socor, Vladimir. "Oil-for-Loans Deal Will Increase Russian Oil Deliveries to China." *Eurasia Daily Monitor* 6, no. 34 (2009).

Soltaganov, V. F. *Nalogovaya politsiya: Vchera, segodnia, zavtra*. Moscow: Dashkov, 2000.

Sperling, Valerie. *Organizing Women in Contemporary Russia: Engendering Transition*. Cambridge: Cambridge University Press, 1999.

———. *Altered States: The Globalization of Accountability*. Cambridge: Cambridge University Press, 2009.

Spufford, Francis. *Red Plenty*. London: Faber and Faber, 2010.

Stalin, Joseph. "O zadachakh khozyaistvennikov: Rech' na pervoi Vsesoyuznoi konferentsii rabotnikov sotsialisticheskoi promyshlennosti, 4 fevralya 1931g." In *Voprosy Leninizma*, by Joseph Stalin, 355–63. Moscow: Gospolitizdat, 1952.

Stern, Jonathan P. *The Future of Russian Gas and Gazprom*. Oxford: Oxford University Press, 2005.

Stulberg, Adam N. *Well-Oiled Diplomacy: Strategic Manipulation and Russia's Energy Statecraft in Eurasia*. Albany: State University of New York Press, 2007.

Sundstrom, Lisa McIntosh. "Women's NGOs in Russia: Struggling from the Margins." *Demokratizatsiya* 10, no. 2 (2002): 7–24.

Tanzi, Vito. "Creating Effective Tax Administrations: the Experience of Russia and Georgia." In *Reforming the State: Fiscal and Welfare Reform in Post-Socialist Countries*, edited by János Kornai, Stephan Haggard, and Robert R. Kaufman, 53–74. Cambridge: Cambridge University Press, 2001.

Taylor, Brian D. *State Building in Putin's Russia: Policing and Coercion after Communism*. Cambridge: Cambridge University Press, 2011.

Teplova, Tatyana. "Welfare State Transformation, Childcare, and Women's Work in Russia." *Social Politics: International Studies in Gender, State and Society* 14, no. 3 (2007): 284–322.

Terent'ev, I. "Agrarnaya reforma i krest'yanskie (fermerskie) khozyaistva." *Ekonomist* 7 (1996): 92–95.

Tikhomirov, Vladimir. "Capital Flight from Post-Soviet Russia." *Europe-Asia Studies* 49, no. 4 (1997): 591–615.

———. *The Political Economy of Post-Soviet Russia.* Basingstoke: Macmillan, 2000.

———. "The Second Collapse of the Soviet Economy: Myths and Realities of Russian Reform." *Europe-Asia Studies* 52, no. 2 (2000): 207–35.

Tilly, Charles. "War Making and State Making as Organized Crime." In *Bringing the State Back In,* edited by Peter Evans, Dietrich Rueschemeyer, and Theda Skocpol, 169–91. Cambridge: Cambridge University Press, 1985.

Tolkushkin, A. I. *Istoriia nalogov v Rossii.* Moscow: Iurist, 2001.

Tompson, William. "Putin and the 'Oligarchs': A Two-Sided Commitment Problem." In *Leading Russia: Putin in Perspective,* edited by Alex Pravda, 179–202. Oxford: Oxford University Press, 2005.

———. "Putting Yukos in Perspective." *Post-Soviet Affairs* 21, no. 2 (2005): 159–82.

———. "A Frozen Venezuela? The Resource Curse and Russian Politics." In *Russia's Oil and Natural Gas: Bonanza or Curse?,* edited by Michael Ellman, 189–212. London: Anthem Press, 2006.

Transparency International. "CPI Table 2008." 2008. http://goo.gl/JxMpc.

Treisman, Daniel. "Presidential Popularity in a Hybrid Regime: Russia under Yeltsin and Putin." *American Journal of Political Science* 55, no. 3 (2011): 590–609.

———. *The Return: Russia's Journey from Gorbachev to Medvedev.* New York: Free Press, 2011.

Turley, Gerard, and Peter J. Luke. *Transition Economics: Two Decades On.* London: Routledge, 2010.

Ukaz Prezidenta Rossiiskoi Federatsii. "Ob utverzhdenii Kontseptsii demograficheskoi politiki Rossiiskoi Federatsii na period do 2025 roda." 2007. http://goo.gl/KVhsV.

United National Development Programme.*Russia in 2015: Development Goals and Policy Priorities.* Moscow: United National Development Programme, 2005.

United Nations. *Demographic Policy in Russia: From Reflection to Action.* Moscow: United Nations, 2008.

Urban, Michael E. "Conceptualizing Political Power in the USSR: Patterns of Binding and Bonding." *Studies in Comparative Communism* 18, no. 4 (1985): 207–26.

———. *Cultures of Power in Post-Communist Russia.* Cambridge: Cambridge University Press, 2010.

Ustinov, I. N. *Mezhdunarodnie ekonomicheskie otnosheniya Rossii: Entsiklopediya statisticheskaya.* Moscow: Ekonomika, 2004.

Van Atta, Don. "The Return of Individual Farming in Russia." In *The "Farmer Threat": The Political Economy of Agrarian Reform in Post-Soviet Russia,* edited by Don Van Atta, 75–91. Boulder, CO: Westview Press, 1993.

Vasil'eva, Natal'ya. "'Prigovor byl privezen iz Mosgorsuda, ya tochno znayu': Otkrovennoe intervyu o dele Yukosa pomoshchnika sud'i Khamovnicheskogo suda." 2011. http://goo.gl/D9wy.

Vendina, Olga. "New Migration Destinations." In *Transnational Migration to New Regional Centers: Policy Challenges, Practice, and Migrant Experience*, edited by Lauren Herzer, Sarah Dixon Klump, and Mary Elizabeth Malinkin, 85–121. Conference Proceedings, Eurasia Migration Papers 2. Washington, DC: Woodrow Wilson Center International Center for Scholars, 2009.

Vinogradov, Mikhail. "'Novyi kurs' Putina: Pravitelstva poruchili v blizhaishie dva goda syshchestvenno uluchshit' kachestvo zhizni." *Izvestiya*, September 6, 2005.

Visloguzov, Vadim. "National 'Health' Project Interferes with Health Care Reform." *Kommersant*, November 18, 2005 translated in *Current Digest of the Post-Soviet Press* 57, no. 46: 8.

Volkov, Vadim. *Violent Entrepreneurs: The Use of Force in the Making of Russian Capitalism*. Ithaca, NY: Cornell University Press, 2002.

Volkovskii, V. I. *Nalogovie organy i ekonomicheskaya bezopasnost': Rossii.* Moscow: Fond podderzhki uchenikh "nauchnaya perspektiva," 2002.

Vorobyov, Mikhail. "Plan Putina-Medvedeva." *Vremya novostei'*, January 16, 2008.

Waldner, David. *State Building and Late Development*. Ithaca, NY: Cornell University Press, 1999.

Wallerstein, Immanuel. *The Capitalist World-Economy*. Cambridge: Cambridge University Press, 1979.

Wegren, Stephen K. *Agriculture and the State in Soviet and Post-Soviet Russia*. Pittsburgh, PA: Pittsburgh University Press, 1998.

———. "Russian Agrarian Policy under Putin." *Post-Soviet Geography and Economics* 43, no. 1 (2002): 26–40.

———. 2010. "Russia's Food Policies and Foreign Policy." *Demokratizatsiya: The Journal of Post-Soviet Democratization* 18, no. 3 (2010): 189–207.

———. "Private Farming in Russia: An Emerging Success?" *Post-Soviet Affairs* 27, no. 3 (2011): 211–40.

Weingast, Barry R., and Donald A. Wittman. "The Reach of Political Economy." In *The Oxford Handbook of Political Economy*, edited by Barry R. Weingast and Donald A. Wittman, 3–25. Oxford: Oxford University Press, 2006.

Weissman, Richard L. *Mechanical Trading Systems: Pairing Trader Psychology with Technical Analysis*. New York: Wiley, 2005.

Whitefield, Stephen. *Industrial Power and the Soviet State*. Oxford: Clarendon Press, 1993.

Woodruff, David. *Money Unmade: Barter and the Fate of Russian Capitalism*. Ithaca, NY: Cornell University Press, 1999.

———. "The Expansion of State Ownership in Russia: Cause for Concern?" *Development and Transition* 7 (2007): 11–13.

World Bank. "Key Development Data and Statistics." 2010. http://goo.gl/DqzeE.

———. "Governance Indicators." 2011. http://goo.gl/sU5wU.

———. "Indicators: Russian Federation." 2011. http://goo.gl/H2qAc.

Worth, Owen. "Whatever Happened to the Semi-Periphery?" In *Globalization and the "New" Semi-Peripheries*, edited by Owen Worth and Phoebe Moore, 9–24. Basingstoke: Palgrave Macmillan, 2009.

Wyman, Matthew. *Public Opinion in Postcommunist Russia*. Basingstoke: Macmillan, 1997.

Yakovlev, Andrei. "The Evolution of Business-State Interaction in Russia: From State Capture to Business Capture?" *Europe-Asia Studies* 58, no. 7 (2006): 1033–56.

Yasin, Yevgeny. "Raskhodov malo, nuzhny reformy: Ot pervogo litsa." *Izvestiya*, September 12, 2005.

Yudina, Tatiana. "Labour Migration into Russia: The Response of State and Society." *Current Sociology* 53, no. 4 (2005): 583–606.

Zakharov, Sergei. "Russian Federation: From the First to the Second Demographic Transition." *Demographic Research* 19, no. 24 (2008): 907–72.

Zhurek, Stefan. "Transforming Russian Agriculture: Why Is Privatization so Difficult?" *The Soviet and Post-Soviet Review* 21, no. 2–3 (1994): 253–82.

Zinchenko, A. P. "Tendentsii i problemy ispol'zovaniya proizvodstvennogo potentsiala krest'yanskikh (fermerskikh) khozyaistv." *Ekonomika sel'skokhozyaistvennikh i pererabatyvayushchikh predpriyatiy* 10 (2001): 17–20.

Zubkov, Viktor. "Viktor Zubkov vyravnivaet kooperatsiyu." 2011. http://www.agronews.ru.

Zygar, Mikhail, and Valeri Panyushkin. *Gazprom: Novoe russkoe oruzhie*. Moscow: Zakharov, 2008.

Index

abortion rate, 109, 111

Abramovich, Roman, 154

administrative regime, 70–1, 74, 76, 80, 81, 93. *See also* dual state

agriculture, 10; Bashkortostan and, 126; Central Black Earth federal district and, 127–8, 130; Central federal district and, 107, 127, 130; economic reform in 1990s and, 122, 123–4; food supply and, 121, 126–7, 134, 144; import quotas, 140; Krasnodar kray and, 125, 126, 127, 128, 129, 134, 135; legalisation of private farms, 121; national security and, 132, 144; National Program and, 132–3; Northern Caucasus federal district and, 126–7, 128, 130, 159; Northern federal district and, 130; Northwestern federal district and, 129, 130, 135, 148; Russian Farmer program, 124–5, 141–2, 144; Samara and, 125, 151; Saratov and, 126, 129, 134; Southern federal district and, 134, 135, 137, 139, 142, 144, 148; Stavropol' kray and, 125, 126, 129, 134, 135–6; Tatarstan and, 126;

underdevelopment of private farming in North, 127–8; Urals federal district and, 127, 130; Volga federal district and, 126, 128, 129, 130, 134, 136–9, 142; Volgograd and, 125, 126, 128, 129, 134, 135. *See also* private farming

Alfa-Access-Renova, 155

All-Russian Confederation of Labor, 182

appointment of state officials to boards of major enterprises, 87–88

Association of Peasant Farms and Agricultural Cooperatives in Russia (AKKOR), 122, 125, 139, 141, 145, 148; corporatist policies, 142; regional leaders, 143

August 1998 economic crisis, 24, 31, 33, 35–6, 39, 52, 57, 153, 177, 188, 193

Avtovaz, 60, 61, 63, 67

banks, 33–4, 44

Balzer, Marjorie Mandelstam, 179

Barnes, Andrew, 10

barter, 22, 31, 44, 55, 56. *See also* nonmonetary exchange

Bashkortostan, 67, 126

deprivatization, 87
Deripaska, Oleg, 80
development. *See* economic growth
Draganov, Valerii, 82
dual economy, 88
dual state, 69–73, 74, 76, 77, 81, 87,
    88–91, 194
Dudley, Robert, 84, 155
Duma, 85, 92, 110; 2007 election

Easter, Gerald, 5, 7, 10
economic exchange: market, 20;
    particularistic, 21–3, 25, 27–8
economic growth: dependency on
    oil for, 18, 39–40, 44–5; political
    problems of, 194–5; "politician's
    dilemma" and, 195; Soviet patterns
    of, 17–9, 172–3; under Putin, 39–40,
    177–8
economic reform: credible commitment
    and, 26; early failure of, 28–35; in
    1990s, 6, 7, 23–35, 174; partial, 31;
    plateaus of, 30, 38; political problems
    of, 195–6; "politician's dilemma"
    and, 195; taxation and, 53–4
economic sectors: internationalized,
    24–5, 33, 41; nontradable, 24–5, 33;
    state-supporting, 24–5
energy, 10–1, 40; policy, 77; rents,
    captured by Putin, 81. *See also*
    extractive industries; gas; oil
environmental groups, 179
European Bank for Reconstruction and
    Development, 30
European Court of Human Rights
    (ECHR), 83, 91–2, 180
extractive industries, 55, 174–6, 182. *See
    also* oil, gas, metals

factionalism, 8, 36, 70, 71, 73, 74–80,
    87, 93, 183–4, 194; blocking reform,
    196–7. *See also* siloviki
Federal Migration Service, 101–2
Federal Tax Service, 58, 92
Federation of Independent Trade
    Unions, 181–2

financial-industrial groups (FIGs), 34,
    35
fiscal crisis. *See* state
food supply, 121, 126–7,134, 144;
    security and, 10, 121, 132, 139, 144,
    149
foreign borrowings before 2008 crisis, 41
foreign investment, 25, 33, 40, 42, 177,
    188, 193; Russian, 182
Fortescue, Stephen, 80
Fradkov, Mikhail, 59, 61
FSB (Federal Security Service), 75, 79.
    See also siloviki

Gaddy, Clifford, 81
Gaidar, Yegor, 26, 29, 47, 53, 123
Ganev, Vanelin, 193
gas, 5, 14, 31, 39, 47, 58, 85, 154,
    173–6, 197; economic dependency
    on, 43, 153, 170, 173, 180, 197;
    internationalized sector of economy
    and, 25; subsidies to Russian
    economy, 31–3, 40–41; use in
    international politics, 156, 167,
    185. *See also* extractive industries,
    Gazprom, oil
Gazprom, 31, 41, 47, 58, 63, 84–5, 153–4
Gazprom Neft, 153
Geddes, Barbara, 194–5
Georgia, war with, 43, 185
Gerschenkron, Alexander, 3
Gimpleson, V. 181, 183
Glinski, Dmitri, 176
globalization, 170, 174–8
Golikova, Tatiana, 112
Gorbachev, Mikhail, 71, 123, 172, 179
Gordeev, Alexei, 132
governance, 38–9, 77, 191–4. *See also*
    state
Graham, Thomas, 75
Gramsci, Antonio, 71
Gref, German, 59, 68
growth. *See* economic growth
Gryzlov, Boris, 63
Gusinsky, Vladimir, 78, 79
Gutseriev, Mikhail, 80

About the Contributors

Andrew Barnes is assistant professor in the Department of Political Science at Kent State University. His publications include *Owning Russia: The Struggle over Factories, Farms and Power* (2006), as well as many journal articles and book chapters on Russian politics and political economy and on comparative postcommunist political economy.

Paul Christensen is adjunct associate professor in the Department of Political Science at Boston College. His publications include *Russia's Workers in Transition: Labor, Management, and the State Under Gorbachev and Yeltsin* (1999), as well as many articles and papers on Russia in the global political economy and on the labor movement in Russia.

Linda J. Cook is professor in the Department of Political Science at Brown University and an associate of the Davis Center for Russian and Eurasian Studies at Harvard University and of the Watson Institute at Brown. She is the author of *The Soviet Social Contract and Why it Failed* (1993), *Postcommunist Welfare States: Reform Politics in Russia and Eastern Europe* (2007), and numerous other publications on Russian politics, welfare, labor, and representation.

Gerald M. Easter is associate professor in the Department of Political Science at Boston College and an associate of the Davis Center for Russian and Eurasian Studies at Harvard University. His publications include *Reconstructing the State: Personal Networks and Elite Identity in Soviet Russia* (2000) and

Capital, Coercion and Post-Communist State (2012), and articles and chapters on Russian and postcommunist politics and on tax politics in postcommunist countries.

Neil Robinson is senior lecturer in the Department of Politics and Public Administration at the University of Limerick, Ireland. His publications include *Russia: A State of Uncertainty* (2002) and *The Sage Handbook of Comparative Politics* (2009). He is the author of several articles and chapters on Russian politics and political economy.

Richard Sakwa is professor of Russian and European Politics in the Department of Politics and International Relations at the University of Kent, UK, and an associate fellow of the Russia and Eurasia Programme at the Royal Institute of International Affairs. His many publications on Russian and postcommunist politics include most recently *The Quality of Freedom: Khodorkovsky, Putin and the Yukos Affair* (2009) and *The Crisis of Russian Democracy: The Dual State, Factionalism and the Medvedev Succession* (2011), as well as many articles and book chapters on Russian domestic and intrnational politics.

Stephen K. Wegren is professor in the Department of Political Science at Southern Methodist University. He is the author of more than one hundred articles and book chapters on various aspects of political and economic reform in post-communist states, including *Russia's Food Policies and Globalization* (2005), *The Moral Economy Reconsidered: Russia's Search for Agrarian Capitalism*(2005), and *After Putin's Russia: Past Imperfect, Future Uncertain* (2010).